TIDELAND TREASURE

The Naturalist's Guide to the Beaches and Salt Marshes of Hilton Head Island and the Southeastern Coast

Revised Edition

TODD BALLANTINE
Text and Illustrations

University of South Carolina Press

Published in Columbia, South Carolina, by the
University of South Carolina Press

Manufactured in the United States of America

First published in 1983 by Deerfield Publishing,
Hilton Head, South Carolina

Revised Edition 1991
Second Printing 1993

ISBN 0–87249–795–X

For Marianne, Emily and Edan…
My beloved family

Grandfather, Great Spirit,
Fill us with light;
teach us to walk the soft earth
as relatives to all that lives.

Lakota Indian Prayer

Acknowledgments

In 1978, I initiated a weekly feature column called "Tideland Treasure" which appeared in *Island Events* magazine on Hilton Head Island. The tale of the marine world is as expansive as the seas and sounds themselves; so my column ran continuously for five years. My thanks to Vic Johnson and Jolie Donnell for allowing my total freedom of expression in their fine publication.

Readers will notice two or three handwriting styles here. My pen wanders from homey manuscript to Italic Chancery calligraphy. Bear with these different techniques. They reveal my graphic experimentation through the years. Perhaps you will get to know me better through my changing hand. For my training in calligraphy, I am indebted to Harvey Hallenberg.

My parents, Sis and Ralph Ballantine, gave invaluable assistance to the production of this book. Mom pored through reams of pages as proofreader and grammarian. Without Dad's artistic advice, *Tideland Treasure* would never have become a book.

Joe Higgins, a botanist and nature photographer from Tarpon Springs, Florida, presented the cover photograph of American beachgrass in dunes to my wife and me as a wedding present. I thank Joe for his clear lens vision, and approval for use of his art on the cover.

Thanks also to Robin Sumner and the staff at University of South Carolina Press for their encouragement and pointers on book production.

And to all the sandlappers everywhere who read, clipped and collected my columns for half a decade, I appreciate your loyal support.

THB

Foreword

Alabaster, long-winged waders lift gracefully upwards from billowing tufts of marsh grass. Out on the sea an ungainly looking brown pelican peels out of formation and divebombs unsuspecting mullet swimming below. Back in the far reaches of an ox-bow tidal creek, smiling-faced bottlenosed dolphins pop surfaceward with spouting spray... splashing, cavorting and trapping fish with cunning nonchalance. Anywhere nearby, walkers and waders, beachcombers and sunbathers play freely on the shore. Day follows night through the years as the boundless ocean rhythmically pounds the sands like the heartbeat of Mother Earth herself.

Such is the fascinating natural world of the Southeastern barrier islands. Washed, pummeled and windblown on the oceanside, twice daily flooded and drained on the lee, the isles are constantly reshaped and renewed by the sea according to the timeless forces of weather and tides. These are dynamic environments, rich in marine life of every shape, size and habit. When we humans explore and settle the islands, we come face to face with the wonder and mystery of teeming life forms in the primordial waters.

Nowhere is the "man discovers the shore" phenomenon more evident than on Hilton Head Island, South Carolina. Largest of the southern barrier isles (and second in overall size to Long Island, New York), this foot-shaped strand has undergone substantial land development since the 1960's. Visitors, new residents and venerable natives alike are forever intrigued by the coastal creatures in the numberless finned, feathered, crusty, blobbed forms. Highly specialized plants adapting to the long growing season here lend a tropical air to the island. This semitropic bit of botany is enough for a lifetime of study of endemic flora and greenery.

"What is it?" is far and away the most common question voiced on the shores here. This book is my simple attempt to reveal typically observed plants and animals of the beaches and salt marshes of Hilton Head Island and the Southeast coast. *Tideland Treasure* interprets the natural world of Hilton Head for two good reasons. First, I live on the island, and it has shown me what to write about. Second, because it is representative of many beaches and wetlands from Ocean City, New Jersey, to Cape Canaveral, Florida. I purposefully use common names for species in order to make them memorable to casual beachcombers and amateur naturalists. And most important, to children.

Subjects here are common in tidelands and are easily seen in season. Normally, they require no special apparatus to identify or understand other than a child-like desire to know more. I call that Real Science.

You and I become citizens on these shores the moment we bury our toes in sand or pluff mud. So we owe ourselves a conscious appreciation of the natural life around us, and under our feet. The sea, the beaches and the salt marshes hide the priceless bounty of wild creation. May this book be your key to unlocking for yourself this tideland treasure.

Todd Ballantine
Hilton Head Island
1991

Contents

The Sea

Mother Atlantic is at once an inspiration, a provider and an awesome power. Her changing moods will create breezes and comfortable temperatures, making our climate most benign. Lovers and poets take heart under moonbeams dancing across her midnight wave tops. Children tirelessly hurl themselves at her surf.

With the tides she churns into the estuaries and salt marshes, recharging the sun-baked, oxygen-starved communities of life there. Borne on her stirring currents, floating soil and plankton and plants and animal matter settle as marsh mud in tidal wetlands on leeside of the islands. Our colored ocean… honestly described as *olive drab*… is a nutrient-rich "nature soup." Teeming with the essential elements for life, the brackish bouillabaisse provides the foundation for a broad foodweb that supports shrimp, crabs, oysters, fish, dolphins, shorebirds and so much more.

Barrier isles such as Hilton Head are but mere bumps compared with the eternal scale of the sea. The ocean which encircles us grinds out our shoreline geology. Watch a November Nor'easter bite off 20 feet of dune to appreciate the raw horsepower in every rolling wave. Having experienced Hurricane Hugo's mauling of the South Carolina coast, I know that living by the ocean is always a game of chance, and never innocent.

Still, we islanders should do more than respect our Mother. We are truly her children. We must learn from her, and love her.

SALT WATER

A tangy taste of brine is evidence enough for swimmers, surfers & sailors that Atlantic waters surrounding us contain salt. About 1/4 lb. of salt is suspended in a gallon of sea water. If the world's oceans were to dry up, their salts would blanket the continental U.S. 1½ miles deep! 3/4 of the mineral recipe of sea water (chart, right) → is good ol' table salt, or sodium chloride.

SEA WATER

TABLE SALT	77.6%
MAGNESIUM CHLORIDE	10.88%
EPSOM SALTS	4.74%
CALCIUM SULPHATE	3.60%
POTASSIUM SULPHATE	2.47%
LIME	0.34%
TRACE MINERALS	0.51%

Why seas are salty: Rivers & streams channel rainwater to oceans. Draining the mainland, they dissolve salts from rocks & soil, & float it in solution to the seas. Here normal evaporation removes the fresh water but leaves heavier salts behind. Earthquakes, volcanoes & storms stir sea floor sediments, releasing more minerals. So day by day the sea gets saltier. How salty? The open sea measures approx. 35‰ (‰ = the # of dissolved salts per 1000 parts water); the beachfront 30-32‰; the salt marsh 20-25‰.

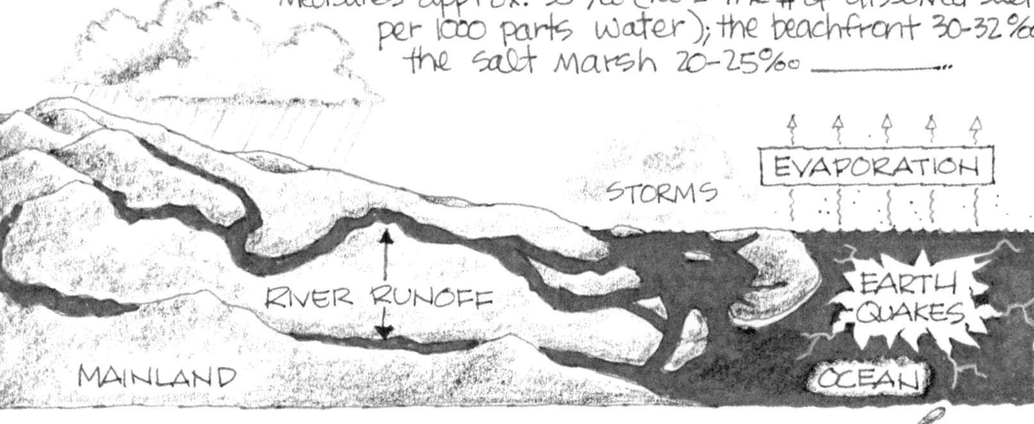

Blood, sweat & tears have a saltish tang, hinting 0.9% salt is found in the human body. But the sea is 3 times saltier. We can't drink the Atlantic because the more concentrated saline water absorbs more fresh water from us than we can get from it! Brinier-blooded marine animals thrive in the sea's mineral bath, however. Sediment-borne salts stirred by winter storms are ingested by microscopic diatoms... 1/300" one-celled plants (phytoplankton). These feed small floating animals (zooplankton) which are eaten step by step by larger & larger animals. Calcium salts in the blood are concentrated by mollusks to crystalize protective shells. For such creatures, salt water is truly the bread & water of life!

DIATOM

← WIND

← WAVE MOVEMENT

- **Swells & ridges** moving across the surface of the sea may take many shapes & sizes. Rollers, "breakers", even "cat's paw" ripples ... most waves result from wind acting on the open ocean. A strong, steady blow forms waves, exerting direct force on the backside & an eddy on the front. This pushing & sucking effect moves the wave forward. The height, distance between ridges (called the "period") & length of waves are determined by wind speed & duration as well as by the "fetch" or distance the wave has traveled. The more massive waves make an oceanic journey of over 500 miles!

The wave moves... the water & bird do not!

- **Watch floating pelicans bob** the sea swells. The big birds stay in one position as the waves advance beneath them. As the wave runs forward (1), they ride up the oncoming front (2). When the crest passes by (3), the pelicans glide back to their original location (4). This up & down, wavetop orbit or "oscillation" reveals water particles do not move forward during wave action; rather, they only travel in a circular motion while the disturbance, caused by winds, moves forward.

- **Breakers** or surf waves form when waves run toward shore. Here the shoals cause the wave to drag bottom sand or rock. Moving more rapidly on the surface than on the bottom, the top-heavy crest rises steeply & soon slams forward in a wall of churning, white water.

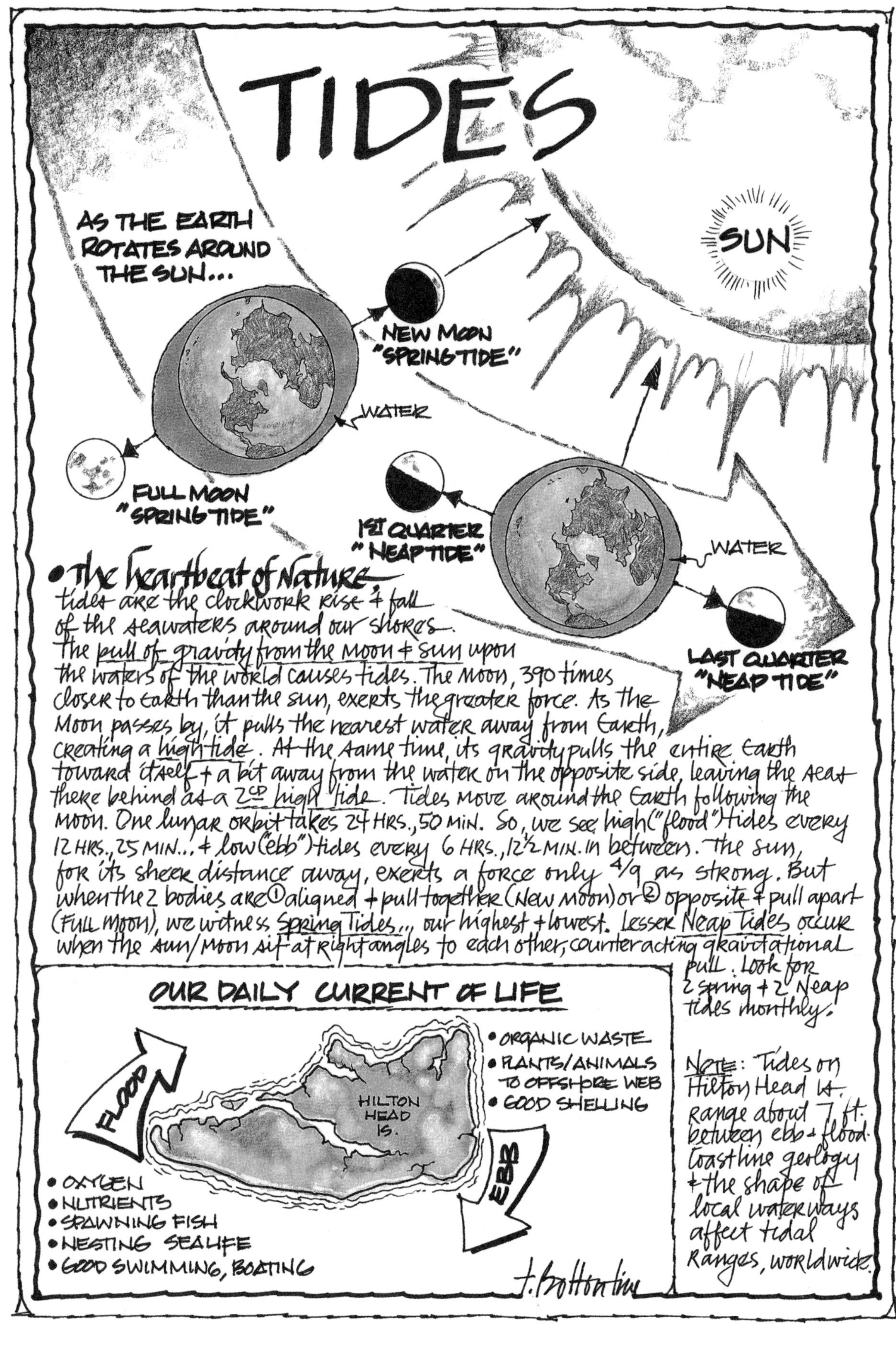

TIDES
AS THE EARTH ROTATES AROUND THE SUN...
SUN
NEW MOON "SPRING TIDE"
WATER
FULL MOON "SPRING TIDE"
1ST QUARTER "NEAP TIDE"
WATER
LAST QUARTER "NEAP TIDE"
• The heartbeat of Nature,
tides are the clockwork rise + fall of the seawaters around our shores. The pull of gravity from the moon + sun upon the waters of the world causes tides. The moon, 390 times closer to earth than the sun, exerts the greater force. As the Moon passes by, it pulls the nearest water away from Earth, creating a high tide. At the same time, its gravity pulls the entire Earth toward itself + a bit away from the water on the opposite side, leaving the seas there behind as a 2nd high tide. Tides move around the Earth following the moon. One lunar orbit takes 24 HRS., 50 MIN. So, we see high ("flood") tides every 12 HRS., 25 MIN... + low ("ebb") tides every 6 HRS., 12½ MIN. in between. The sun, for its sheer distance away, exerts a force only 4/9 as strong. But when the 2 bodies are ① aligned + pull together (New moon) or ② opposite + pull apart (Full moon), we witness Spring Tides... our highest + lowest. Lesser Neap Tides occur when the sun/moon sit at right angles to each other, counteracting gravitational pull. Look for 2 spring + 2 Neap tides monthly.
OUR DAILY CURRENT OF LIFE
FLOOD
HILTON HEAD IS.
EBB
• ORGANIC WASTE
• PLANTS/ANIMALS TO OFFSHORE WEB
• GOOD SHELLING
• OXYGEN
• NUTRIENTS
• SPAWNING FISH
• NESTING SEALIFE
• GOOD SWIMMING, BOATING
Note: Tides on Hilton Head Is. range about 7 ft. between ebb + flood. Coastline geology + the shape of local waterways affect tidal ranges, worldwide.
J. Bottontine

TIDAL CURRENTS

• **To watch the running sea** day after day is to learn of the enormous to & fro power of the tides. The sun & moon exert a gravitational pull on the whole ocean, producing the effect of high & low tides. Tidal currents occur when the incoming or out-going mass of water increases in height & forward motion along the coast. Normally, this "tidal wave" moves about 3 mph., but narrow passages like sounds constrict the water flood. Here the tides can run along at 12 mph.!

SOUND... FASTER CURRENT

OPEN SEA... SLOWER CURRENT

• **The danger of tidal currents** is that they can carry away floating objects in their path. Boaters know that to move forward against the current requires more fuel or sail than to move with it. Swimmers should beware that tides can pull individuals great distances along shore, especially in leeside sounds, creeks or inlets. When 2 tidal currents collide, a turbulent mix of churning water called a "rip" is formed. Here swimming is particularly hazardous! Should you be caught in a tidal current, keep calm & do not fight the tide. Float with the flow & swim slowly toward the beach. You may land some distance downshore... but you will arrive safely...

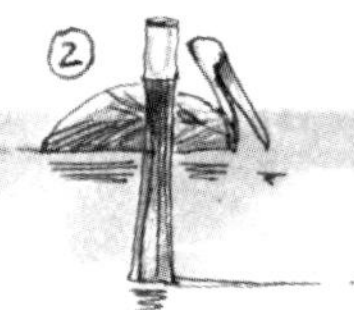

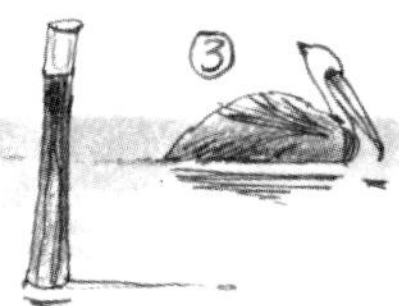

The apparent effortless floating-by of seabirds demonstrates the force of tidal currents.

UNDERTOW!

• **Waders, swimmers & surf fishermen beware** the seaside phenomenon known as an undertow. An undertow is a powerful current below the surface which flows back to sea from the beach. Waves crashing ashore first run quickly up the strand. Simple gravity causes the mass of water to flow back down the slope of the beach, even while the next wave advances forward over it. The most powerful undertow is caused by the steepest shoreface (example... the Cape Hatteras coast).

How an under-tow is caused

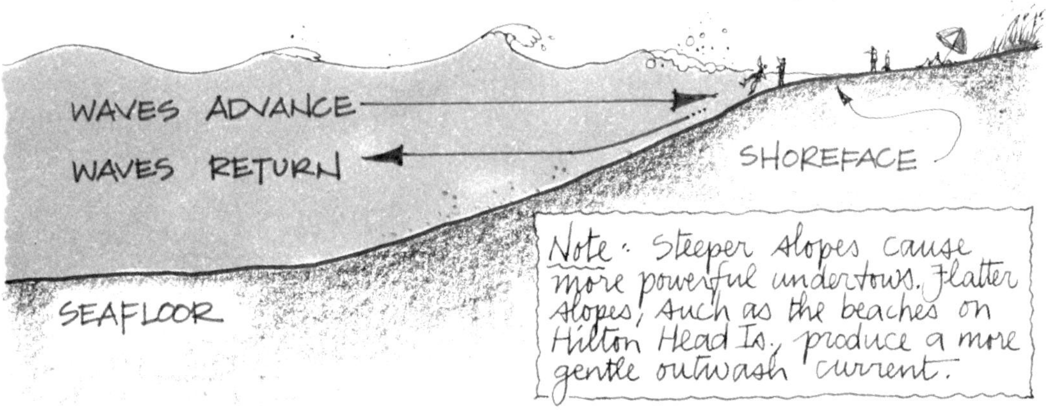

WAVES ADVANCE

WAVES RETURN

SHOREFACE

SEAFLOOR

Note: Steeper slopes cause more powerful undertows. Flatter slopes, such as the beaches on Hilton Head Is., produce a more gentle outwash current.

• **Danger!** Because an undertow is below surface, we who play in the ocean cannot see the current. Following a wave, one can take a spill and be sucked out to sea. If this should occur, remember:

1. An undertow pulls outward from the beach, not downward to the seafloor.
2. Victims should stay calm & float with the current to deeper water.
3. The undertow weakens in deeper water.
4. Swim slowly on the surface back to shore.

NOR'EASTER

● **The big blows** that push across the island from the Fall to April are well-known to "offseason" residents. A form of trade wind, nor'easters (or north-easters) accompany cold fronts with wind velocities to 25 mph & plunge temperatures by 10-20°. Constant stiff breezes stream from the northeast as a portion of an "anticyclone" high pressure zone behind the front. Here winds swirl in a clockwise manner & air currents descend to the center of the swirl. Fall & Spring, nor'easters bring cool, crisp & sunny weather. In the winter, drizzles lasting days are more common——..

NOR'EASTERS ARE FRONTAL WINDS FROM A HIGH PRESSURE CELL

THE PROBLEM WITH NOR'EASTERS: W+T+S+C → E

● Although many of us enjoy the sweater weather nor'easters bring, beachfront property owners fear the winds (W) for the erosion they cause. They blow for long (48 hrs. or more) stretches, non-stop. This pushes tides (T) onto shore & up in marsh creeks which does not allow ebb tides to recede entirely. So the following tide accumulates on top of the last, creating near flooding conditions. Wind-whipped surf (S), fueled by the tidal surplus, pounds at seawalls & dunes. Sand & even rocks are eroded & carried southward by the littoral or longshore current (C). All these factors of the nor'easter lead to significant erosion (E). The hardest hit areas seem to be the beaches between Folly Creek & the Holiday Inn——..

THE COLORED OCEAN

● **The pea green poridge** color of Southern seawater may surprise & even offend first time visitors to the Atlantic barrier isles. Why the murky water? Especially in Summertime, the ocean here is laden with diatoms. These are microscopic, one-celled plants ("phytoplankton") whose populations explode in warming water. Their chlorophyll-rich bodies give the sea a greenish tint. The brownish color is caused by abundant detritus (decayed plants & animals) floating in from leeside salt marshes. Current-borne silt from rivers emptying into nearby estuaries also muddies up the mix... a stirring of the ocean, the land & living & dead sealife which forms a nutritious but colorful Nature soup!

Diatoms

3 causes of the Ocean's color—...

Detritus

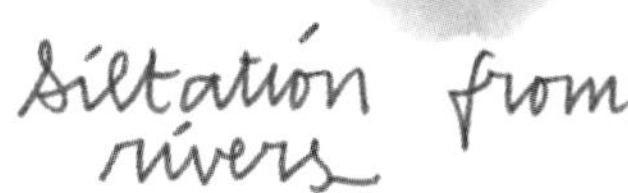

● **Blue seas are beautiful to view**, but in fact they are quite empty of ocean life. The aquamarine, postcard-perfect hue of Bahamian seas are caused by the scattering of light among water molecules unfettered by oceanic debris or nutrients like diatoms. The water disperses light particles in a manner similar to a blue sky. But compared to "South Carolina soup", those tropic seas are a watery desert in terms of their content of microscopic, living matter!

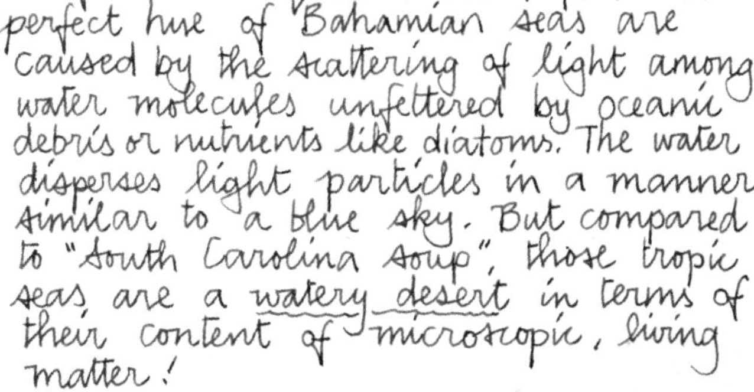

Where the Atlantic is greenest

PLANKTON

Invisible to the naked eye, but thick as soup in our waters are legions of drifting plants & animals called plankton. The name, plankton comes from the Greek word for "wandering". Plankton reproduces, feeds & dies on sea currents. Most lives in the ocean's sunny upper layers, using oil droplets or horny body projections to float, or by swimming with whip-like tails. Populations are dense in estuaries. There, abundant drainage from mainland soils supplies the plant plankton needed mineral salts. Fed this fertilizer, the organisms multiply incredibly (50 times more plankton abounds near the coast than in the open sea), turning our saltwater pea-green. Consumed by all animals... either directly or through the foodchain, plankton is the staple that sustains the world's sealife.

DINOFLAGELLATE

DIATOM

COCCOLITHOPHORE

◀ PHYTOPLANKTON:

Tiny, floating plants ("phyto") make up 80% of all plantlife on earth, counting numbers of organisms. Utilizing sunlight & dissolved nutrients, they create oxygen & carbohydrates eaten by tens of thousands of marine animals. DIATOMS are singular or long chains of silica shells joined like a box. They're most numerous. DINOFLAGELLATES are armored by cellulose cells. Most "swim" by whipping their "flagella" tails. COCCOLITHOPHORES, the sea's smallest, are made of calcium carbonate.

COPEPOD

ZOOPLANKTON ▶

These science-fiction animals graze on phytoplankton or each other. They're eaten by creatures ranging from menhaden to blue whales. Some are temporary plankton, like the larva of brittle stars & squirrel fish. Others are permanent, such as the common copepod (a 1/10" crustacean) & the well-known jellyfishes...

SQUIRREL FISH LARVA

JELLYFISH

BIOLUMINESCENCE

• **A star burst of night lights** in the summer surf is always a delight & a mystery to after-sundown beachwalkers. Seen as a sparkling show of, white, pin-point flashes, the phenomenon usually appears at waters edge, underfoot on tide flats, or to boaters in lee-side creeks. Bioluminescence is the name given to this odd effect. It is created by certain sea animals which produce light chemically without heat—.

NOCTICULA▸

• **The littlest lamplight** is a common one-celled zooplankton called, Nocticula (meaning, "light of the night"). The 1/50" flagellate which navigates using a whip-like "tail" frequents inshore waters, May to October. In season, it is so numerous that millions fill a single quart of seawater! Fish schooling thru their populations appear as eerie, glowing, zig-zag streaks in the evening waters. Nocticula makes "cold light" by a glandular release of enzymes which act on other internal substances, to produce a 3rd chemical and light energy. For such micro-creatures, bioluminescence serves no real function—.

• **Many animals of the sea & land are bioluminescent.** Some do use their body-glow to communicate or lure prey. Here is a sample of other creatures which produce this strange, heatless light.

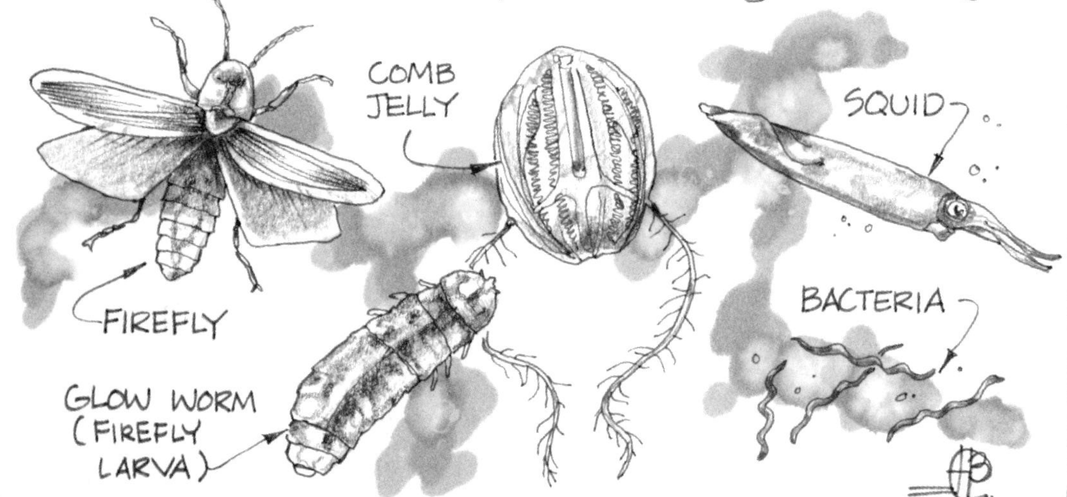

BARRIER ISLANDS

• **A broken necklace of sand isles** runs parallel to the Atlantic & Gulf coasts. Geologists call these tidewater landforms barrier islands. Like an outer line of defense, they protect the mainland from the effects of sea storms. It is estimated that there are 295 major barrier islands in the 18 coastal states, from Maine to Texas. Generally the terrain of a barrier isle is characterized by: ① A dynamic beach system with offshore bars, pounding surf & shifting or eroding beaches; ② a series of grassy dunes behind the beach; ③ maritime forests (see pp. 60-61) with wetlands in the interiors; ④ salt or tidal marshes on the lee side, facing the mainland. The classic shape of barrier islands is elongated with one end typically wider than the other (see the illustration, below).

Note: With 35 barrier islands (144,150 acres), South Carolina is 2nd in the number of islands to Florida (80).

• **The large barrier islands of the south**, including Kiawah, Pawley's & Hunting Islands, SC & Georgia's Sea Islands owe their origens to melting ice. When the Pleistocene Epoch ended 10,000 years ago, the great continental ice sheets thawed, causing the sea level to rise. Ridges & hills that once extended eastward on the mainland were cut off by the tidal surge. Lowlands & river valleys were inundated. Eventually, only high zones were left standing as isolated islands in the new, higher seas. Sedimentation from seaward-flowing rivers constantly adds material to the lee or baysides, building the cordgrass & mud prairies in our spacious saltmarshes. Meanwhile, storms & currents erode sand from the sandy seashores.

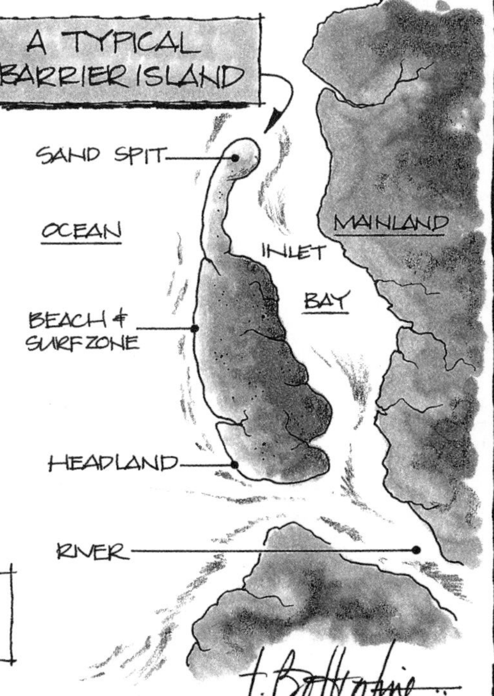

Note: Hilton Head Island is only half barrier island. Page 19 tells why...

COASTAL BREEZES

• **Lady's winds** – our land & sea breezes – make life more pleasant for residents of coastlines & barrier islands. They moderate the stickiest of summer's dogday hotspells. Even the bite of wintry chill is tempered by the warming blow. Weatherwatchers know that breezes here shift like clockwork, blowing onshore in daytime & offshore at night. This effect is caused by differing surface temperatures of the land & ocean.

Onshore Breezes...

• The morning sun bakes the landmass which heats faster than the sea. The air above it heats, expands & rises upwards. Cool air currents from the ocean flow landward to replace the risen hot air. So, as the day grows brighter, onshore breezes increase.

Note: Land gains & loses heat more quickly. Seawater stays at a more constant temperature.

Offshore Breezes...

• After sundown, the landmass quickly loses its heat. Soon it is cooler than the sea. Warmer sea air, retaining heat, expands & rises upwards. Cool air from the coast rushes seaward to replace the risen warm air. So, as the night grows later, offshore breezes increase.

The Beach

Hilton Head Island has broad, flat sand beaches with long tidepools, making for hours of recreational souvenir hunting and dawdling fun for children. Yet, the shore on neighboring Daufuskie Island, less than 2 miles away, is a clayey driftwood museum. Edisto Beach State Park, South Carolina, is *the* beach for finding fossils in these parts. Out on windswept Cape Hatteras, the steep yellow strand is a graveyard of shipwrecks. And so goes the wondrous diversity of seashores: No one beach copies another.

Even on Hilton Head, we have our nearly wilderness beaches, beaches stacked high with "armor" (rock revetments to fend off waves from homes), muddy clamming beaches, best birding beaches, dolphin watching beaches and of course, crowded sunbathing beaches. I have included a five-part section called "Beach Walks" to show the diversity here. Apply the lessons learned to similar shores in the Southeast.

When the tides run from flood to ebb, you will find mysterious and weird flotsam awash on the soggy sandflats. Pick it up... the slimier the better... and study it. There is nothing commonplace about the blobs and gobs on our shores. They wriggle and tickle and pinch and swell and shrink and sag, and boy can they smell bad after cooking all morning in the southern sun.

A show-off tan can be a side benefit, or a sunburn the curse, of beachcombing; so remember to apply good quality sunblock before heading outdoors. At day's end, pebbly mementos of your excursion will tumble out of sandals, bathing suits and hair. One way or the other, you will never forget our beaches.

They are the gems of the first water.

BEACH WALKS...PART I
DOLPHIN HEAD

MARSH | PINE ISLAND | BEACH | PORT ROYAL SOUND

THE VIEW NORTH

PINCKNEY ISLAND

DAW'S ISLAND

OVERWASH ZONE

OLD MARSH GRASS PEAT

RIP-RAP

• **Hilton Head's Northern Frontier** is the fragile ribbon of sand called Dolphin Head. Located in Hilton Head Plantation, this strand is hemmed by Port Royal Sound (north) & Bear Creek saltmarsh (south). The beach, a razor's edge between quiet cordgrass meadows & the churning sea, is an ephemeral moment in geologic time. With each tide, the sea floods & the sand rolls back into the marsh.

• **Dolphin Head** names the high bluffs overlooking Port Royal Sound ... home for Atlantic bottlenosed dolphins. The bluffs have eroded dramatically. Once the homesite for William Elliott's Myrtle Bank plantation house, the land has lost 250 ft. since 1860. Elliott's once-proud foundation now lies crumbling in the tideflat, offshore. Waterfront property owners have built a sloped, "rip-rap" stone seawall to slow erosion. But storm waves & currents, diverted by the rocks, have pounded the open beach with a vengeance. The sidewalk-wide strand leads to Pine Island. Centuries past, this 1 acre hammock probably adjoined the bluffs. During spring tides & storms, the sea now washes over the beach & into the marsh, turning the wetland into a bay.

• **Beachcombing Dolphin Head:** Sun-bleached oyster rakes, clusters of dead shells cemented with calcium, abound. Colorful sea whip corals hold fast to the bigger oysters. Weathered, rust-brown mud lumps (2-5"), eroded from the bluffs, litter the shore. Blackish periwinkle snails scavenge in tidepools. Deer tracks are sign that whitetails browse the marsh & Pine Island greenery.

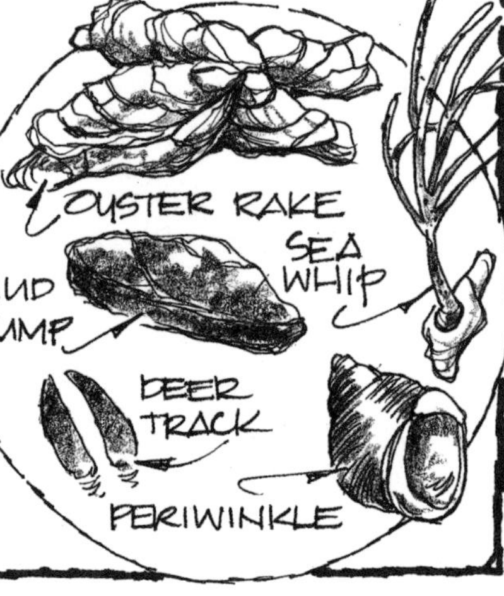

OYSTER RAKE

SEA WHIP

MUD LUMP

DEER TRACK

PERIWINKLE

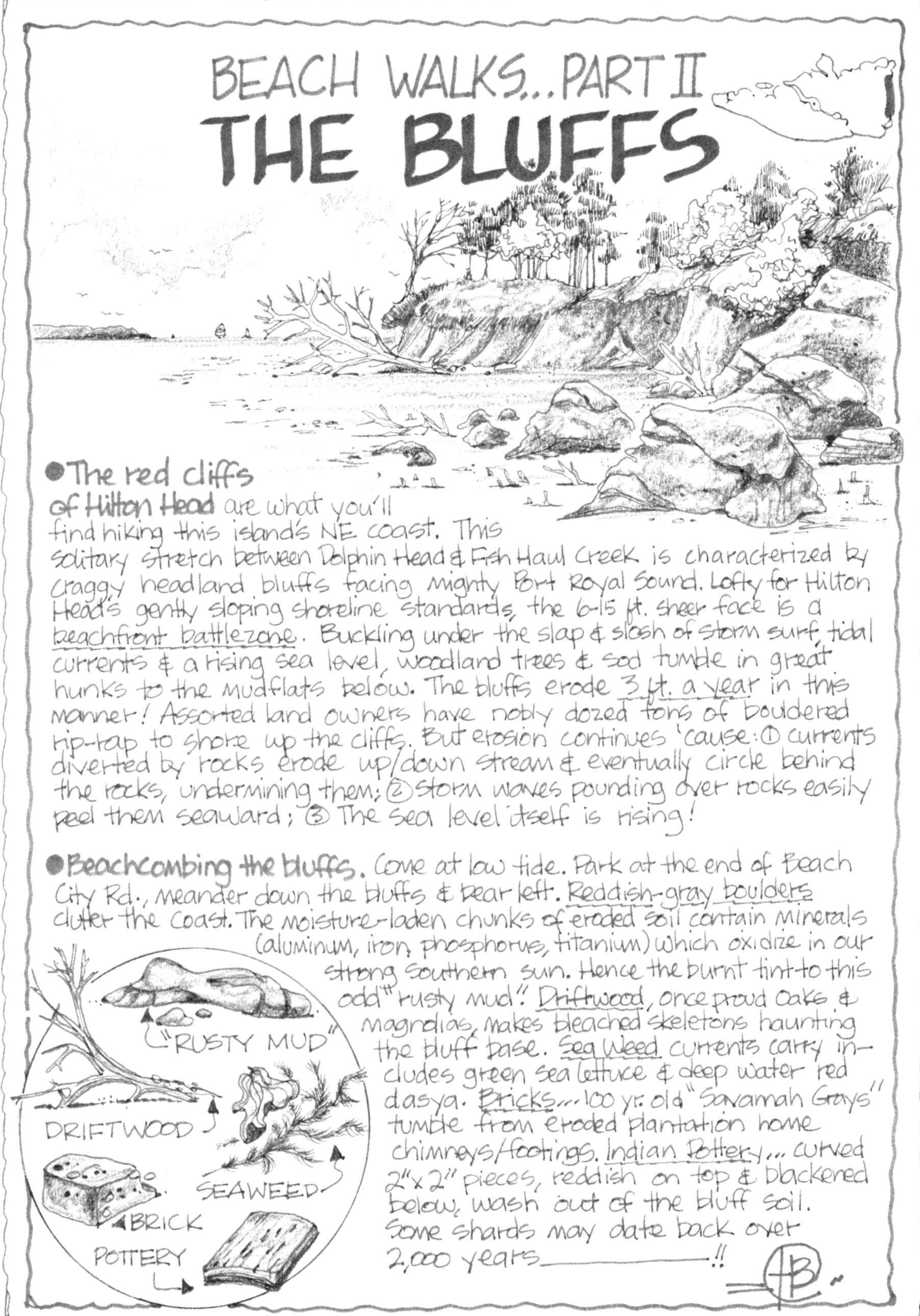

BEACH WALKS... PART II
THE BLUFFS

●The red cliffs of Hilton Head are what you'll find hiking this island's NE coast. This solitary stretch between Dolphin Head & Fish Haul Creek is characterized by craggy headland bluffs facing mighty Port Royal Sound. Lofty for Hilton Head's gently sloping shoreline standards, the 6-15 ft. sheer face is a beachfront battlezone. Buckling under the slap & slosh of storm surf, tidal currents & a rising sea level, woodland trees & sod tumble in great hunks to the mudflats below. The bluffs erode 3 ft. a year in this manner! Assorted land owners have nobly dozed tons of bouldered rip-rap to shore up the cliffs. But erosion continues 'cause: ① currents diverted by rocks erode up/down stream & eventually circle behind the rocks, undermining them; ② storm waves pounding over rocks easily peel them seaward; ③ The sea level itself is rising!

●Beachcombing the bluffs. Come at low tide. Park at the end of Beach City Rd., meander down the bluffs & bear left. Reddish-gray boulders clutter the coast. The moisture-laden chunks of eroded soil contain minerals (aluminum, iron, phosphorus, titanium) which oxidize in our strong southern sun. Hence the burnt tint to this odd "rusty mud"! Driftwood, once proud oaks & magnolias, makes bleached skeletons haunting the bluff base. Sea Weed currents carry includes green sea lettuce & deep water red dasya. Bricks... 100 yr. old "Savannah Grays" tumble from eroded plantation home chimneys/footings. Indian Pottery... curved 2"x2" pieces, reddish on top & blackened below, wash out of the bluff soil. Some shards may date back over 2,000 years——!!

BEACH WALKS...PART III
"HILTON HEAD"

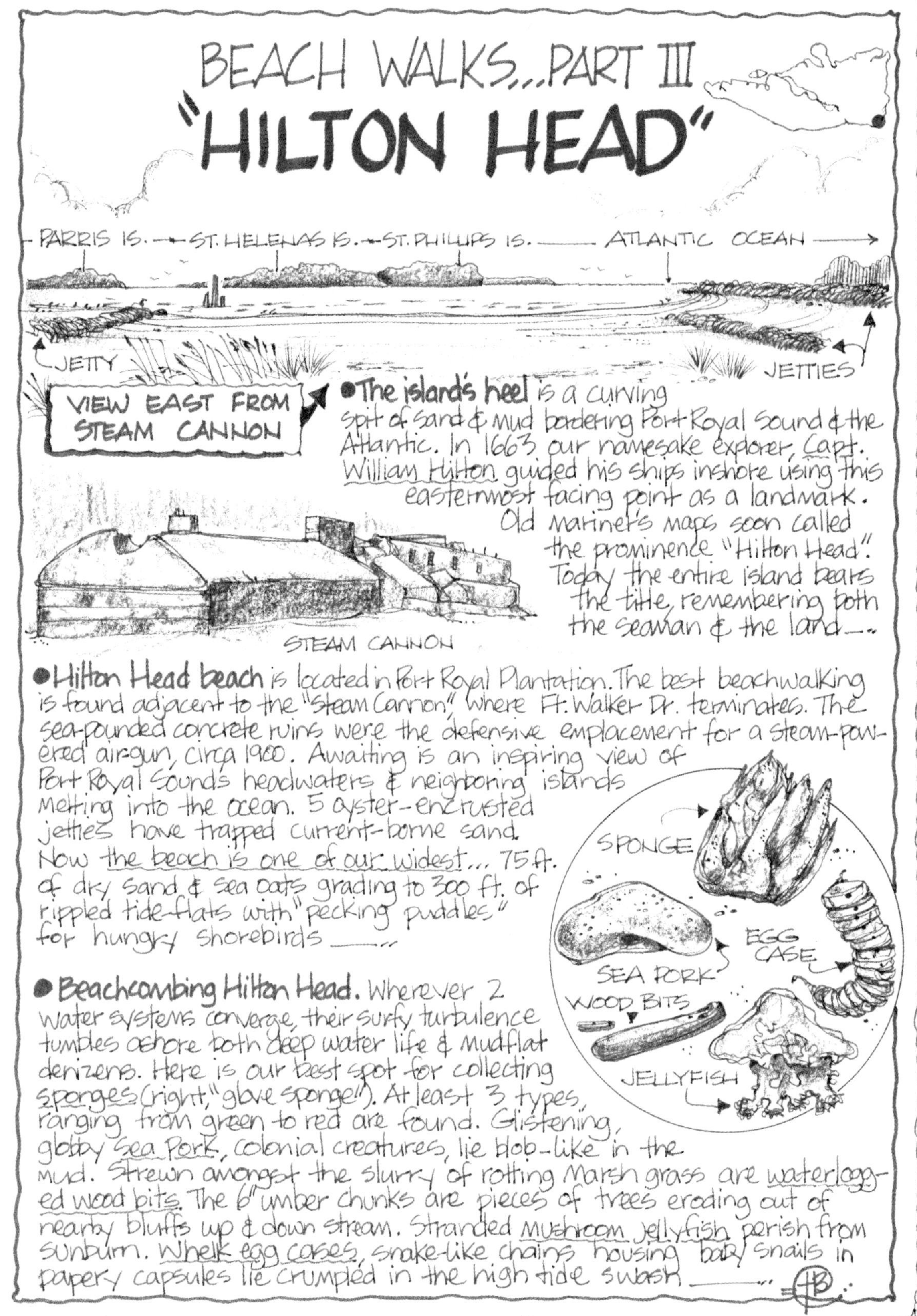

• **The island's heel** is a curving spit of sand & mud bordering Port Royal Sound & the Atlantic. In 1663 our namesake explorer, Capt. William Hilton guided his ships inshore using this easternmost facing point as a landmark. Old mariner's maps soon called the prominence "Hilton Head". Today the entire island bears the title, remembering both the seaman & the land....

• **Hilton Head beach** is located in Port Royal Plantation. The best beachwalking is found adjacent to the "Steam Cannon," where Ft. Walker Dr. terminates. The sea-pounded concrete ruins were the defensive emplacement for a steam-powered airgun, circa 1900. Awaiting is an inspiring view of Port Royal Sound's headwaters & neighboring islands melting into the ocean. 5 oyster-encrusted jetties have trapped current-borne sand. Now the beach is one of our widest... 75 ft. of dry sand & sea oats grading to 300 ft. of rippled tide-flats with "pecking puddles" for hungry shorebirds ....

• **Beachcombing Hilton Head.** Wherever 2 water systems converge, their surfy turbulence tumbles ashore both deep water life & mudflat denizens. Here is our best spot for collecting sponges (right, "glove sponge"). At least 3 types, ranging from green to red are found. Glistening, globby Sea Pork, colonial creatures, lie blob-like in the mud. Strewn amongst the slurry of rotting marsh grass are waterlogged wood bits. The 6" umber chunks are pieces of trees eroding out of nearby bluffs up & down stream. Stranded Mushroom Jellyfish perish from sunburn. Whelk egg cases, snake-like chains housing baby snails in papery capsules lie crumpled in the high tide swash ....

BEACH WALKS...PART IV
THE ROCKS
●The beach that isn't, the shoreline called "North Forest Beach" is submerged under 10 ft. of seawater at high tide. Stretching between Heron St. & Yucca St. is frontage suffering extreme erosion. A southbound "littoral drift" current & a rising sea level has peeled dunes back inland 10 ft. a year! To barricade their dangling homes, most residents here have constructed colossal rock seawalls to rebuff attacking waves. So the effect of this strand at ebb is a low, flat valley hemmed by 15 ft. craggy cliffs & the angry sea, squared off like 2 menacing armies awaiting their appointed tidal battle....
PALM STUB
●Rock crevice ecology. Seawalls here are built by grading sand banks, laying on a thick black nylon mesh & weighting it down with tremendous aggregate boulders. Big rocks measure 6 ft. across. But high surf floating suspended sand, dirt & salt hay chips off small pebbles, 10 to a fistful. The gravely debris packs the crevices, making protected hideaways for odd 'critters like Sea roaches (1¼"). These long-tailed, brown reminders of cockroaches slither the rocks eating rotting flotsam....
GREENBRIAR TUBER
SEA ROACH
ARK SHELL
TWIG
●Beachcombing by the rocks. Hike up from the "public Beach"... clambering down the slippery rocks is dangerous! Scavenge the sea wall base & nearby tide pools. Rolling across the sand is fluffy foam. Water pounding the rocks like boiling milk forms this bubbly blend of silt & sea salts. Potato-like greenbriar tubers (2-6") pile up. These knobby root systems from a spiny climbing vine, eroded from dunes, are considered edible cooked. Where no seawalls exist, Yaupon Holly bushes tumble beachward, their spindly twigs perishing from exposure. Eroded, too, are palm trees, "no-see-ums" swarming their stringy root stubs. Found shells include graceful ark & coquina clams, moon snails....

BEACH WALKS...PART V

SOUTH BEACH

● **The toe end** to our foot-shaped Island is called "South Beach" on Sea Pines maps. Bending around south to west from Painted Bunting Rd. to Braddock's Cove Creek, it's a wide-open sand spit formed by 2 coastal currents. Here a southbound longshore current, floating sand eroded from No. Forest Beach, slams into Calibogue Sound's rip tide outflow. The 2 streams neutralize each other & sand is dumped in place at the mouth of the Sound. Created is Hilton Heads widest beach & a turbulent shoalwater feeding ground where romp gamefish, pelicans, osprey & dolphin ——→.

● **South Beach is swelling!** From 1968-80 this strand widened 400 ft., with 12 ft. of verticle height! In one night Hurricane David ('79) layed down a "big berm" of soft, clean sand 5 ft. high, 50 ft. wide & 600 yds. long at the high water line. 4 breakwater jetties are all but buried now & look like single file concrete grave stones. Shorebirds skitter sand flats where dolphin dove a decade ago. Breakers on the horizon 3 mi. out from Bald Eagle Rd. show where sand bars will build up our South Beach spit of the future——!

● **South Beachcombing.** Park at South Beach Village, wander beachward via the Raquet Club paths. Here collect nerf-ball sized cones dropped by tremendous "yellow pines" flat-topped by salt air. The high beach's steep slope is caused by Calibogue Sound's cutting, sideways currents. Search the squeeky-fine sand (only the lightest grains float on currents) for fingery Codmium or sponge seaweed, sunburned brown. The shore flattens as you hike toward the Atlantic, revealing bleached sand dollars, many crunched by surf. Sea Cucumbers shrink at your touch. Littering the flats is a 'pasta' of broken clam worm tubes, & "chocolate jimmies"... fecal pellets from burrowed sand shrimp——...

THE SHAPE
OF HILTON HEAD ISLAND

● **Coastal contours** on Hilton Head Island have been moving since time immemorial. The island's peculiar footshape is the product of erosion in 2 distinct geologic periods. In the Pleistocene Epoch (1.75 million–10,000 years ago), higher sea levels deposited sand on the northern sector. As recently as the Holocene Epoch (5,000–10,000 years ago), rising sea level deposited a barrier fringe on the Pleistocene core... forming the areas from Port Royal Plantation to Sea Pines.

SPIT
② HOLOCENE FRINGE (BARRIER ISLAND)
① PLEISTOCENE CORE (SEA ISLAND)
BROAD CR.
*CURRENTS
NORTH

① **Ancient Hilton Head** (Dark area): A crescent-shaped plateau that impeded waves & collected sand, this Sea Island extended perhaps a mile N.E. into Port Royal Sound & So. into Broad Creek.

② **Present Hilton Head** (Light area): Storm waves & longshore currents* erode northern headlands & transport most of the sand southward. The southern "toe" of this Barrier Island is a "spit" of sand that the currents drop. Broad Creek is now a landlocked tidal marsh.

③ **Future Hilton Head** (Dark area): Rising sea levels & storms will erode the beachfront from Dolphin Head to northern Sea Pines (light area). Unless this shoreline is "nourished" with new-pumped sand, it could recede as much as 100 yards. Waters will tear at dunes, rock revetments & unfortunately, homes & hotels. The currents will send the loose sand south. The spit at South Beach could accrete (grow) miles into Calibogue Sound. The island would become narrower & longer. And 10,000 years from now? Some predict higher seas will submerge this Sea/Barrier isle entirely. Then, Hilton Head will be hailed as a resort most attractive to snorklers!

J. Bottomley

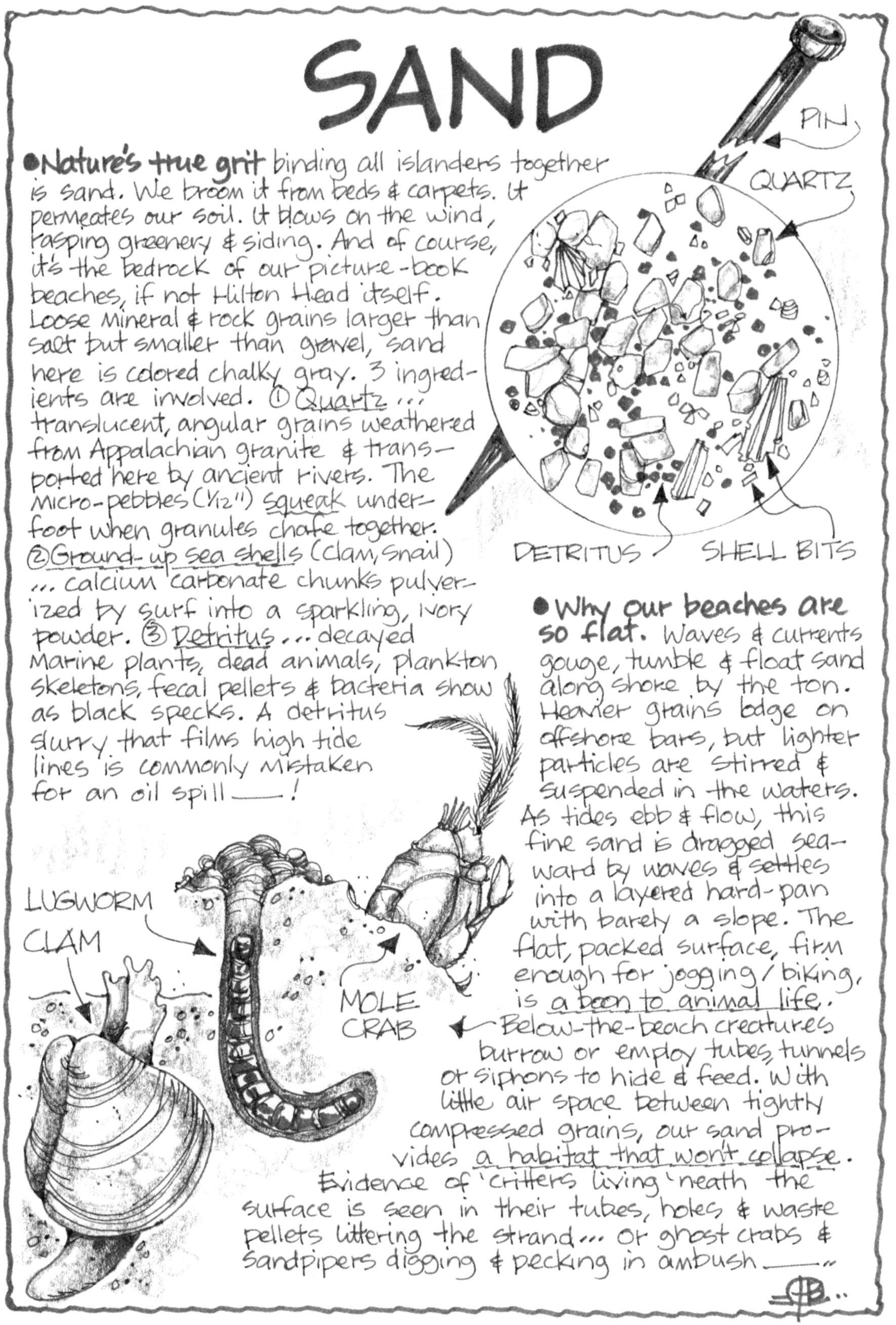
SAND
PIN
QUARTZ
DETRITUS
SHELL BITS
Nature's true grit binding all islanders together is sand. We broom it from beds & carpets. It permeates our soil. It blows on the wind, rasping greenery & siding. And of course, it's the bedrock of our picture-book beaches, if not Hilton Head itself. Loose mineral & rock grains larger than salt but smaller than gravel, sand here is colored chalky gray. 3 ingredients are involved. ① Quartz ... translucent, angular grains weathered from Appalachian granite & transported here by ancient rivers. The micro-pebbles (1/12") squeak underfoot when granules chafe together. ② Ground-up sea shells (clam, snail) ... calcium carbonate chunks pulverized by surf into a sparkling, ivory powder. ③ Detritus ... decayed marine plants, dead animals, plankton skeletons, fecal pellets & bacteria show as black specks. A detritus slurry that films high tide lines is commonly mistaken for an oil spill —!
Why our beaches are so flat. Waves & currents gouge, tumble & float sand along shore by the ton. Heavier grains lodge on offshore bars, but lighter particles are stirred & suspended in the waters. As tides ebb & flow, this fine sand is dragged seaward by waves & settles into a layered hard-pan with barely a slope. The flat, packed surface, firm enough for jogging / biking, is a boon to animal life.
LUGWORM
CLAM
MOLE CRAB
Below-the-beach creatures burrow or employ tubes, tunnels or siphons to hide & feed. With little air space between tightly compressed grains, our sand provides a habitat that won't collapse. Evidence of 'critters living 'neath the surface is seen in their tubes, holes & waste pellets littering the strand ... or ghost crabs & sandpipers digging & pecking in ambush —..

SAND PATTERNS

● **SWASH LINES...** When uprushing waves skim up the beach, a thin film of water bulldozes a line of sand & flotsam ahead of itself. After the swash sinks into sand & slides back seaward, arcing debris formations remain at the high water mark like a "scorecard of wave action." Watch scavenger shorebirds tip-toe single file along these breadlines of beach morsels. Hunt here for shells...

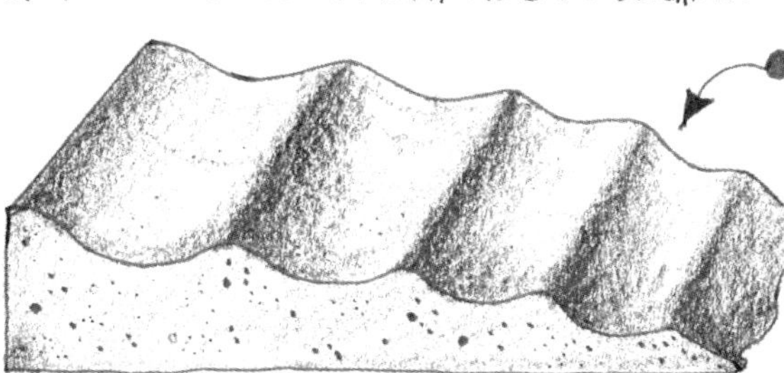

● **RIPPLE MARKS...** Show as small waves in the sand on low tide flats. Ripples form under the back & forth motion of high tide water moving across shoal sand. Average onshore ripple measures 2–3" crest to crest.

● **PINHOLES & SAND DOMES...** High tide's premier waves invade dry beach sand. Air trapped between grains bubbles out thru' pin-head sized holes. The 2nd wave's swash seals off escaping air under a crust of wet sand. Air pressure inside pumps up a sandy dome (inset, right). It collapses easily if you tap it with your toe—...

● **RILLS...** Miniature river deltas draining high tide swash back to the sea. Rills float out debris, shells & animals, thus make good beachcombing—...

● **CUSPS** (top view, right)... Odd concave, crescent-shaped depressions evenly spaced across the wet beach. They may form when uprushing swash excavates this small bay, dredging the center on the ebb. Successive waves surge in, deepening cusps.

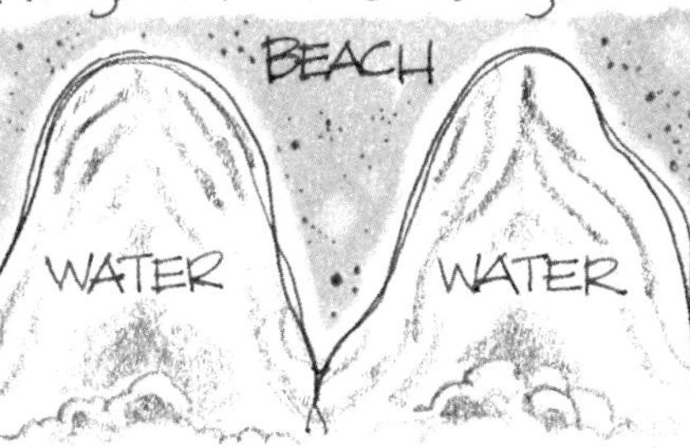

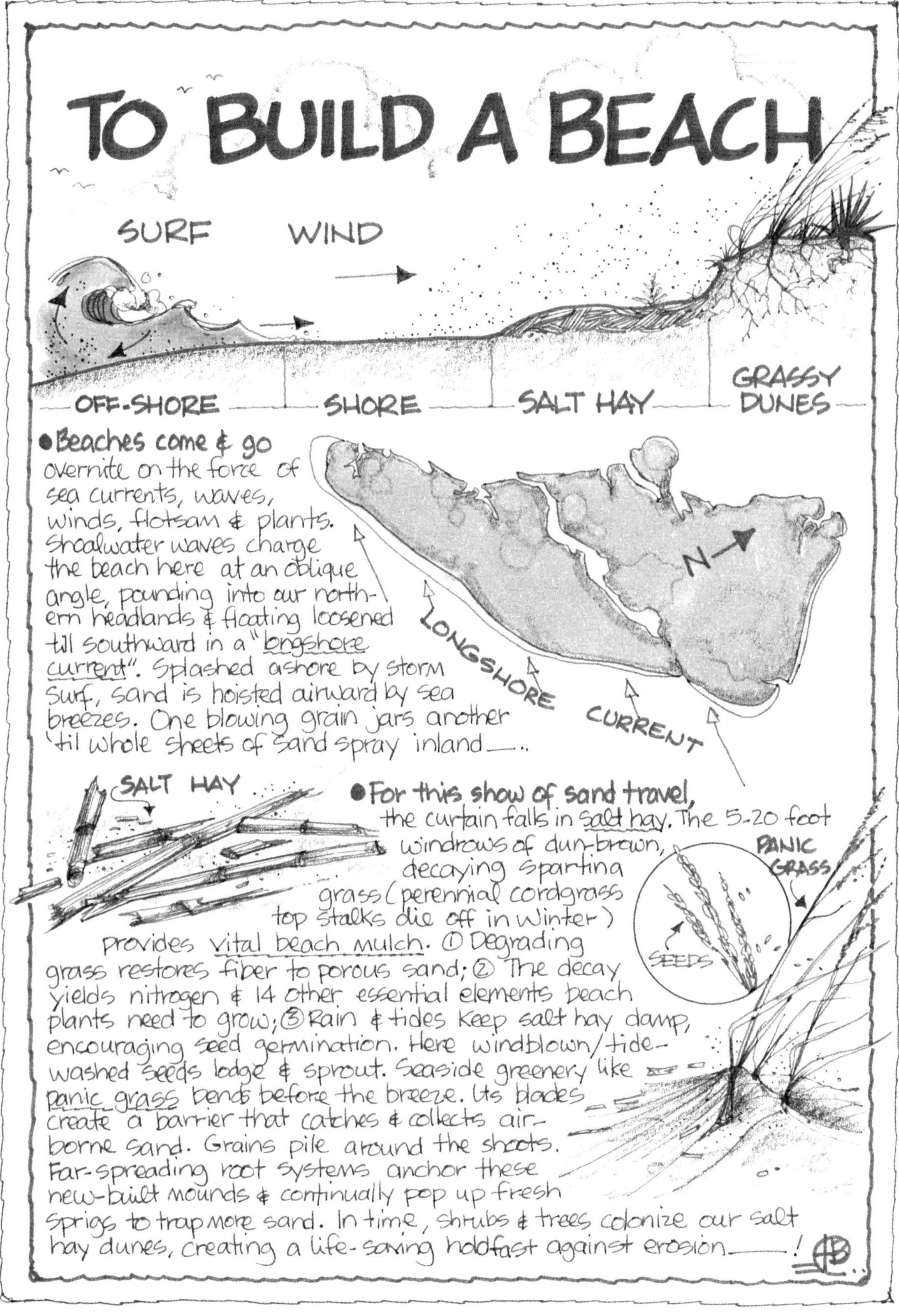
TO BUILD A BEACH
SURF
WIND
OFF-SHORE
SHORE
SALT HAY
GRASSY DUNES
●Beaches come & go
overnite on the force of sea currents, waves, winds, flotsam & plants. Shoalwater waves charge the beach here at an oblique angle, pounding into our northern headlands & floating loosened till southward in a "longshore current". Splashed ashore by storm surf, sand is hoisted airward by sea breezes. One blowing grain jars another 'til whole sheets of sand spray inland——..
N
LONGSHORE
CURRENT
SALT HAY
●For this show of sand travel,
the curtain falls in salt hay. The 5-20 foot windrows of dun-brown, decaying spartina grass (perennial cordgrass top stalks die off in winter) provides vital beach mulch. ① Degrading grass restores fiber to porous sand; ② The decay yields nitrogen & 14 other essential elements beach plants need to grow; ③ Rain & tides keep salt hay damp, encouraging seed germination. Here windblown/tide-washed seeds lodge & sprout. Seaside greenery like panic grass bends before the breeze. Its blades create a barrier that catches & collects airborne sand. Grains pile around the shoots. Far-spreading root systems anchor these new-built mounds & continually pop up fresh sprigs to trap more sand. In time, shrubs & trees colonize our salt hay dunes, creating a life-saving holdfast against erosion——!
PANIC GRASS
SEEDS

The Night Beach

• **A sandy secret** that sunbathers never know is how fascinating wildlife becomes in the shore & shoals after dark—

Owls hunt rats in the dunes, chuck-wills-widows catch moths on the wing.

Raccoons scavenge tide pools. Cotton rats raid grass, seeds. Even deer venture forth to graze sea oats.

Ghost crabs scurry up & down the strand to scavenge the tidal wrack—

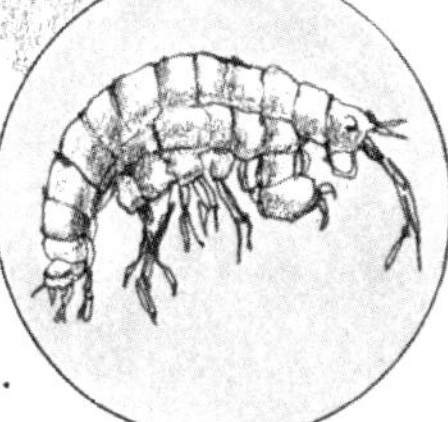

Beach hoppers emerge from burrows to feed on dead seashore matter.

* Sea hares are snails without shells!

Skates, dogfish, kilifish, squid & sea hares* feed in shallow water at low tide.

Mysid shrimps, isopods and copepods float from the sea floor to the surface in the protective dark.

Surface-dwelling during daytime, plant plankton settle into deeper water—

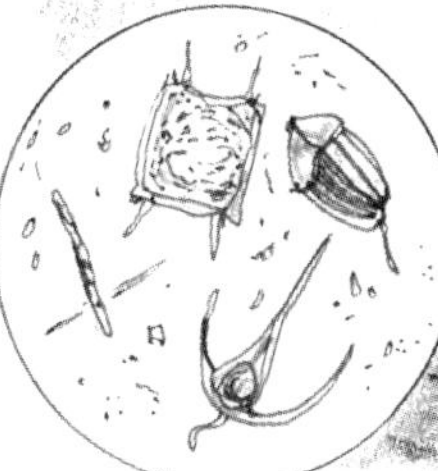

AUTUMN The BEACH

Falling temperatures bring a cooling in the air & water. Along the shore, Summer's frenzy of living activity matures to a season of storms, wildflower colors, & the comings and goings of familiar seaside animals.

Autumn Activity...

Plant plankton "blooms" or grows rapidly, nourished by stirrings of dissolved nutrients in seawater during storms.

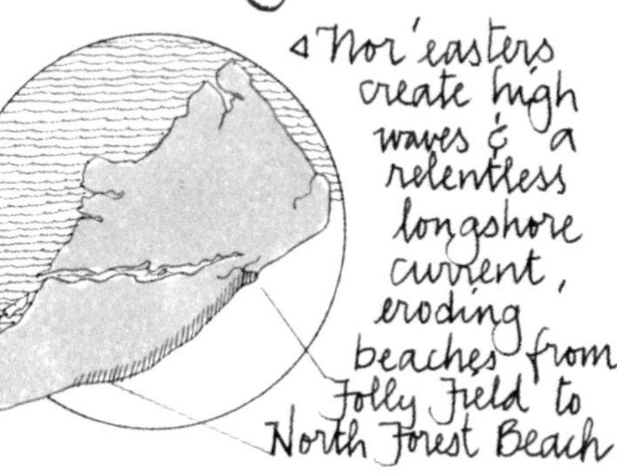

Nor'easters create high waves & a relentless longshore current, eroding beaches from Folly Field to North Forest Beach.

Migrating birds & butterflies, fill the skies of the Atlantic Flyway with wild wing-beats and bright color.

Swimming crabs migrate into deeper waters offshore, where temperatures are more constant.

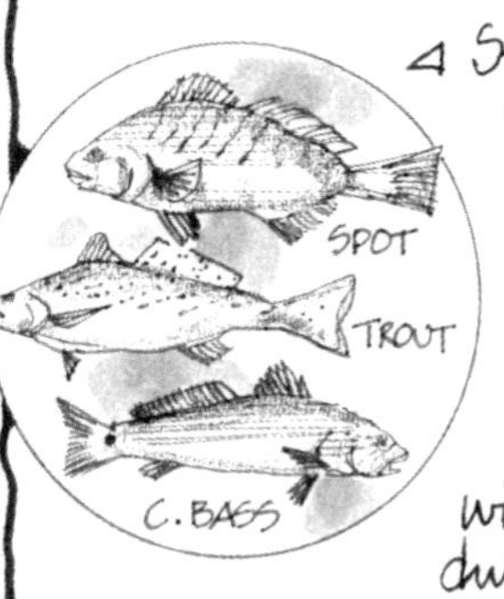

Spots, trout & channel bass migrate into surf & inshore creeks as waters cool. Fishing there will be superb during Fall months!

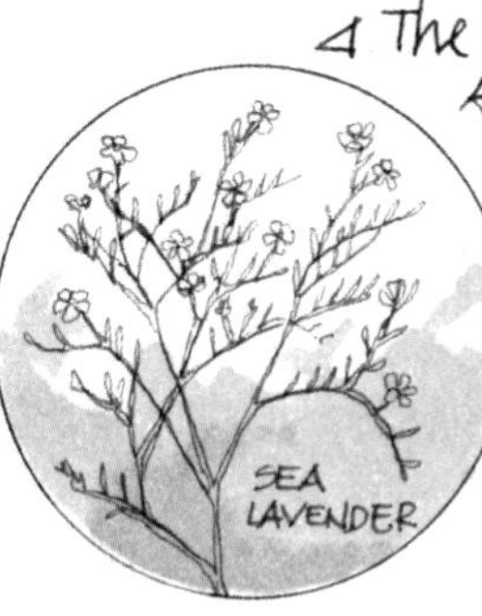

The rainbow of sea-side flower colors includes salt myrtle (white); sea oxeye, gold-enrod & camph-orweed (yellow); sea oats (gold); sea lavender (lavender).

LIFE ON THE
WINTER BEACH
The wild beauty of the wide-open beach, untrammeled by umbrellas, radio blare & broiling crowds beckons to nature lovers when cold times come here. Weekly Nor'Westers blow in clear, bright days & high-pressure skies offer miles-away visibility. Watch for Cormorant formations 100 yds. out or Scoter ducks dotting the horizon, above—
Erosion.. storm surf pummels our weak dunes, peeling away grassy edges. Wind & waves spread sands into powdery piles on the high beach, pound it rock-hard at waterside.
Driftwood.. uprooted by eroding waves, timber intricately sculpted by surf, sand blast & burrowing ship worms tumbles ashore.
Sentinel Gulls brave the blow, heads pointed windward, awaiting wave-washed morsels. These scavengers aren't too proud to raid nearby dumpsters or to gulp palm berries! Note dragging tracks in sand.
A
B
C
D
E
Flotsam torn loose by currents & surf, includes Ⓐ Seaweeds snarled with Ⓑ Magenta or yellow Sea Whip Coral; Ⓒ Piles of Coquina Clams; Ⓓ Cast-off Crab claws; Ⓔ A macaroni of clam worm tubes. Rotting flotsam nourishes below-sand creatures.
A
B
First Spring Plants sprout. Hardy Ⓐ Sea Rocket, a rubbery-leaved mustard, grows at high tide lines. Ⓑ Mingled with dune grasses, Thistles send out rosettes of 6" prickly leaves.

SLOUGHS

● **One of the islands' most unique natural systems** has one of the oddest names... the slough. Pronounced sloo, a slough is a linear depression or bottomland usually filled with water, mud & aquatic plants. Today these wet swales commonly run parallel to & are located west of the seashore. Ridges isolate the slough to the east & west. Sloughs originated as ancient shorelines during the last "Ice Age" (approx. 10,000 years ago). When the sea level dropped (due to glacial refreezing), these low zones of wave action were stranded inland. New beaches formed to the east as the sea receded. What were ancient dunes are now forested ridges containing the slough.

W
E
Salt Marsh
Ridge
Slough
Ridge
Slough
Ridge
Dunes/Shore
Sea

● **The 2-way life cycle of a slough... wet & dry.**

Note: The roller-coaster topography of a barrier island reveals sloughs lying parallel to today's dunes & shore.

Wet period (Mar-Sept., Dec-Jan.): During normal rain, nor'easters, even hurricanes, sloughs collect "runoff" water. Wetlands (marshes/swamps/bogs) are formed. These provide breeding grounds for frogs, insects, crayfish & fish. Woodland plants invading the slough are drowned-out, establishing an open-water environment.

Dry Period (Sept-Dec., Feb-Mar.): Water levels fall due to insoak, plant transpiration & evaporation. Fish/frogs concentrate in the shrinking pools & are hunted by wading birds. Some sloughs "vanish" or completely dry-up. Open-water plants are exposed & die. Once again the slough bed is cleared. As the year's leaves, stems & twigs decompose, valuable nutrients are restored to the soil.

SLOUGHS... A BOON TO MAN

• **Natural wetlands forming between dunes & ridges** are far too often overlooked as useful & too commonly dredged, filled & forever destroyed on "developing" barrier islands. However, citizens here must realize how these sloughs perform critical functions which affect our very lives. For the 4 reasons below, marshes, swamps & bogs must be conserved.

① **Flood Control**: Low-lying troughs absorb & retrain rainfall & hurricane surge which would flood houses/roads. In drier weather, wetlands release their store of water to nearby creeks.

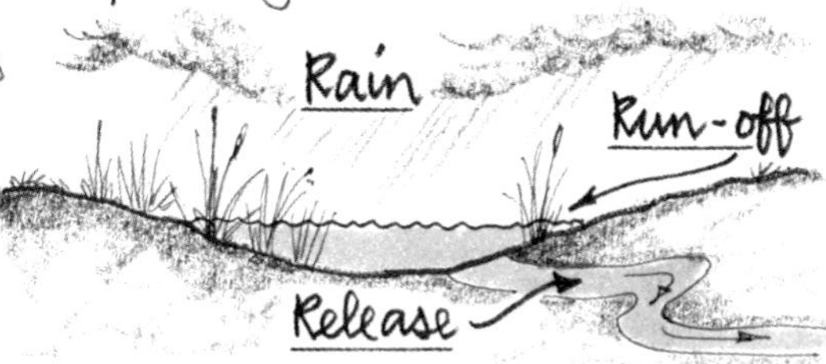

② **Pollution Cleansing**: Sewage, pesticides, chemical fertilizers, heavy metals & animal wastes are trapped by slough plantlife. Bound in the mesh of roots & oxygen-poor soil, pollutants like nitrates are transformed into harmless substances by bacteria. The water seeping underground would be filtered free of dangerous compounds by the slough.

③ **Groundwater Recharge**: Collected surface water percolates into the soil to underground reservoirs, restoring shallow supplies needed by plants, & perhaps deeper (artesian) sources consumed by humans.

④ **Recreation**: Fishing, photography & nature study are easily available quite near the beach to all who make the small effort to visit sloughs, the barrier isles' hiddenmost resource.

How to go BEACHCOMBING

• The sea island coast is a rich nursery of plant & animal life. Amateur naturalists & shorewalkers may collect a trove of colorful shells & live marine creatures by treading the broad sandflats between the tides. Beachcombing here is cheap & easy outdoor recreation, as well as an aerobic exercise for all ages. For best results, follow the simple pointers below which highlight clothing, locations & equipment to take.

What to wear	Tools to take	Where to look
Summer: A sunhat, T-shirt, bathing suit & sneakers if near oysters. Winter: layered clothing, gloves & hat. Always: sunglasses.	Trowel or kitchen knife for digging; bucket & jars for collecting specimens; magnifying glass; field glasses & field guides.	Sandflats between high & low tide, especially following storms; tidal pools; inlet mud-flats; wrack (debris) at high tide line.

Three marine lifestyles to search...

Anchorers

Crawlers

Clams
Worms, shrimp.
Mole crabs

Burrowers

Note: Fresh marine specimens may be preserved in rubbing alcohol. Clean snails & clams by boiling the shells. Starfish & sand dollars may be sun-dried.

TIDE POOL
ECOLOGY
From Port Royal Sound to South Beach, tide pools are created when along-the-shore currents excavate bottom sand as they run their course parallel to the coast, at high tide. When seawaters ebb, long drainage "puddles" filled with marine life will sculpt the beach. Surf-scattered plants & animals are now trapped within the steep walls of the mini-lagoons. As the mid-day sun cooks the shoals to 100°, the water evaporates, gets shallower & turns saltier. Some creatures burrow in the soft bottom silt, but most get sluggish in the brine & in turn are eaten by larger animals from the pool or the beach. So,,, these little creeks make tidewater aquariums where beachcombers can explore the quick & violent circles of life & death here on the strand,,
Marine snails, Hermit Crabs and fingerling fish schools invade pools to hunt seaweed & insect larvae washed ashore,,
Cast up by wind & surf, Jellyfish pursue fish in the deeper pools, but will die on the sand when waters drain!
The mobile, agressive meat-eaters, like Atlantic Blue Crabs & starfish outmaneuver smaller crawling 'critters ... and may clean out the pool before it ever dries up —!
Scavenger birds such as Gulls or Fish Crows eat anything which hasn't dug in for safety 'neath the pool —!

INDIAN ARTIFACTS..

..ON THE SHORE!

• What do beachcombing & Indian lore have in common? On Hilton Head, a lot! As the pounding surf continues to erode our northern headlands, exposed mudbanks tumble-out artifacts which intimate aborigines abided here perhaps 4,000 years ago! Navigating along deep tidal creeks, harvesting bounties of shellfish, & tapping abundant fresh-water springs, the natives may have been kin to our "Escamacu" tribe, first reported by 16th century Conquistadors. This hunter-gardener-villager race vanished soon after 1715, but the fragments below hint at their lifestyle. Who were they? What's your guess? Search bluffs/banks for bits 'n pieces of Indian artifacts in the dark-shaded areas on this Island Map →..

INDIAN SPRING
DOLPHIN HEAD
SKULL CREEK MARSHES
SPANISH WELLS
FISH HAUL CREEK AREA
FT. WALKER BEACH
SEA PINES INDIAN SHELL RING

◄ **PROJECTILE POINTS..** Used on spears or arrows, are "flaked" (chipped) stone, 2-6" long. May be 1,000-4,000 yrs. old.

BONE TOOLS▼ Like ① an awl for punching hides, or ② a fish hook for catching lunch! 300-3,000 yrs. old.

▲ **POTTERY..** Made from marsh "clay", sand, even palm fibers. ① PUNCATED (holes by stabbing) is up to 3,500 yrs. old. ② CORD-MARKED (long, deep lines), up to 1,500 yrs. old. ③ FINE CORD MARKED (criss-crossed), 300-1,000 yrs. Note.. Shards are charred on one side from firing.

▲ **SHELL TOOLS..** Hoes & "pick axes" were fashioned by jamming a pole thru chipped holes in Whelk shells. Unnaturally large 4" holes are a clue.

CLAY PIPES► 2" long, used in ceremonies for "peace pipe" herbal smokes. Date back 800-4,000 yrs.__.

The Salt Marsh

The first time I crossed the bridges from the mainland to Hilton Head Island, I was awestruck by the verdant, tall grass prairies bordering the curling channels and creeks, below. This also may be your first introduction to the salt marsh... John and Mildred Teal's "green ribbon of soft, salty, wet, low-lying land"... where the earth melts into the back waters.

These leeside wetlands breathe life with the coming and going of tides. Marshes are flooded to grasstops at high tide, and drained down to glistening mudflats with shallow "salt pan" pools at low tide. The sheer population of plants and animals that can abide in this habitat of mixing and flushing water is staggering. Biologists estimate that salt marshes and their estuary watersheds produce five to ten tons of organic matter per acre annually, compared to one and a half to five tons per acre in the most fertile agricultural soil. One acre alone of cordgrass marsh can support one million fiddler crabs.

Newcomers here commonly mistake the salt marshes for foul smelling, muck-ridden places, worth vicarious appreciation only from a patio or cruise boat. Yet, if these tidelands somehow vanished, most animals portrayed in this book would not exist on or near the island. The bedrock foundation of the marine foodchain are the countless species of plankton and invertebrates that mature in the mud, grasses and streams. Without our wet nurseries, places like Hilton Head might appear picturesque, and to some, tidier. But they would be biologically barren.

The federal Coastal Zone Management Act thankfully conserves and protects our salt marshes for boaters, fishermen, shrimpers, nature-lovers and tourists to enjoy. If you have not visited the marsh lately, take *Tideland Treasure* and go.

The breadbasket of the barrier isles is worth the discovery.

THE SALT MARSH

- **A chartreuse swash** of waving grass praries, steaming mudflats & forever winding, high-banked creeks is the wetland world of the salt marsh. These low-lying, border environments are found in estuaries and in-shore zones between barrier islands & the mainland. Salt marshes form in silt deltas which deposit at river mouths. Saltwater tolerant plants colonize the muck & trap further sediment running off islands following rains. The seasonal death & decay of stems & leaves builds the soggy peat soil of the marsh, called muck. Protecting the marsh on the oceanside are the barrier islands like Hilton Head. They act as tremendous sandbars, absorbing surf & strong winds. Tidal currents are diverted around the islands' ends where they gently bathe & flush the fertile salt marshes with a clockwork supply of salt water—.

HILTON HEAD ISLAND'S SALT MARSHES ■

- **THE TIDES ARE THE HEARTBEAT OF MARSHLIFE.**

◂ **At High Tide:** Every 6 hrs., 6 min., tides flood in. This nearly covers grasses, stirs up bottom nutrients (thereby supplying shellfish with food) & carries along oceanic fish & plankton to feed & breed.

▸ **At Low Tide:** Ebbing waters (1-3 knots) transport a tan slurry of dissolved nutrients, marsh grass & small animals (dead & alive) to nourish the offshore food chain. Now upland animals like raccoons, wading birds & deer invade the exposed flats to hunt fish, insects, bivalves, crabs & snails & to forage marsh plants.

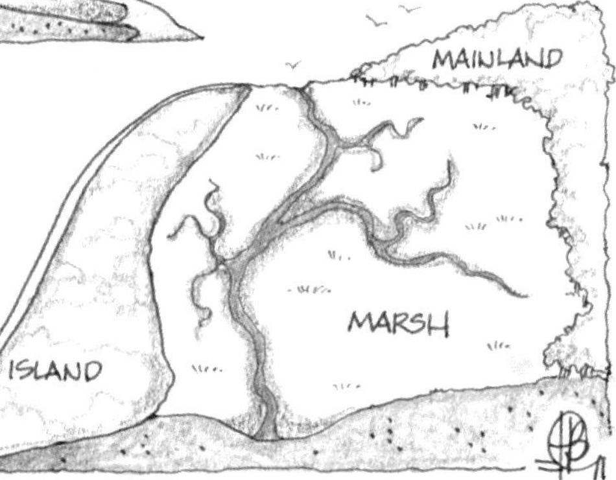

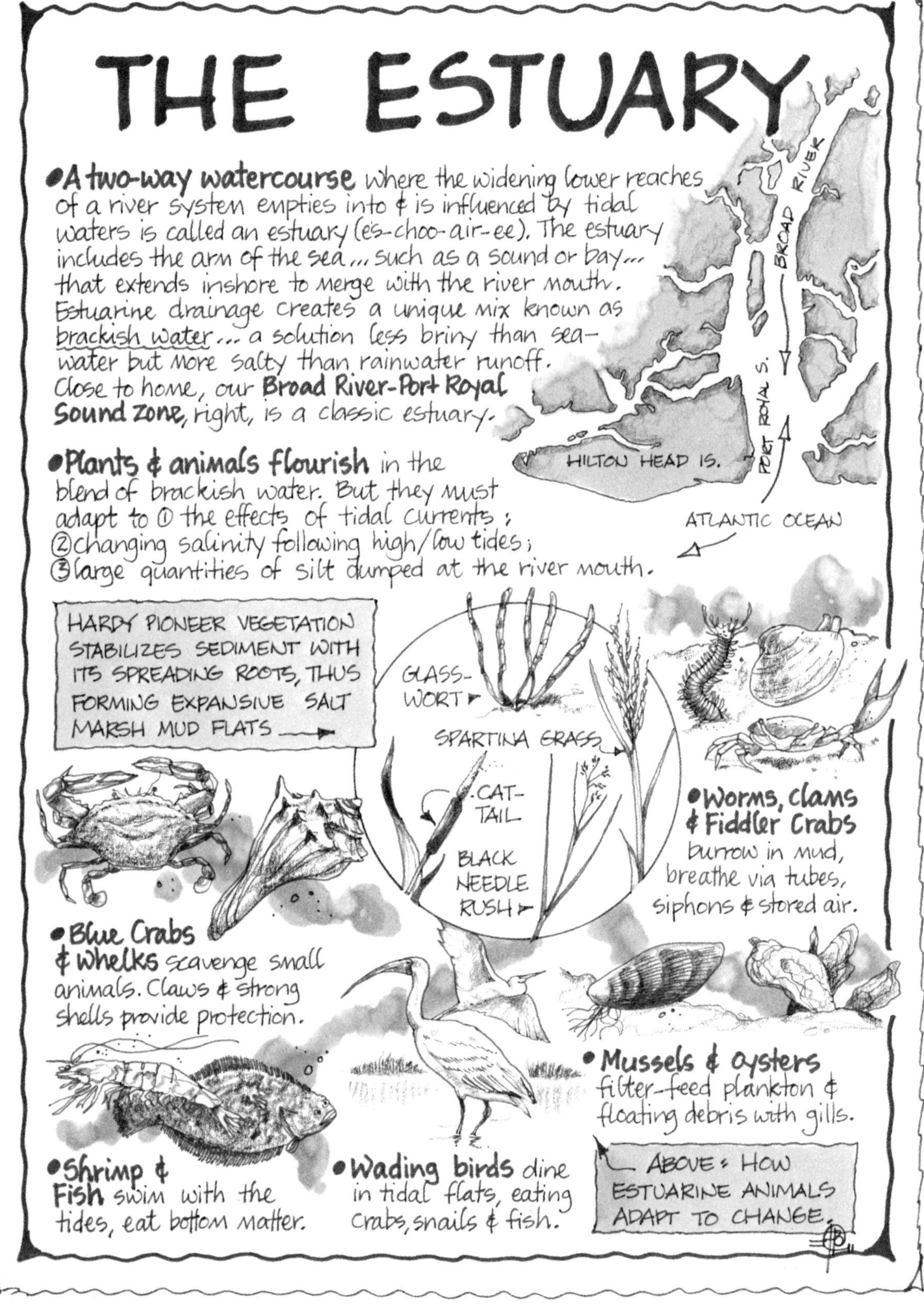
THE ESTUARY
• A two-way watercourse where the widening lower reaches of a river system empties into & is influenced by tidal waters is called an estuary (es-choo-air-ee). The estuary includes the arm of the sea ... such as a sound or bay ... that extends inshore to merge with the river mouth. Estuarine drainage creates a unique mix known as brackish water ... a solution less briny than seawater but more salty than rainwater runoff. Close to home, our Broad River-Port Royal Sound zone, right, is a classic estuary.
BROAD RIVER
PORT ROYAL S.
HILTON HEAD IS.
ATLANTIC OCEAN
• Plants & animals flourish in the blend of brackish water. But they must adapt to ① the effects of tidal currents; ② changing salinity following high/low tides; ③ large quantities of silt dumped at the river mouth.
HARDY PIONEER VEGETATION STABILIZES SEDIMENT WITH ITS SPREADING ROOTS, THUS FORMING EXPANSIVE SALT MARSH MUD FLATS
GLASS-WORT
SPARTINA GRASS
CAT-TAIL
BLACK NEEDLE RUSH
• Worms, clams & Fiddler Crabs burrow in mud, breathe via tubes, siphons & stored air.
• Blue Crabs & Whelks scavenge small animals. Claws & strong shells provide protection.
• Mussels & oysters filter-feed plankton & floating debris with gills.
• Shrimp & Fish swim with the tides, eat bottom matter.
• Wading birds dine in tidal flats, eating crabs, snails & fish.
ABOVE: HOW ESTUARINE ANIMALS ADAPT TO CHANGE.

SPRING IN THE SALT MARSH
●The greening of the salt marsh is ushered in by the 1st Spring rains of March. Winds shifting back to the SW push in storms which drench sleepy seedlings here, & carry a burden of minerals & nutritious debris from melting Mountain snows down rivers & into the coastal estuaries. Feeding on this fertilizer, salt water plankton & mud creek algaes bloom thick as soup... attracting whole hosts of hungry marine creatures inshore. Note these signs of rebirth...
●Cordgrass sprouts anew. Long-spreading roots pop up new 8 in. shoots from the mulch of dead "hay" stubble.
●Insects like ⓐ"No-see-um" midges, ⓑmosquitos, ⓒ deerflies, hatch from larva in marsh pools. Some suck blood, still others suck plant stems... all provide food for migrant birds & marshbound fish...
ⓐ
ⓑ
ⓒ
(LONG-BILLED MARSH WREN)
●Wrens, Sparrows, Rails & Marsh Hawks breed. Nests are elevated in marsh plants to guard against the danger of flooding.
ⓐ
ⓑ
●Once marsh creeks heat up over 60°, ⓐ Fiddler Crabs populate mudbanks by the millions to feed & mate. Air-breathing ⓑ Periwinkle Snails hike up grass stems at high tide. After tides run, watch for Herons/Egrets hunting these easy catches...
ⓐ
ⓑ
●Marsh music rings forth from backwoods ⓐ tree frogs, ⓑ crickets, & male birds. The rythym-makers will be Snapping Shrimp who click out the beat with their big claw!
J. Bottontine...

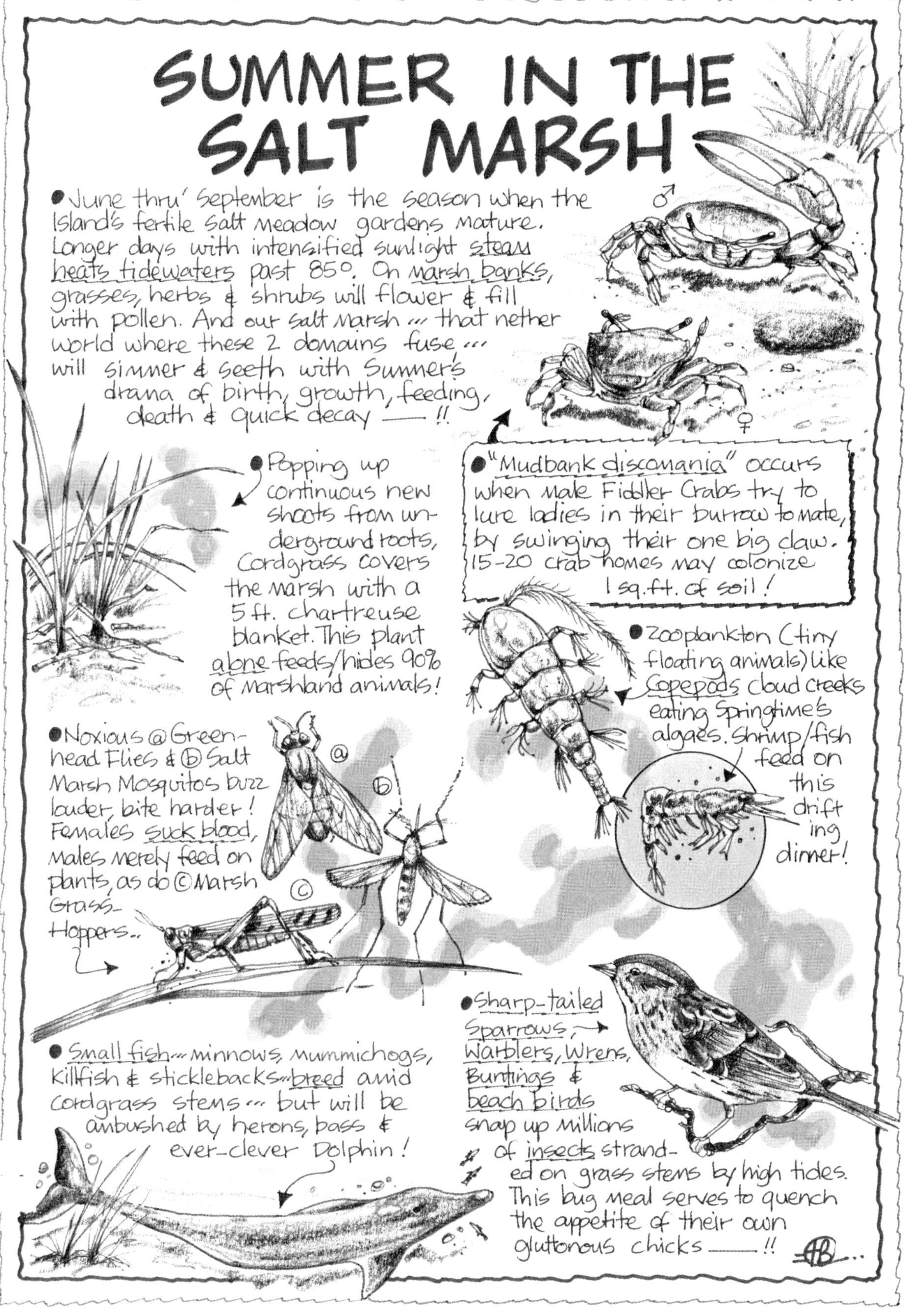
SUMMER IN THE SALT MARSH
●June thru' September is the season when the Island's fertile salt meadow gardens mature. Longer days with intensified sunlight steam heats tidewaters past 85°. On marsh banks, grasses, herbs & shrubs will flower & fill with pollen. And our salt marsh ... that nether world where these 2 domains fuse ... will simmer & seeth with Summer's drama of birth, growth, feeding, death & quick decay —— !!
♂
♀
●"Mudbank discomania" occurs when male Fiddler Crabs try to lure ladies in their burrow to mate, by swinging their one big claw. 15-20 crab homes may colonize 1 sq.ft. of soil!
●Popping up continuous new shoots from underground roots, Cordgrass covers the marsh with a 5 ft. chartreuse blanket. This plant alone feeds/hides 90% of marshland animals!
●Zooplankton (tiny floating animals) like Copepods cloud creeks eating Springtime's algaes. Shrimp/fish feed on this drifting dinner!
●Noxious ⓐ Greenhead Flies & ⓑ Salt Marsh Mosquitos buzz louder, bite harder! Females suck blood, males merely feed on plants, as do ⓒ Marsh Grass-Hoppers..
ⓐ
ⓑ
ⓒ
●Sharp-tailed Sparrows, Warblers, Wrens, Buntings & beach birds snap up millions of insects stranded on grass stems by high tides. This bug meal serves to quench the appetite of their own gluttonous chicks —— !!
●Small fish ... minnows, mummichogs, killfish & sticklebacks ... breed amid cordgrass stems ... but will be ambushed by herons, bass & ever-clever Dolphin!
AB ...

AUTUMN IN THE SALT MARSH
● As October breezes 'thru, & November nudges ever-nearer, the Island's salt marshes explode with a frenzy of animal travel & the harvest of golden grains. The wash of ochre in the grasses signals shorter days & greater chill. W-NW cold fronts will cool shallow marsh creeks faster than offshore waters. Most marine life will school seaward to avoid coming freezes & to dine on the "plankton bloom" stirred-up by storms there. Fleeing the frost, enticed by the Fall foodstuffs here, scores of resident & visiting wildlife flock to the fertile salt marshes 'til Thanksgiving. Watch for these signs of life:
SEEDS
A
B
① Marsh insects like (A) Mosquitos & (B) biting Midges mate/lay eggs in the moist mud. The clutch will lie dormant 'til awakened by Spring rains.
② "Bug eggs" are welcome chow for stay-around fish*. So watch for wading birds hunting fish!
* MUMMICHOG
③ Cordgrass goes to seed. "Spartina", this 6' grass of the creeks sets tussocks of straw colored seeds on the wind/tide, yellowing the entire marsh along the way.
④ Seed-eaters like Sparrows & Meadow Voles come out of hiding to gobble the cordgrass cereal. Watch as more & more marsh hawks hover above the stalks, eyeing easy prey ——..
⑤ Exit the crabs. Most crabs like the Blue (A) head for the warmer Atlantic bottom. Fiddler Crabs (B) crawl in burrows & go into a sleepy stupor 'til April.
A
B
⑥ Migrating Birds. Like this Tree Swallow, wading birds, shorebirds, hawks, rails & ducks sail southward via the Atlantic Flyway and stopover here——.
t. Boltontine

WINTER IN THE SALT MARSH
●Life is lean in our Dec-Feb. marshes. Few marine plants or animals can survive the frigid 45° creek waters. Yet, at low tide, the sun sizzles exposed banks to 80°, so mud algaes continue to produce a subsistence food for burrowed fish/shellfish. Watch winter's wetlands for recycling, scavenging & sky-high migrations.
●Cordgrass dies back, building nutritious peat from its rotting stems & fertilizing estuarine/ocean plankton with its minerals. Color the marsh drab brown!
A
B
C
●Stem-sucking (A) Chinch Bugs, (B) Plant-Hoppers, & (C) Grasshoppers glean grass heaps... attracting insect-eating birdlife, like the Myrtle warbler above, from field & forest.
A
B
●'Coon Capers... ea.'nite, Raccoons paw-up (A) Oysters, (B) Clams & (C) too-cold Crabs from mudbanks. Many marsh 'coons nest by March near creeks, building dens from shells & piles of dead "hay".
●Fish like (A) Mummichog & (B) Killfish dig into mud-bottom insulation, or swim torpidly in creeks, making 'em prime pickings for solitary wading birds & shorebirds!
A
B
C
"BOTTOMS UP" FOR BLACK DUCKS
●Ducks & even Geese over-winter here to nibble on roots, shoots & seeds of rushes & cordgrass "cereal". At left, a common dusk & dawn dabbler.

SALT MARSH SOUNDS

• **To listen is to learn** that the salt marsh is a dynamic always-alive environment. The comings & goings of tides, the play of breezes across the grasses, the cacaphony of animal noises & even the gurgling muck produces a natural timbre welcomed daily by many islanders. Here are 5 of the more common salt marsh sounds to enjoy....

▸ **Wind on Spartina**... the sway & scrape of salt grass stems is rythmically reminiscent of rustling prarie wheat.

▾ **A loud hyena cackle**... is heard from unseen Clapper rails winging thru' grass stalk jungles.

▾ **Fiddler Crab feet** crackle in the mudflats as herds of hundreds advance before tides or human feet.

▸ **A sharp "pop!"** is made by the pistol shrimp which snaps its claws loudly together. This stuns prey which is then dragged inside the shrimp's burrow.

◂ **A soft "plop"** sounds when air bubbles escape from marsh banks submerged by incoming tides.

SALT MARSH SMELLS

• **A special aroma** that fills the island air is one of the first sensations experienced by new visitors here. This natural pungency is commonly mistaken for air pollution, but salt marsh smells are quite natural to coastal zones. To familiarize yourself with this "essence o' estuary", learn to sniff out some of its main ingredients, shown below...

① **Saltwater**: The mineral mix including table salt, magnesium, epsom, calcium, potassium & lime is borne to all sectors by prevailing breezes.

② **Chlorophyll**: Marshland plants such as Spartina grass (right) exude a green leafy smell, especially following Spring rains.

Spartina

③ **Decay**: As plants & animals decompose, they release gaseous nitrogen into the air & ammonia compounds to the marsh muds.

④ **Sulfur**: Hydrogen sulfide (H_2S), slightly reminiscent of rotten eggs, occurs when marsh mud is dug or disturbed. "Anaerobic" (oxygen lacking) bacteria utilize H_2S gas in their life cycles, in the deep, black layers of muck.

* Note: Sulfur dioxide (SO_2), a rancid malodor that wafts on muggy Southwesterly winds is an air pollutant, not a normal marsh smell. It originates from power plants & paper mills in Savannah...

MARSH MUD
Muck. That slimy black mud we see... and smell... in our salt marshes is commonly ignored, cursed or dredged, but it plays a vital role in our island's ecology. Marsh mud forms when ① upland topsoil is carried to creeks by rivers & rain runoff. As the creeks drain into sounds, the fine silt settles on steep stream banks where the current force is slower. Over time the mud sediments reduce channel flow to a shallow, meandering trickle. Now ② marsh plants such as cord-grass (Spartina arterniflora) begin to colonize the stable muck, spreading from running roots. ③ Marsh animals such as oysters, snails & fiddler crabs feed, breed & die in marsh bank communities. Their waste & corpses add rich organic material to the marsh mud.
HOW MARSH MUD FORMS
MARSH CREEK CROSS SECTION
STEEP BANK
DRAIN COURSE
Why marsh mud smells bad. The fine-packed sediments are oxygen-poor. Here native "anaerobic" bacteria decays bottom matter & releases hydrogen sulfide (H2S)... a poisonous gas smelling of rotten eggs. The muck stench is worst on warm, windy days or when the mud is disturbed!
VARIETIES OF MARSH MUD SEEN ON HILTON HEAD IS.
"RUSTY MUD" formed when the muck's iron is oxidized.
SALT MARSH CREEKS & MUD FLATS.
"BEACH BALLS" form when waves tumble eroded mud seaward, picking up shells.
"SWASH LINES" on beach made of marsh debris.

● **Few animals are visible** in our saltmarsh mudflats, at 1st glance. Deposited in stagnating stream curves or deltas where creeks empty into more turbid waters, these sediment fields are a harsh habitat. 2-6 ft. of salty, silty tidal wash floods & ebbs. The always soggy soil is low in oxygen, high in hydrogen sulfide gas. Open flats sunscald to 140°. So to survive here, small creatures burrow in the mud for protection. They'll filter-feed on floating particles or scavenge "detritus" (surface debris). Predators swim/fly in & out with the bi-daily tides... feasting en route on the muck & grass menagerie abounding here.

A typical mudflat forms where a salt creek curves, depositing mud on the inside of the curve & cutting a bank on the outside...

● **Oysters & clams** filter & siphon in floating detritus.

● **Fiddler crabs, snails & worms** burrow in mud, eat detritus.

● **Insects** breed in pools. Larvae feed on plants & small animals.

● **Starfish, oysterdrills & oystercatchers** attack bivalves.

● **Fish** consume insect larvae at high tide.

● **Birds** like Egrets, Rails, Gulls & sandpipers feed upon any crawling or floating 'critters in sight!

DETRITUS

• **A brackish slurry** of decomposed marsh grass & animal matter in a solution of algae & bacteria is found everywhere in the salt marsh. Floating in the tidal bath or glistening along creek banks, this mixture is called detritus, a French term meaning "disintegrated matter". Detritus is composed of 95% dead spartina grass & 5% algae, bacteria & fungi with a pinch of animal waste & carrion. Tall spartina "cordgrass" adds debris when mature outer leaves fall; the standing stalk dies following seed dispersal; stems are trampled by marsh animals; plants die from rain washout or freezing. Abundant fungi & bacteria decompose the grass & waste into soft, micro-particles. Tides are the great stirrer & spreader which deposits layers of detritus to all quarters of the marsh...

HOW DETRITUS IS PRODUCED

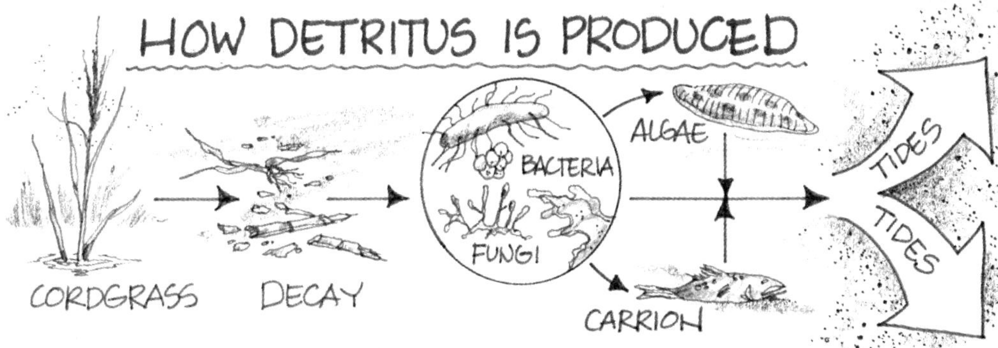

• **Detritus is a Nature's Soup** of nourishment & energy for all salt marsh organisms. It fertilizes the marsh because decomposer bacteria fix nitrogen in surface layers of the mud, making this valuable nutrient available for continued plant growth. All small tideland animals called "detritovores" either filter detritus from currents or gobble it directly in mud. Detritovores are in turn preyed upon by larger animals... fish, birds, terrapin, otter, raccoon, dolphin & even man...

Oysters
Shrimp
FILTER-FEEDERS
Mullet
Nematodes
Insects
Mud Snails
MUD-EATERS
Fiddler Crabs
DETRITOVORES

H. Ballentine

HAMMOCKS

• **Small tree islands** embraced on all sides by wide-open salt marshes are known locally as hammocks. These 1-2 acre microzoic mounds stick out of cordgrass meadows as eye-catching but unreachable forested protuberances. The term hammock is derived from the Indians' "hammocka", meaning 'garden place'... an image appropriate to these green-shadowed enclaves unique with their own special plant life, shown in these border sketches.

• **How hammocks form:**

1. Some hammocks are the last remaining pleistocene-era dune ridges which are isolated by the rising sea level.

2. More commonly, others form at the mouths of estuarine creeks. Here water-borne sediment accumulates around some refuse as a bar or "sill". Salt tolerant seeds germinate in the muck & build layers of soil with their rotting leaves. "Maritime" shrubs & trees thrive in the hammock humus. The increasing elevation of the isle decreases the killing effect that salt water has on roots & leaves. Over time, the hammock interior seems a jungle-like mass of twisting, tangled, vining evergreens, while the exterior is ringed with a sentinel colony of high marsh vegetation.

HAMMOCK ECOLOGY

DENSE COVER FOR NESTING, ROOSTING

SALT MARSH FOOD SOURCES

HIGH GROUND STORM REFUGE

● **Salt marsh hammocks are miniature wildlife refuges** for many birds & mammals of the barrier islands. Although they are located on the protected lee-side of the island, the forested humps still may sit as far as ½ mile from the nearest high ground. Enclosed by the dynamic wetland world of flood & ebb, the hammock habitats provide for 3 vital wildlife needs... cover, nesting & food.

● **COVER**: During spring tides & storms, the dense, tangled greenery is used for safe hide-aways & roosting perches by species such as those at the left.

● **NESTING**: Animals capable of swimming to & from hammocks migrate there to raise their young. Standing dead trees, stout branches & the camouflage of a thick understory provide safe nest spots. The sheer distance to the "mainland" is protection against predators. Animals that nest here, right. →

● **FEEDING**: Wading birds hob-nob on hammocks while hunting fiddler crabs/snails in nearby marsh banks. Perching birds sup on fruits from vines & shrubs. Marshland insect hordes attract birds like flycatchers, swallows & woodpeckers.....

The Plants

Maritime vegetation is a case study in survival. Sea, salt, sand, flood tides, erosion, desiccating heat, intense windchill and even ice forever test coastal plants for sheer endurance. The tough algae, fungi, herbs, shrubs and trees by our beaches and salt marshes are strange looking. They have transformed themselves to take sustenance from nature, and at the same time fight her for their lives.

Some kinds of seaweed attach themselves to the ocean floor with a specialized "holdfast" for support in quixotic currents. In the marsh, plants must withstand a regimen of flooding by potentially lethal quantities of salt in the tides. Twisted and stunted beachside plants, called *hallophytes,* bend before the blast of breeze. But none of these fail for fertility.

Seasoned islanders appreciate this passion play of plant survival. We welcome the autumnal return of yellow blossoms spatter-painting dune swales, golden grains against the blue sky, and the shimmer of sunlight on new leaves. The rise of one community of wild plants forecasts the arrival of others on successive days ahead.

Such tidelandscapes, recognized year after year, lend the warm glow of permanence and surety to all who come to know their many hues and quirks.

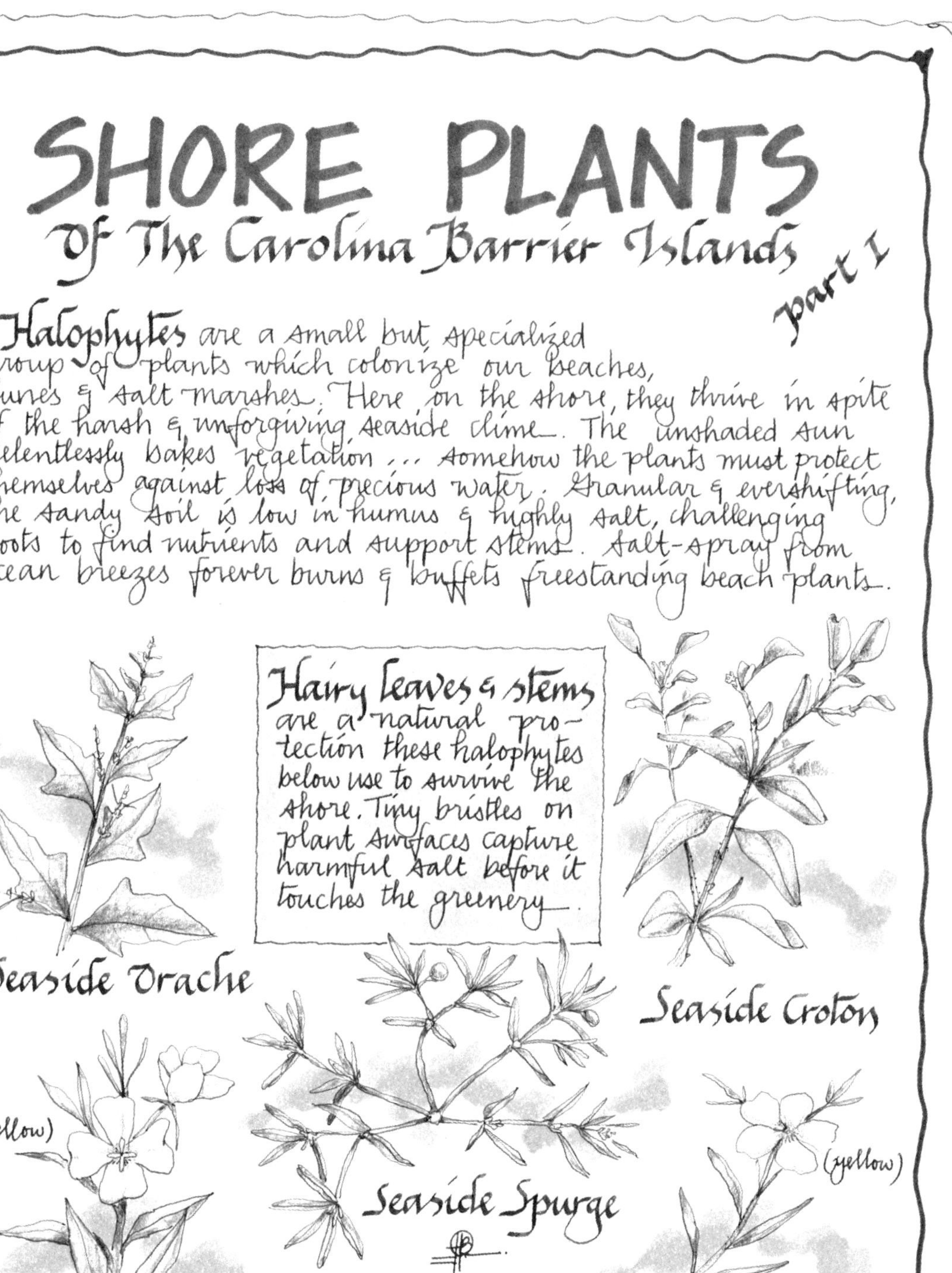
SHORE PLANTS
Of The Carolina Barrier Islands
part I
• Halophytes are a small but specialized group of plants which colonize our beaches, dunes & salt marshes. Here, on the shore, they thrive in spite of the harsh & unforgiving seaside clime. The unshaded sun relentlessly bakes vegetation ... somehow the plants must protect themselves against loss of precious water. Granular & evershifting, the sandy soil is low in humus & highly salt, challenging roots to find nutrients and support stems. Salt-spray from ocean breezes forever burns & buffets freestanding beach plants.
Hairy leaves & stems are a natural protection these halophytes below use to survive the shore. Tiny bristles on plant surfaces capture harmful salt before it touches the greenery.
Seaside Orache
Seaside Croton
(yellow)
(yellow)
Seaside Spurge
Evening Primrose
(opens at sundown...)
Rockrose

SHORE PLANTS
Of The Carolina Barrier Islands
Part II

• **Stickers, prickers & thorns** characterize a group of all too familiar shoreside plants. Each species bears sharp spines on the leaves, stems or fruits, which can stab the feet & limbs of casual duneswalkers. These barbs afford protection against marauding herbivores (plant-eating animals) or capture sand & salt which damages plant tissues. Prickly fruits (sandspur, cactus) allows the plant to disperse its seeds when they latch on to fur ... or to your feet! So, to save your skin ... get to know these spiked hallophytes from a distance!

SHORE PLANTS
Of The Carolina Barrier Islands
Part III
Beach Pennywort
Morning Glory
• Vines & creeping stems are a self-defense mechanism for select plants near shore. To escape the killing effect of seawind & saltspray, they keep their leafy heads down. Some lie flat on the sand, growing along the surface in an outreach for sunlight. Others twine themselves around nearby shrubs or grasses for stem support & foliage protection. Here are shown 5 common "creepers, crawlers & climbers" by the sea ___."
Wild Bamboo
(One of 8 "Smilax" species)
Lippia
Poison Ivy

SHORE PLANTS

Of The Carolina Barrier Islands

Part IV

• **Succulent plants** are common on the dunes and beach, above the tidal swash line. Know them by their thick, fleshy leaves which conserve moisture, waxy, extra-sturdy "cuticle" cells on the epidermis (leaf surface) reflect sunlight & resist sand or salt spray, thereby avoiding dessication ... the deadly loss of water from the interior plant tissues caused by the arid environment of the seashore...

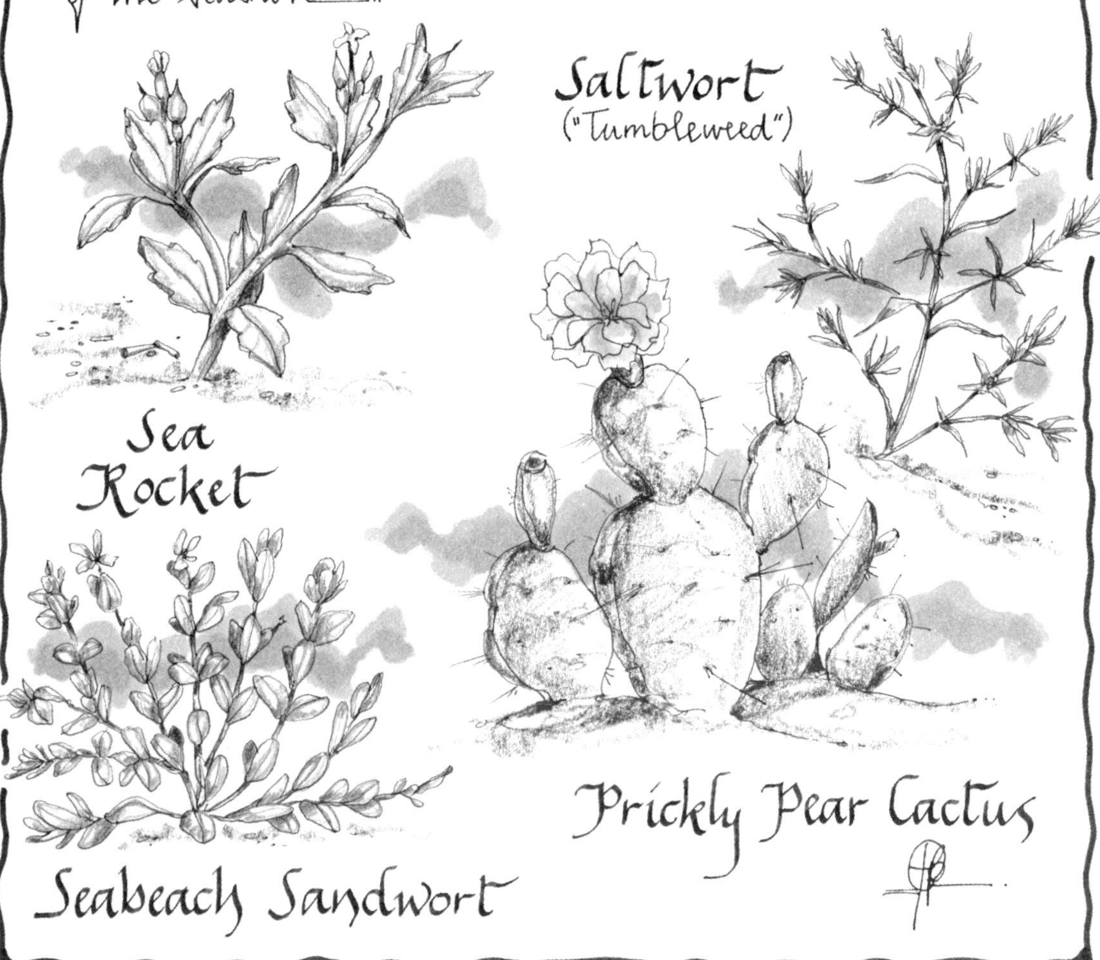

SHORE PLANTS
of The Carolina Barrier Islands
Part V

• **Fungi and lichens** are non-flowering plants lacking roots, stems or leaves. Although the great majority of their populations are found in our nearby maritime forests, some species do eke out a living in dune sands, grasses & shrubs near the ocean.

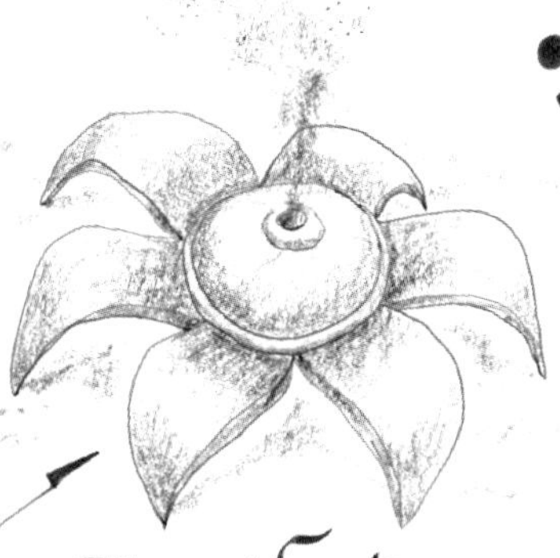

Earthstar
(Exploding spores)

• **Fungi** do not produce their own food through photosynthesis. Instead, they subsist on decaying organic matter such as dead grass or animals. Nitrogen & other valuable nutrients are released to the air & sandy soil as the fungi decompose their hosts.

Stinkhorn
(Attracting flies)

• **Lichens** are "sandwich plants" living together in symbiosis, or mutual benefit. The fungi supplies support, water & minerals. The green algae produces food used by both plants. See these lichens on tree bark & in shaded grottos between dune ridges.

Pale Shield Lichen

Reindeer Lichen

FALL FLOWERS
OF THE BEACH

"Flower power" rules the dunes during Sept-Oct. Here a select group of hardy herbs has survived Summer's scald, the nitrogen-poor soil, & the lack of cover, and now splashes ridges & swales with violet, magenta, yellow & creamy blooms. Note these plants own deep roots to anchor in the soft, shell sand, or crawl as vines rather than risk their soft stems standing before the wind. Their stiff, leathery leaves fend off the killing salt-spray. By the Autumnal Equinox (Sept. 22), legions of bees & migrant butterflies will swarm to this larder of nectar, adding an extra dash of pigment to the beach-front bouquet!

① **BUTTERFLY PEA** .. Pale violet 1½" flowers with white midribs grow on bushy vines. Leaves always found in threes.

⑤ **CAMPHOR-WEED** .. This branching yellow aster blankets the dunes in gold. Note crinkly rough leaves.

② **MORNING GLORY** .. This creamy 3" bell tinted with yellow inside welcomes the dawn, closes by supper. A vine plant.

⑥ **YELLOW GOATS BEARD** .. Looks like a 1 ft. dandelion with long, grassy leaves. Like #2, flowers close up by evening.

③ **SAND SPUR** .. Is actually a grass with sharp-spined bur-blooms. Bristles help transport green seeds on animal fur or your toes!

④ **COLIC ROOT** .. Tiny ⅛" white flowers hug a 1½ ft. free-standing stalk. Blooms look bulbous. A rosette of leaves grows at sand level.

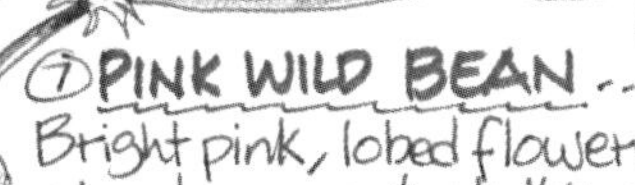

⑦ **PINK WILD BEAN** .. Bright pink, lobed flowers stand on erect stalks off trailing vines. Sports pencil-straight pea pods. Leaves in threes...

SHORE SNACKS

Edible Seaside Plants

Sea Rocket
Use tangy leaves & seed pods in salads or as a cooked vegetable in Spring.

Sea Lettuce
Collect this green sea-weed from sand bottoms. Wash, chop & add to salads.

Prickly Pear
Pick reddish cactus fruits with gloves. Peel away the thick skin & enjoy the sweet pulp.

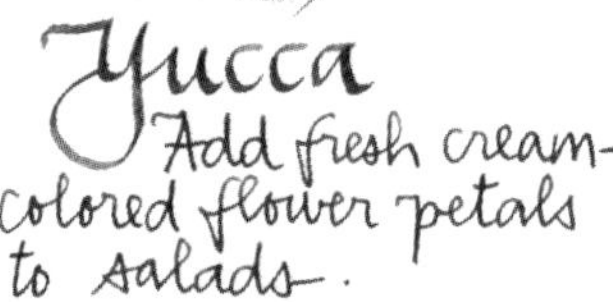

Yucca
Add fresh cream-colored flower petals to salads.

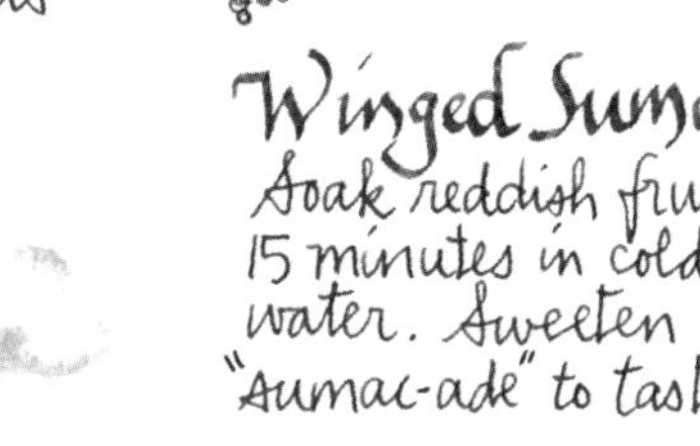

Bull Thistle
Remove spines from flower stems. Cut open. Eat raw or add to salads like celery.

Winged Sumac
Soak reddish fruits 15 minutes in cold water. Sweeten "sumac-ade" to taste.

Dewberry... Eat blackberry-like fruits with milk & honey. Add fresh shoots to salads.

Brambles sprawl dune grasses.

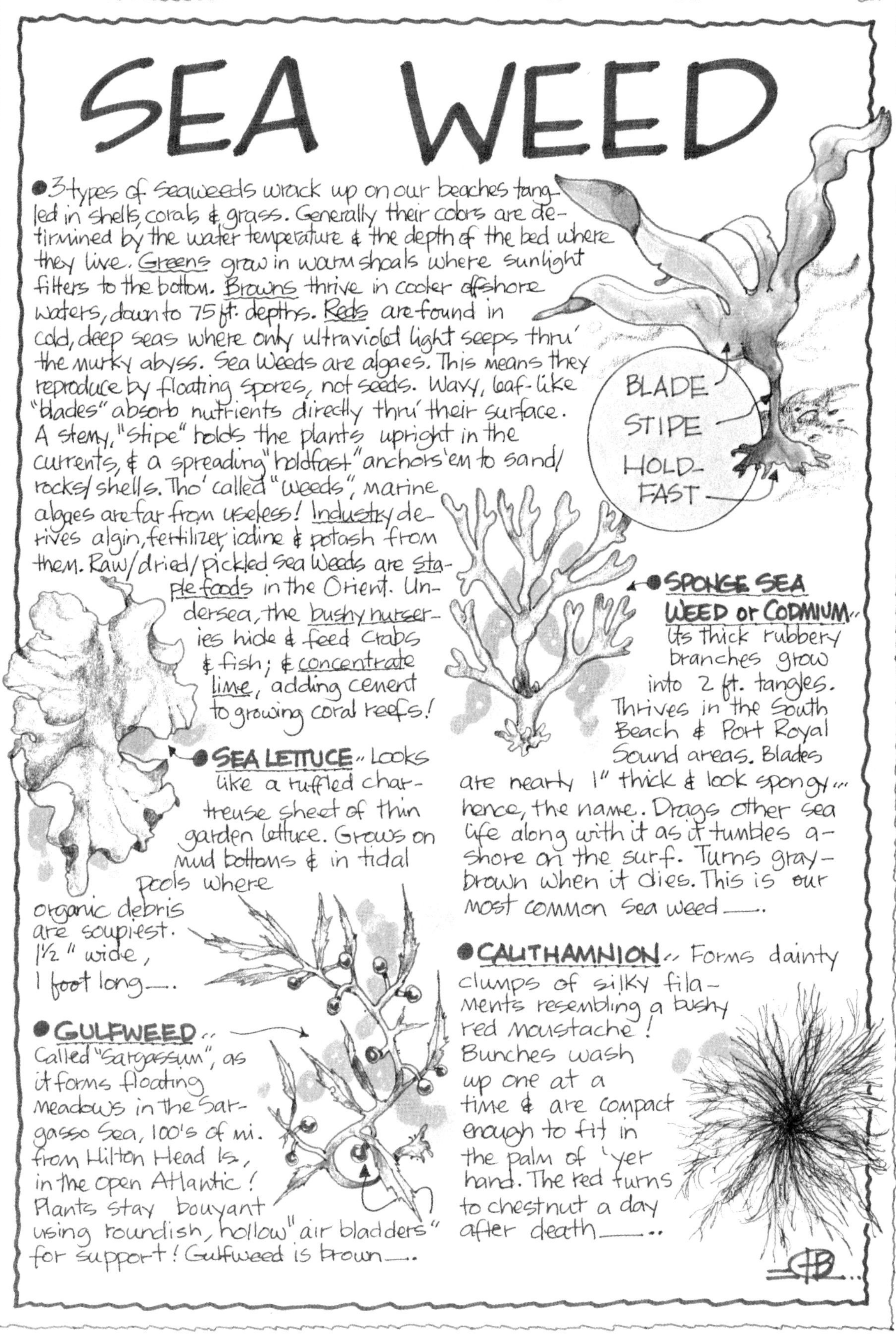
SEA WEED
●3 types of Seaweeds wrack up on our beaches tangled in shells, corals & grass. Generally their colors are determined by the water temperature & the depth of the bed where they live. Greens grow in warm shoals where sunlight filters to the bottom. Browns thrive in cooler offshore waters, down to 75 ft. depths. Reds are found in cold, deep seas where only ultraviolet light seeps thru' the murky abyss. Sea Weeds are algaes. This means they reproduce by floating spores, not seeds. Wavy, leaf-like "blades" absorb nutrients directly thru' their surface. A stemy, "stipe" holds the plants upright in the currents, & a spreading "holdfast" anchors 'em to sand/rocks/shells. Tho' called "weeds", marine algaes are far from useless! Industry derives algin, fertilizer, iodine & potash from them. Raw/dried/pickled Sea Weeds are staple foods in the Orient. Undersea, the bushy nurseries hide & feed crabs & fish; & concentrate lime, adding cement to growing coral reefs!
BLADE
STIPE
HOLD-FAST
●SPONGE SEA WEED or CODMIUM.. Its thick rubbery branches grow into 2 ft. tangles. Thrives in the South Beach & Port Royal Sound areas. Blades are nearly 1" thick & look spongy... hence, the name. Drags other sea life along with it as it tumbles ashore on the surf. Turns gray-brown when it dies. This is our most common sea weed—.
●SEA LETTUCE.. Looks like a ruffled chartreuse sheet of thin garden lettuce. Grows on mud bottoms & in tidal pools where organic debris are soupiest. 1½" wide, 1 foot long—.
●GULFWEED.. Called "Sargassum", as it forms floating meadows in the Sargasso Sea, 100's of mi. from Hilton Head Is., in the open Atlantic! Plants stay bouyant using roundish, "hollow" air bladders" for support! Gulfweed is brown—.
●CALLITHAMNION.. Forms dainty clumps of silky filaments resembling a bushy red moustache! Bunches wash up one at a time & are compact enough to fit in the palm of 'yer hand. The red turns to chestnut a day after death—..
GB..

BEACH GRASSES

● Wear shoes when you hike across the dunes to the beach. For here reign the beach grasses which flourish in extra-thick & often downright prickly blankets during Fall. These herbs alone can survive the blistering salt-spray, drenching spring tides, scalding heat & arid soil, for 5 good reasons. ① Flowering seed spikes produce 100's of seeds. ② Stickers, wings & parachutes launch seeds, ③ which can lie dormant for years 'til growing conditions are just right. ④ New sprigs sprout from running root-stocks (#'s 1-4) or ⑤ bulby root tubers that also reservoir water during drought (#5). Enjoy these 5 duneland denizens on your way to the shore...

SEED
FLOWER

① BITTER PANIC GRASS.. Bluish-green, the 4 ft. tall grass is topped with a 12" long seed spike. Has tiny orange seeds...

SEED

③ BROOMSEDGE.. A 3 ft. tall kin to sorghum. Turns dune swales rusty red in September. Seeds fly on silky white wings.

SEEDS

SEED SPIKE

SPUR

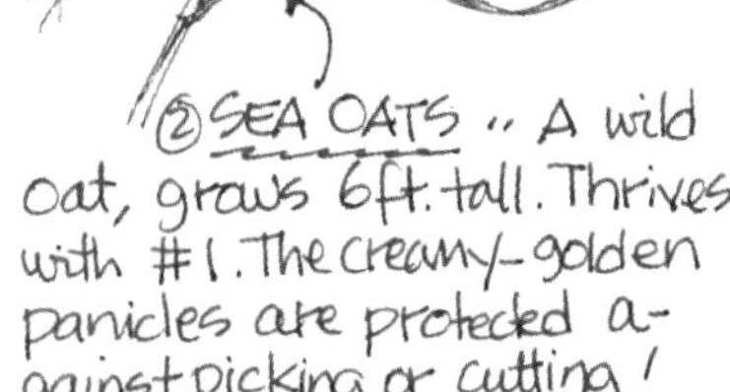

② SEA OATS .. A wild oat, grows 6 ft. tall. Thrives with #1. The creamy-golden panicles are protected against picking or cutting!

⑤ NUTGRASS .. Is actually a 12" sedge (its leaves have 3 edges, not 2 like grass blades). Thrives in fertile salt hay, near high tide lines.

④ SANDSPUR .. Grows in a 1 ft high rosette. Spiny burs lie like land mines 'neath the sand, can puncture bare feet! Inside rest 2 fleshy seeds.

.. WHERE THE GRASSES GROW ..

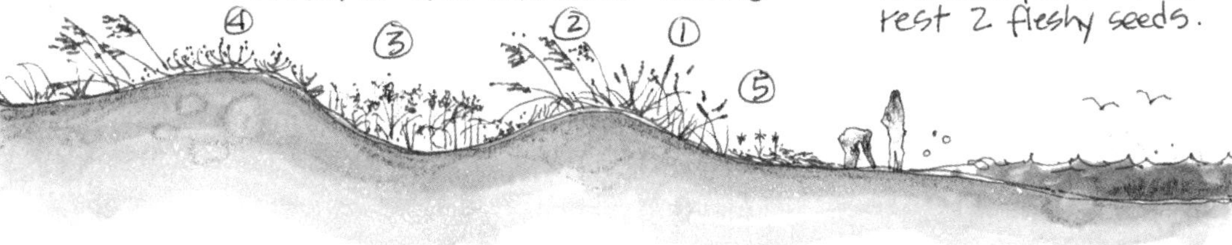

SEA OATS
European explorers, so enamored with the amber waves of Sea Oats adorning the dunes, named these SC.-Ga. islands the "Golden Isles". Wild relatives to the cultivated grain, hardy Sea Oats colonize the open sand closest to the sea. "Spikelets" of tawny seeds dangle chest-high, all on one side of a roundish, green stem. This pliant plant is one of the few that can bend, but not break, before the blast of burning salt spray.
Palish Oat panicles pop-out in June & brown-up by October, when hungry animals or storm winds send seeds groundward. New plants sprout in spring 'neath 10" of beach debris fertilizer. Yearling sprigs first catch blowing sand, building small dunes. Growing Oats send roots 8ft. in all directions & continue to grab grains in mid-air, adding bulk to the dunes the plants build. Sea Oats are so valuable in sandbagging the shore against erosion that SC. law makes digging, cutting or picking the plant (without the owner's permission) ILLEGAL!
SPARROWS
DEER
DOVES
Note.. Wildlife travels far & wide to the beach to eat & spread seeds, or munch the long leaves of Sea Oats, our golden grainery!
MARSH RABBITS
CARDINALS
BOAT-TAILED GRACKLES
CHINCH BUGS

YUCCA

Spanish Bayonet is one of coastal Carolina's most familiar Yuccas... a group of shrubs & trees in the lily family. Islanders plant Yuccas as ornamental borders, but back dunes & sandy openings are hot habitats where they flourish naturally. Maturing to 12 ft. heights, the woody trunk bristles with an awesome array of stiff dagger-shaped leaves. The 2½ ft. long blades are tipped with a sharp spike which will poke painfully upon contact. Beware! May-July, Yucca flowers top a head-high stalk jutting out of the pom-pom of leaves. 6 petaled & creamy white, the blossom clusters contrast radiantly with neighboring shoreline greenery & waft a sweet fragrance on our moist summer air. By July 4th bunches of cucumber shaped fruits appear. These 2-4" green capsules are packed with fibrous pulp & about a dozen black seeds...

Moths make the moves in Yucca ecology. The 1" female Yucca Moth (Tegeticula), camouflaged white, comes to feed on the flower nectar. As she does, by chance she gathers a big ball of pollen which she carries to nearby Yucca blossoms, causing cross-fertilization. Here she lays 1-2 eggs in the ovary. When fruits ripen, the larva emerges to eat the seeds. But these caterpillars can't gobble the whole cache, so many seeds fall to the ground to germinate!

Yucca uses. Deer relish the fruit pulp. They stretch their long necks over the "bayonet" leaves to reach the meat. Plucked flower petals are delightful add-ins to salads. Baskets, sandals, rope & mats are products Indians made from leaf fibers. The thick roots are a ready store of moisture & are used in soapmaking...

SHRUBS
OF THE DUNES

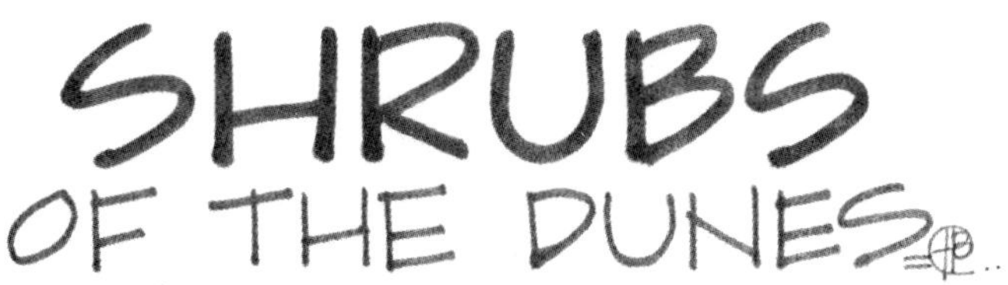

● **As sentinels against salt, wind & sun,** duneland shrubs require special adaptations. Their stiff, extra-waxy leaves fend off burning salt spray & sunscald. Broad roots spread far laterally, giving support in nor'easter gales. Where the sand's ground temperature soars to 140°, these roots must be thick & woody to retain precious groundwater.

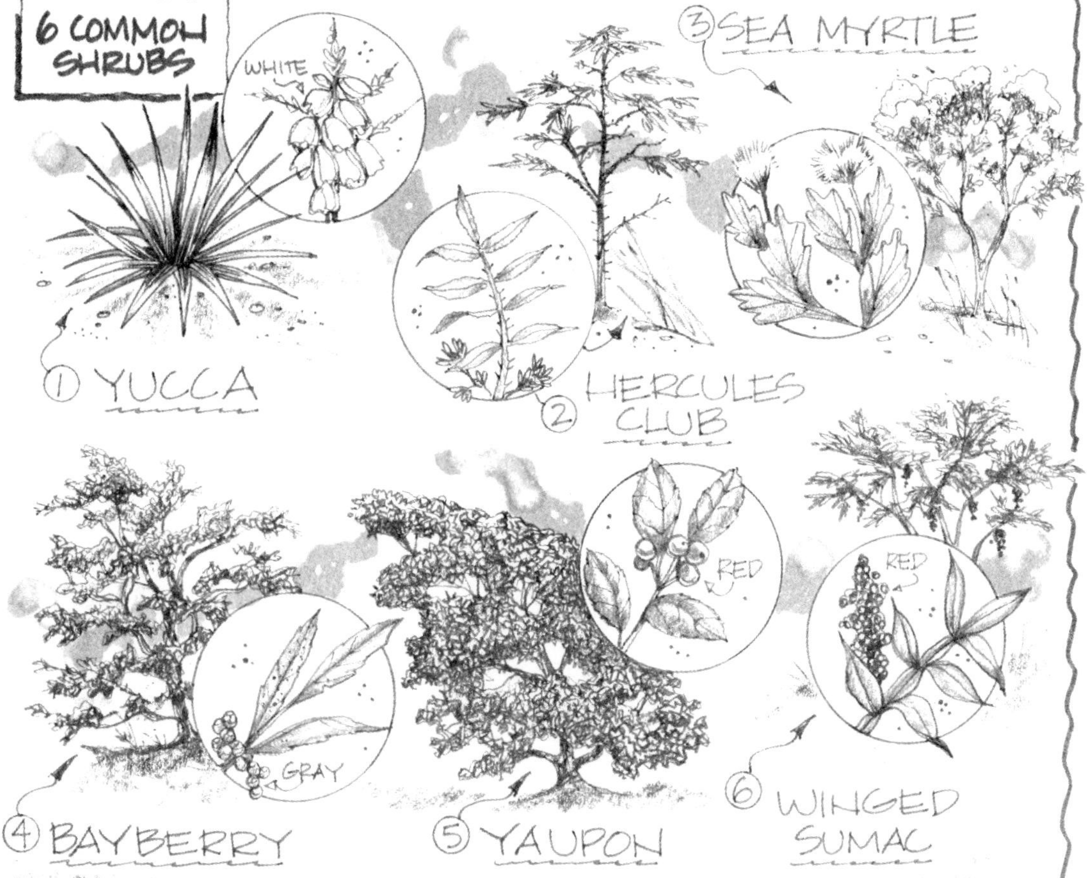

6 COMMON SHRUBS
WHITE
① YUCCA
② HERCULES CLUB
③ SEA MYRTLE
RED
RED
GRAY
④ BAYBERRY
⑤ YAUPON
⑥ WINGED SUMAC

WHERE THE SHRUBS GROW...

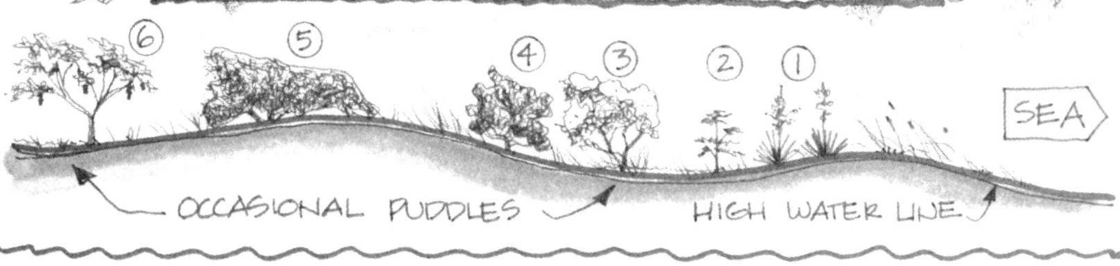

6
5
4
3
2
1
SEA
OCCASIONAL PUDDLES
HIGH WATER LINE

TREES OF THE DUNES

● **Walking inland from the beach,** one notices dune shrubbery giving way to a phalanx of evergreen trees. When bushes' leaf litter decays, it mulches the arrid, fast-draining sand. Windblown & animal-borne tree seeds will sprout 'neath the damp debris & shading foliage. To survive in the face of seawinds & dry sand is the specialty of "beach trees". Leafage is tough... a waxy cellulose coating, stiff needles or leathery fronds will resist salt. Roots spread wide for support but must tap down to reach water. Duneland trees drink from an upwelling "lens" of fresh ground-water which floats near-surface above saltwater invading subsoils from the sea. These 3 hardy species are the most commonly observed ocean-side timber —..

● **LIVE OAK...** Broad fissured trunk, wide-spread crown. 2-5" leaves are dark green, stiff & waxy. Hardiest, most salt-resistent island oak.

● **PALMETTO...** 20-40' tall, with or without thatch of old, dead leafstalks on the trunk. Pliable 6-7' fan-like fronds bend with the wind. Note center midrib on the frond.

● **SLASH PINE...** thrives in moist sand zones. Needles in 2 & 3. Cones are 2-6" & tipped with sharp curved prickles. Grows 80-100' with a roundish crown.

SALT PRUNING

● **Dwarfed trees & shrubs** along the beachfront are the peculiar victims of what is called "salt spray". When the Atlantic's roiling surf explodes, seawater droplets are tossed aloft & blown ashore by winds. Included in the spray is sodium chloride (table salt), a killer mineral which burns needles/leaves of exposed dune vegetation. Salt spray whips up the face of the foredune & "prunes" woody plants at an upward angle, flattening their crowns & causing lower branches to sprawl along the swale sand for safety—.

HBallantine

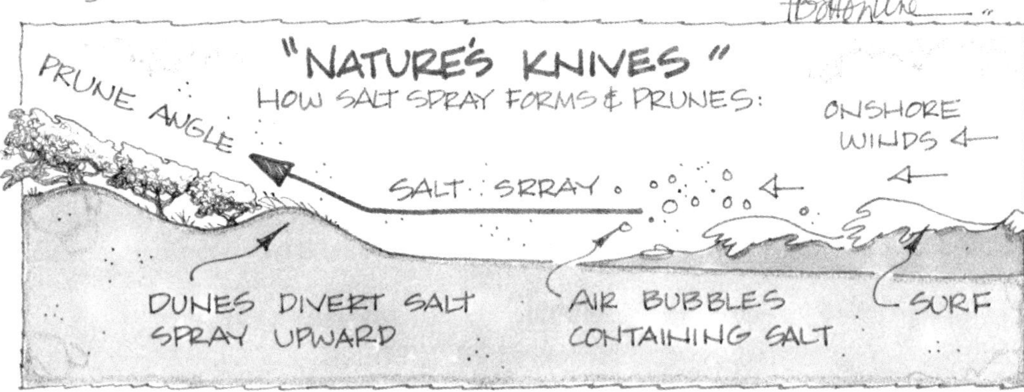

THE EFFECTS OF SALT SPRAY

● **STUNTING...** Evergreen oaks, bayberries & yaupons flatten noticeably on the windward side. Bottom branches reach out horizontally.

● **MISSING MIDRIB...** Pines' center branches are killed by spray, but the crown & lower limbs stay alive.

● **WILDLIFE COVER...** Rodents, lizards & sparrows hide & feed 'neath the protective low-growth shrubbery.

MARITIME FOREST

● **The woodlands near the sea** are a unique plant association called the maritime forest. Trees & shrubs here are specially adapted for survival in sandy soil, dune-swale topography & strong sea breezes laden with salt spray & sand. Well-developed root systems anchor them in the soft soil & tap deep for groundwater. Support against the wind is provided by strong trunks with twisting branches. Broadleaf evergreen leaves or needles are extra-thick, fending off salt-sand blast while absorbing sunlight year-round.

● **More maritime woods** are found in Sea Pines Plantation than elsewhere on Hilton Head. Vast tracts have been destroyed by golf courses, commercial developments & road building, with their clear-cutting or paving techniques. Remaining maritime forests should be preserved because they ① give aesthetic pleasure, ② reduce dust, fog, vapor, ③ shade extensive acreage, cooling the island amid summer's heat, ④ provide a noise buffer, ⑤ offer outdoor recreation opportunities & ⑥ provide a rich habitat for diverse wildlife.

WHERE THE WOODS ARE...

Atlantic Ocean

● **How maritime forests grow.** ① Hardy shrubs, palms & dwarf oaks guard the seaside border. ② Live oak, magnolia & slash pine fill the canopy. Branches interlock to form a dense green blanket, allowing little light to plants below. ③ Big-leaved palms & red bay grow 'neath lower limbs of #2. ④ Understory shrubs are sparse, but yaupon holly thrives.

HOW THE MARITIME FOREST SERVES WILDLIFE

• **The deep woods near the sea**, known as the Maritime Forest, are populated by a rich association of island animals. Hosts of mammals, birds, reptiles, amphibians, insects & others spend entire life cycles here because the everchanging landscape provides 4 necessities for habitat: food, cover, water & nest sites.

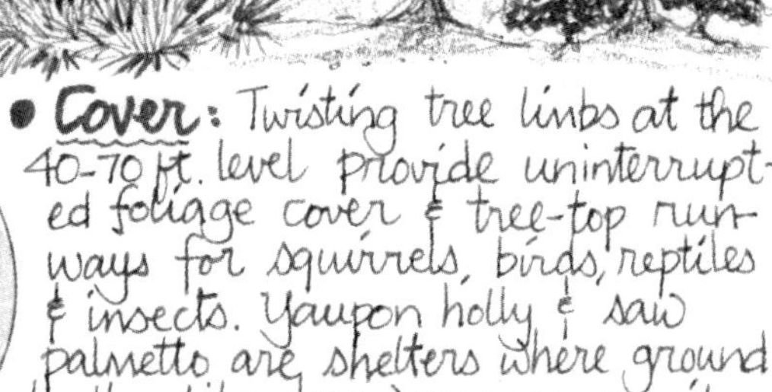

• **Food**: Live Oak acorns or "mast" annually feed deer, squirrels, gray fox, 'coons, wild turkey, mallards, wood ducks, quail, dove, woodpeckers, nuthatches, brown thrashers, towhees, thrushes, jays. Berries feed many birds & mammals. Insects are an ever-present edible for lizards, toads, frogs & birds like vireos or warblers.

Mast
Insects
Fruits

• **Cover**: Twisting tree limbs at the 40-70 ft. level provide uninterrupted foliage cover & tree-top runways for squirrels, birds, reptiles & insects. Yaupon holly & saw palmetto are shelters where ground dwellers like deer, 'possum, quail & snakes hide, rest or hunt.

• **Water**: Natural wetlands found in low swales ("sloughs") between dunes may flood March–September, forming marshes & swamps. Here woodland animals seek drinking water. Fish, frogs, reptiles, birds, marsh rabbits & insects breed here. Wading birds migrate in to feed.

Wetland
Dune
Dune

• **Nesting**: The Maritime Forest is "nature's living room" on the barrier isles. Many animal classes nest in/on strong oak/magnolia limbs, softening the roost with spanish moss, lichens, leaves & bark bits. Deadwood dens are used by squirrels, 'coons, woodpeckers, owls & others.

COASTAL PINES

• **"Yellow pines"** are the most abundant green growth of the southern barrier isles. Their pole-straight branchless trunks topped with silvery umbrella crowns are seen in all habitats here. Each pine species is specially adapted to different areas: loblolly - moist zones; shortleaf - light, dry soils; longleaf & slash - high sand ridges; pond - marsh borders; spruce - salt marsh side bluffs.

anatomy of a pine.

• **Loblolly pines** are most abundant here. A fast-growing volunteer of cut-over fields, low dunes & marsh hammocks, it loves moist depressions called "loblollies", hence its common name. It can top 75 ft. in 30 years! Bark on mature trees makes scaly cinnamon-colored plates. 6-9" needles are yellow-green. They'll drop after the 2nd season. Cones are 2-6" long & are tipped with triangular spines on the scales. In late winter all islanders get to know these pines by their pollen. Noticeable clusters of yellow male flowers crowd lower branches Feb. to Mar... female blooms grow higher up. Seasonal winds breeze their pollen far'n wide, lemon-dusting lagoons & automobiles overnight. The airborne granules are a source of great sniffling for just about everyone in the weeks before the Spring Equinox ——!

• **Pines provide** for island wildlife in many ways. ① Quail, dove, wild turkey, songbirds & squirrels eat the nutritous, fat-rich seeds. ② Deer browse on needles & twigs. ③ Rodents, deer fawns & gamebirds hide 'neath the bushy cover of young trees. ④ Mature pines are nest sites for mourning doves & are roosts for migrating robins ——"

LIVE OAK

• **The grand old tree** of the Deep South is the majestic Live Oak. From coastal Virginia to Florida, it thrives in the sandy soils and salt marsh bluffs of barrier islands. Live oaks are not towering timber... they grow to only 40-50 ft. tall. But they are known to reach outward 3 times as far! Supported by a buttressed trunk (3-4 ft. diameter), broad-spreading limbs arch out horizontally in a twisting ballet of growth fashioned by seawinds & an eternal stretch for light in deep maritime woods. Some branches droop to the ground. Its round-topped crown makes the live oak look like an overgrown shrub from a distance.

• **Why "live" oak?** Simply, this oak is evergreen. The 2-5" elliptical leaves are extra hardy. A waxy cellulose covering protects them against salt spray, sunscald & even occasional freezes. Some leaves do fall in March when new buds nudge 'em off the stem, but the entire tree is never without greenery. Hence the slang, "live" oak. Note: Flowers appear in Mar.-Apr. Smallish 1" acorns are produced by Thanksgiving. They cover the forest floor in December, having rattled groundward thru limbs & leaves in Nor'easter gales.

• **The useful Live Oak** has been a boon to man & wildlife here. Indians ate the sweet nut meat after soaking out tannic acid. In the era of the great sailing ships, the U.S. Navy used the curved limbs to brace vessels' ribs & "knees". Today the popular ornamentals shade city streets & offer climb-alls for kids' playgrounds. Limbs are tree-top runways for mammals, birds, lizards & tree frogs. Squirrels & birds nest in junctions of the sturdy trunk, using everpresent Spanish moss for cushioning. Winter's "mast" of acorns feeds deer (50% of their diet), 'coons, squirrels, wild turkeys, quail, woodpeckers & many songbirds.

PALMETTOS

• **Palmetto, cabbage palm & sabal palm** are each names used by Carolinians to describe our state tree. The palmetto (sabal palmetto) is a true palm tree which thrives along the coast from SC–FLA. Here the humid clime (45-60" annual rain), the 300 day growing period & the never-frozen soil provides terrarium-like conditions for growth. Mature palmettos stand 60 ft. tall with a 1-2 ft. trunk diameter. They can live to 75 years. Note: palmettos are not to be confused with **saw palm**, a shrub palm with fan-like fronds.

• **Long, drooping fronds** (6 ft. long) identify the palmetto. Each frond's leathery blade forms from a central midrib on the stalk, amid sprays of thread-like cellulose fibers. A leathery covering is a specialization these employ to withstand sunscald, frost & salt winds. Young trees wear a "thatched skirt" of dead leaf stalks clinging to the trunk. In time, decay & climbing animals peel away this criss-cross cover, revealing splintery gray bark on straight, mature trunks. In May, tiny lemon-colored flowers bloom on a dangling cluster or "spathe". Certainly each blossom will be abuzz with spring's pollen-hungry honey bees. Oval indigo fruits ripen thru autumn. Enclosed within is a single brown seed, 2/3 the guts of the drupe.

• **Palmetto power...** How our palm trees help the environment: ① Fruits are food for 'coons, crows, mockingbirds & gulls. ② Dead trees are dens for boring woodpeckers, or squirrels nesting in soft, inner fibers. ③ Dead frond slash offers cover for snakes (never reach under a frond without looking first!), lizards & insects, & it rebuilds humus in sandy soil. ④ Long, stringy roots bind soil in unstable zones like dunes or marsh hammocks. Thus they help resist erosion.

SAW PALMETTO

● **The shrub palm** of the southern barrier islands is called the saw palmetto. Sharp saw spikes arming the stem of the frond name this plant... it is spiny enough to slice leather! Islanders can't miss seeing the saw palmetto. It thrives as 5 ft. high dense scrub growth: ① in swales between sand dunes; ② in the open air of "Florida scrub" pine woods; ③ 'neath live oaks in the shady maritime forest. Fronds make a ◂ fan-shape, 2 ft. in diameter. But unlike those of palmetto trees, saw palm leaves radiate out from the base of the leafstalk. The root is the reason saw palmettos are shrubby. It spreads laterally underground, sending fresh green fronds upward every few inches. This hairy "rhizome" root is known to ripple asphalt bike/golf cart paths!

● **The value of saw palmettos to the island environment:**

① **Like a snow fence,** shrub-growths catch blowing sand to build dunes.

② **Shrubs are cover** for ground-dwelling deer, reptiles & birds. Predators are cut on the stem's spines.

③ **Fruits** (dark blue) feed coons, squirrels, robins & mockingbirds.

④ **Fire-resistant roots** sprout shoots following forest fires, quickly recolonizing woodlands.

⑤ **Indians** used the dried fruits as a sedative to treat infection & to aid digestion. Seeds were eaten. Inner root bark made a poultice to relieve skin ulcers, snake & insect bites.

• "The salt marsh evergreen" might be a good nickname for our Southern Red Cedar. For this is the 20-50' Juniper with the whispy, viridian-green crown, colonizing brackish mudbanks & wettish sand/oyster spits. Along estuaries, tides & high winds often topple the tree, causing it to sprawl out across the tideland turf.. its arms reaching to the sun & its crown laid flat from salt spray. In protected climes, Red Cedars achieve a drooping "Christmas Tree" pyramid form. Its 1/8" scale-like leaves (not needles!) are closely pressed in opposite pairs & stay on the twig 5-6 years before browning up. To age the tree, note the trunk. By the time the shredded, rust-red bole measures 2 feet across, this slow-grower may be over 200 years old!

I. Bottomlane

Note: Lovers of lime, So. Red Cedars thrive wherever calcium-rich shells abound. See 'em stand in "Shell Rings" & Tabby ruins, they indicate a high-PH soil.

CEDAR WAX-WING

CONE

The aromatic sap in the twigs & bark is a rich magenta!

• Cedar pollen (from separate ♂ flowers) & happy honeybees fill the air here 'round Valentine's Day. Fertilized ♀ blooms mature into fleshy-round cones. The 1/4" sweet fruits look chalky-blue from a covering of waxy powder. So relished are the berries as a wildlife food, that one bird, the Cedar Waxwing, is even named for its cone cravings! Oct.-Dec. watch Waxwings, finches, tree swallows, warblers & mockingbirds raze the fruits, then roost nights in the thick greenery. Deer also enjoy the twigs & leaves. A popular ornamental, this Cedar has historically yielded moth-repellant oils, wood shavings for animal bedding, & lumber for cabinetry, cigar boxes, siding & graphite pencils.

SPANISH MOSS

• **Old man's beard** might be a more useful name for Spanish moss, for it is neither Spanish, nor a moss! Rather, it's a stringy gray, rootless herb that drapes live oaks, cypresses & gums with woolly festoons. Their natural platforms of knarled, horizontal limbs provide the best foothold for the "moss" which slides off spindly pines or bushy palms. Contrary to popular misconception, Spanish moss does not kill our beautiful hardwoods & is definitely not a parasite. It merely hangs from trees to drink in rainwater, absorb sunlight & take up dust or minerals leaching from its chosen branch. Growing entirely in the air, sapping nothing from its host, Spanish moss is called an "epiphyte" or air plant. The only damage it may cause a tree is to cover up blossoms or fruits (ie. pecans), or when its rain-soaked weight causes old, weak limbs to snap—.

Note: Special hairs coat the rootless tendrils to sop-up nutrients as weather changes. In dry spells, the thirsty plant goes furry-gray as these hairs open out like doors to catch water. After rains, the doors shut to conserve moisture. The plant, now 75% water, looks rubbery green.

FLOWER
PARACHUTES
SEED POD

• **A well-traveled member** of the pineapple family, Spanish moss ranges from coastal Virginia to Argentina. Here, the plant blooms April–July, its blossoms filling our warm evenings with a delicate fragrance. Miniscule seeds breeze along on hairy "parachutes," then bounce off the slippery top foliage & tumble to already dead/rotting boughs below. There the moss settles in bark fissures & flourishes in the garden of deadwood. 'Cause this naturally occurs on leafless limbs, the plant appears to have strangled the tree—!

• **Deer, wild turkey & horses eat** this epiphyte. But it's as a nest bedding that "long moss" has greatest value. It makes the home cushy for owls, egrets, mockingbirds, squirrels & more. Herbalists use it as tea to relieve rheumatism, abcesses & birth pains. Henry Ford stuffed seats in his 1st model T's with this treeline upholstery!

POISON IVY
"Leaves of 3, let 'em be!" is gospel woodlore to remember when hiking to the beach or thru the forest. Commonly confused for wild grape vines twining trees or free-standing shrubs, Poison Ivy is an all too common plant menace here Mar.-Oct. Human contact with its leaves, vines & fruits produces an annoying, itchy rash. The plant tissues are loaded with urishiol, a poisonous oil similar to carbolic acid, irritating to the skin. This oil may be brushed on your skin from other folks clothes, or from roaving dog & cats. 1 of 20 people are immune to poison ivy, however ——.
WAXY-WHITE BERRIES
A poison Ivy remedy! The smartest thing to do is avoid the plant. Learn to spot the familiar 3 leaflets usually smooth-edged, sprouting from pine straw, making tangled shrubs or flourishing out of a hairy central vine on pines/oaks. Urishiol takes about 3 hours to do skin damage. Wash exposed areas with soap & cold water. If itching develops into lines of clear bubbly blisters, scrub the spot... even popping the bumps (this won't spread the infection)... with a cloth soaked in apple cider vinegar. This may sting a few seconds, but it's worth it. The vinegar dries up "the itch" in hours!
Poison Ivy is food for these birds (winter berries) & for deer (leaves & branches). Animals aren't allergic to ivy, as constant consumption produces a blood immunity!
DEER
FLICKER
CAT BIRD
HERMIT THRUSH
YELLOW-BELLIED SAPSUCKER

SOME SIMPLE

SALT MARSH PLANTS

● To grow green in the salt marsh, plants must work for a living! Twice-a-day flood tides lace foliage with burning salt. Yet rains & nearby lagoons also bring a bath of fresh water. Low tide mud banks bake at 140°, then cool down to 70-80° when waters return. By adapting strong, spreading roots & thick, weather-proof leaves, these simple seven survive our salt marshes,,,, and do their job stabilizing soggy soil & hiding/feeding animal life ranging from Oysters to Fiddler Crabs ——..

① CORDGRASS (Spartina arterniflora) is the marsh! The head-high grass dominates tide covered marsh banks. 1" wide leaves grow 1½ ft. long. Goes to seed by October.

② SALT MEADOW CORDGRASS (Spartina patens) only grows knee-high on drier marsh flats where tides merely trickle. Leaves are thinner (1/16") & shorter than Spartina arterniflora.

③ BLACK NEEDLE RUSH grows waist-high at the highest tide line. Hollow, sharp-pointed stems are tinted dusty gray ——.

④ SEA OXE-EYE DAISY.. Yellow blooms bush up just behind the needle rushes, beginning June. Leaves are stiff enough to support Willet nests —.

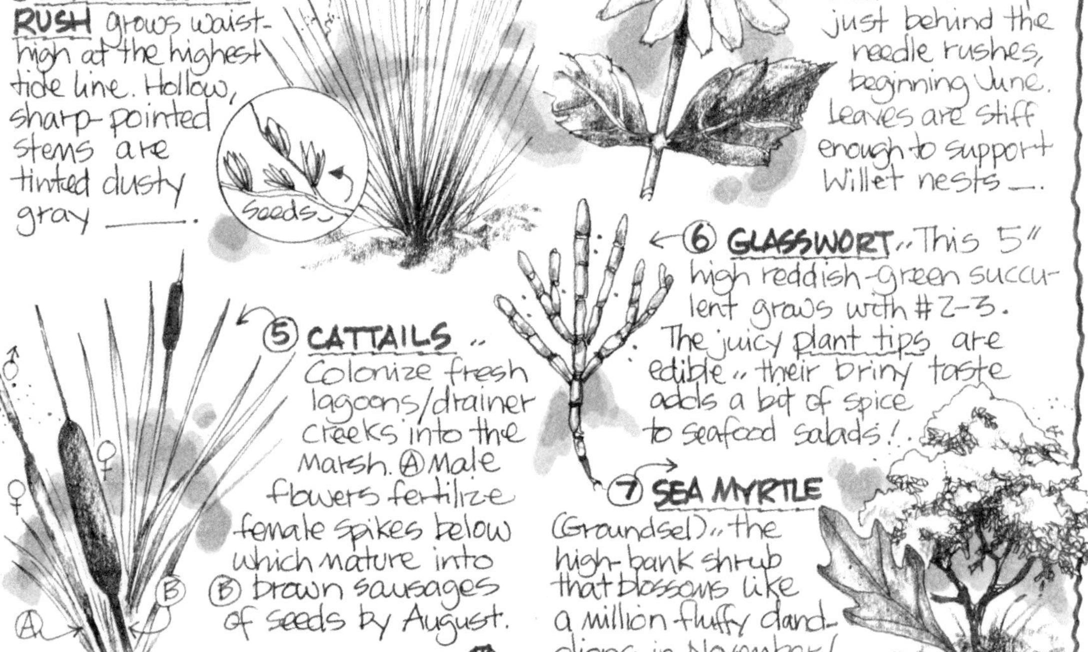

⑤ CATTAILS.. Colonize fresh lagoons/drainer creeks into the marsh. Ⓐ Male flowers fertilize female spikes below which mature into Ⓑ brown sausages of seeds by August.

⑥ GLASSWORT.. This 5" high reddish-green succulent grows with #2-3. The juicy plant tips are edible.. their briny taste adds a bit of spice to seafood salads!

⑦ SEA MYRTLE (Groundsel).. the high-bank shrub that blossoms like a million fluffy dandelions in November!

SALT MARSH SHRUBS

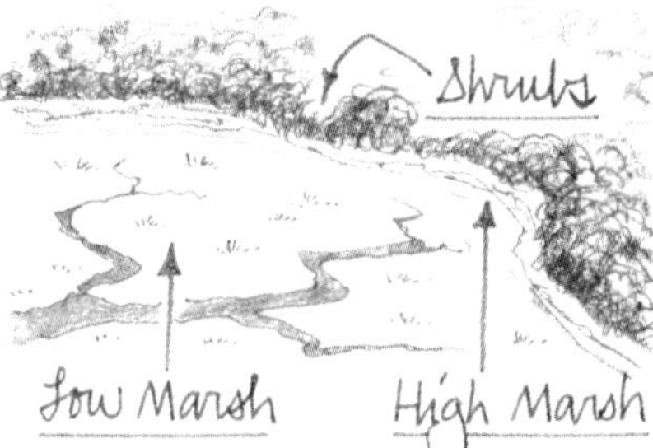

• **A phalanx of bushes & small trees** colonizes the perimeter of the "high marsh". Here plants are seldom flooded except during unusual Spring tides or storms. Beyond their stand lies the brackish wetzone of cordgrass & salt creeks. These shrubs must adapt to strong wind, salt spray, burning sun & sandy soil. They adjust by employing pliant branches which bend before the breezes. The shrubs grow horizontally into dense thickets rather than upwards into shearing winds. Protection against salt & sun is provided by a waxy coat of cellulose on the leaves, which feel stiff to the touch. Behind this thick green cloak, needed water is stored. Shallow root systems form a wide-spreading network 'neath the soil to absorb maximum rainfall trickling thru the sand. Below are shown the 4 most seen saltmarsh shrubs.

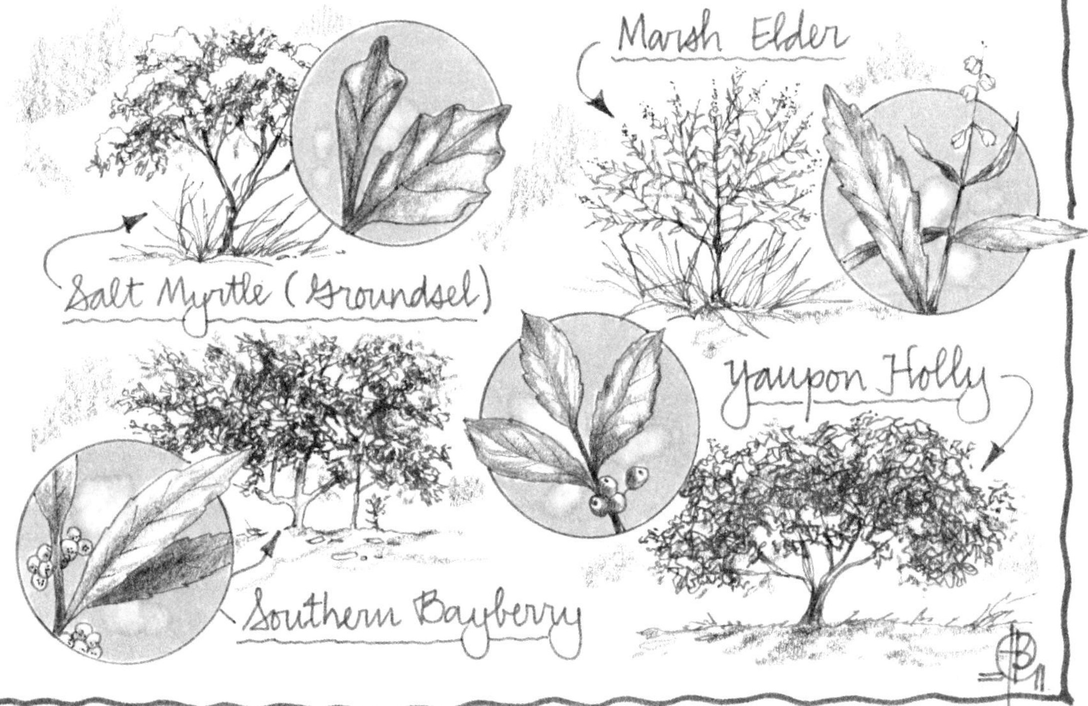

SEA MYRTLE

(GROUNDSEL, SALT MYRTLE, SILVERLING)

FEMALE (TOP) + MALE (BOTTOM) FLOWERS

- **Snow-white, billowing blooms** on coastal sea myrtles are a sure-fire forcaster of coming frost. These are the 10-15 ft. tall shrubs bordering roadsides, saltmarshes, ponds + grown-over landfills. From late October through December, watch the bushes turn out feathery flowers like a million dandelions in one, branching boquet. The ivory fluff in the flora is made by female blossoms, with tiny seeds attached to tufts of silky hairs carried far + wide on Autumn winds. Male flowers are yellow. They appear on separate shrubs + spread their pollen on the wind.

- **Sea myrtles are kin to Sagebrush,** those gnarled, 4 ft. desert bushes, out West. Study a myrtle trunk... you'll see the connection. Twisted + woody, it must stand up to Nor'easters whipping across open water. Or crunch the gray, green, toothy leaves. The pungent aroma reminds you of the "sage" in sagebrush. Lowcountry herbalists say this resin (in leaves + roots) is a treatment in tea for colds, coughs + stomachaches. Hence the nickname: "Consumption weed". Watch for honey bees among the blossoms. The honey they make from sea myrtle nectar has a strong, wild flavor + is especially popular in the South.

J. Ballantine

EARLY SPRING WILDFLOWERS

● What a welcome sight it is to see fields, roadsides & wetlands sprinkled with Spring's 1st spots of color! Wildflowers... 10's of 1000's of their windsown seeds nap dormantly thru Dec-Feb chills 'til March drizzles, stronger sun & warmer earth sparks 'em to pop up almost overnite! Get to know these "Spring Six"... ea. bloom tells a tale of the soil, drainage & light patterns of its specific Island habitat..

① **INNOCENCE**.. A perennial kin to bluets. The tiny, 4 petaled white blossoms grow from dense rosette mats right at the margin where shading Oaks, Sweet Gums & Sassafrass meet clearings. Loves to root in grass. Our earliest bloomer—.

④ **BLUE TOADFLAX**.. Delicate lavender & white flowers with 2 petals above, 3 below. Stands 12" high. Thrives in open sun, sandy soil & fill dirt habitats. Commonly grows near both #1 and #2 —.

③ **BULL THISTLE**.. That 3 ft. tall plant in the ditches with the tennis ball-sized white/violet blooms. Celery-like stems are covered by down, but the leaves bite like cactus!

② **SHEEP SORREL**.. Knee-high reddish flower stalks blanket fallow fields & hi-way shoulders. Likes acid soil... if it sprouts in your garden, add nitrogen!

⑤ **SOW THISTLE**.. 4-6 dandelion-like yellow flowers top 2 ft. high masses of prickly leaves. A typical thistle, it loves wet soil, open sun.

⑥ **LIFE EVERLASTING**.. Fluffy "pussy toes" blooms tip branchy, green, 1-3 ft. clusters, on roadsides.

The Animals

Consider the horseshoe crab. The armored arthropod has been trudging from shoals to shore and back for well over four hundred million years with very little evolutionary change in its physique. How is it that a primitive citizen of the sea like *Limulus* has successfully maintained its lifestyle for 400 million years? The answer lies in the tidelands themselves.

All reaches of our coast...the beach, the inlets, marshes and estuaries... are an edge between the mighty ocean and the land. The sea islands stand as a barrier to the sea, and these two elements are forever intermingling. The currents and tides bring or steal the sands, and erode the soils of the high grounds. The marshes and estuaries are piled deep with a rich bed of nutrient silt, borne by the moving waters. Here, both microscopic and tremendous-sized animals from the sea and land will migrate to breed, grow, hunt and die.

The sea beach may seem like a cemetery of wave-stranded animals and cast-off shells. Nearby tidepools offer refuge for a wealth of nearshore creatures abandoned by the sea. They hustle around these warm puddles, oblivious that their moments are numbered in their draining, shrinking world. A few yards seaward lie the shoals where a saltwater aquarium of spined, legged, tentacled, shelled and finned animals abide day and night. The salt marsh with its matrix of creeks, canals, mud banks and flats is a living pasture for the entire wetworld foodchain.

The sea currents which swirl around or pass by the islands are highways of migration for coastal animals. Fish follow on the trail of blooming plankton. Larger fish and dolphin prey on their swelling populations. Birds wing the wavy crests and treetops along the coast in seasonal pursuit of food and nesting space.

Many of these waterside wayfarers, along with the resident species of the sands, waves and marsh grasses, are easily observed by islanders. The animals we experience on a beachcombing excursion or fishing outing may be visitors to our world as much as we are to theirs. Yet all are due our appreciation and conservation, for we are each kindred creatures in the whole of creation.

ANIMALS LIVING IN THE LITTORAL

MEAN HIGH TIDE ... MEAN LOW TIDE

← THE LITTORAL BEACH →

● **The beach between tides,** called the littoral, is a hidden garden of animal life. Some harried creatures do scavenge low tide flotsam, risking air exposure, sunburn & shorebird hunters. But the majority hides below the surface safe from surf & predators, feeding on organic matter currents trickle down thru sand grains. Here are 3 ways life gets by in this everchanging world of wet & dry —...

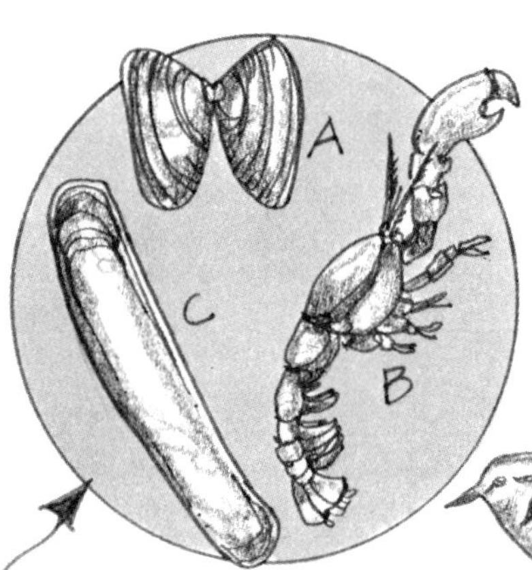

PLOVER

● **Burrowing** animals like Ⓐ coquina clams, Ⓑ ghost shrimp & Ⓒ jacknife clams dig 1-18" under beach sand. Breath thru siphons & holes —...

A B C D E

GULL

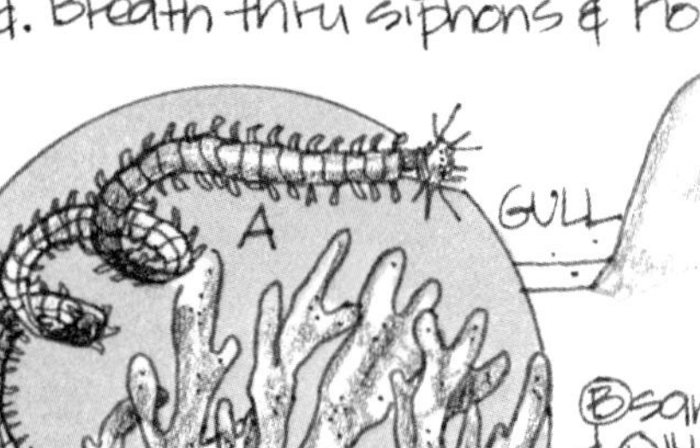

● **Crawling** Ⓐ fiddler crabs, Ⓑ sand dollars, Ⓒ starfish, Ⓓ hermit crabs & Ⓔ "beach fleas" scavenge swash lines, hide in debris, old shells & sand for defense.

● **Anchoring** helps Ⓐ clam worms & Ⓑ finger sponges exist. The worm is footed in a self-made tube, the sponge attached to driftwood & rocks.

B

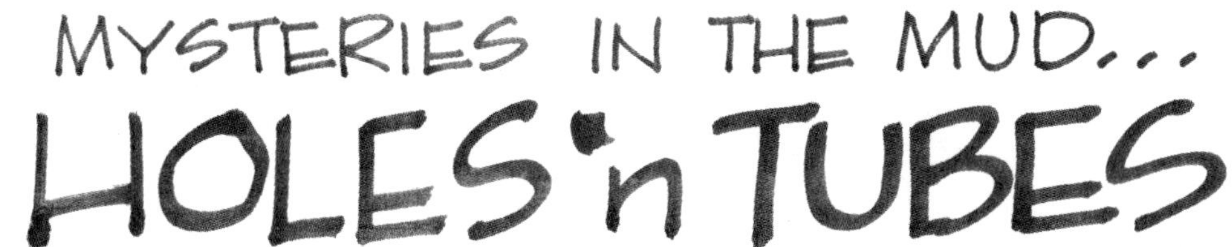

• The wide, wet flats between the highest wave swash & the lowest ebb tide are a dangerous domain for small sea creatures. To duck enemies, escape the pounding surf & yet still suck in food & oxygen, many marine animals burrow down into the shelter of the subterranean mud. Why not stop on your next beach trek to study these hide-away-hosts' "front doors"?... those familiar but mysterious holes, tubes, tunnels & tracks...

• **MUD or GHOST SHRIMP**.. This big-clawed, 2" cream-colored shrimp digs down 1½ ft! Sucks drifting organic matter into its burrow. Expels waste pellets that look like "chocolate jimmies" sprinkled about the hole... Burrows are "U" shaped with 2 entrances...

• **CLAM WORM**.. Gyrates within a mucus & sand hollow tube to pump in plankton & small prey. These macaroni-like chambers poke up 1" & break off in the waves. Pieces pile up like wet noodles at low tide!

TUBE "NOODLES"

• **GHOST CRAB**.. Digs "gopher holes" from the wave line all the way back into the dry sand dunes. The 2" tannish speedster usually hides 3 ft. down during sunlight & runs to the sea at night to wet gills & feed. Holes show both the sand-ball diggings & crab tracks around the entry...

• **OLIVE SNAIL**.. This 2½" cylindrical snail is typical of its large footed (gastropod) kin. It digs fast & deep, leaving a trough-trail & a narrow, pushed-up "mole tunnel" in the tidal muds...

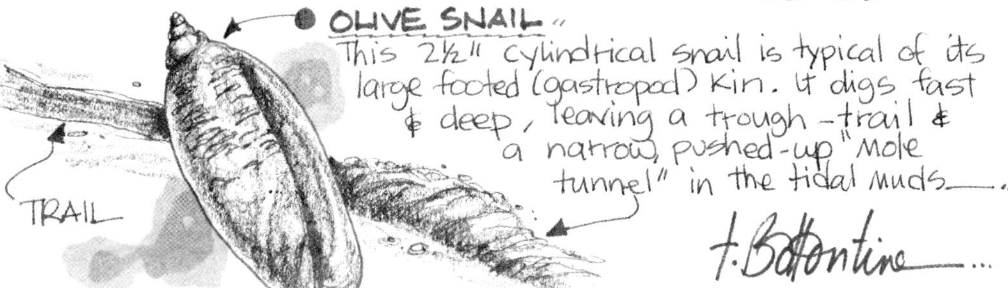

T. Ballantine...

SAND TRAILS

•**Stalking the strand** are countless creatures of the sea which come ashore to hunt, build homes or lay eggs. Especially in the morning, tidal-flats bear dragging, tiptoed, clawed, webbed, tunnel or pellet tracks left by marine visitors. Watch for & follow these mystery markings ... a surprise may await you at the trail's end!

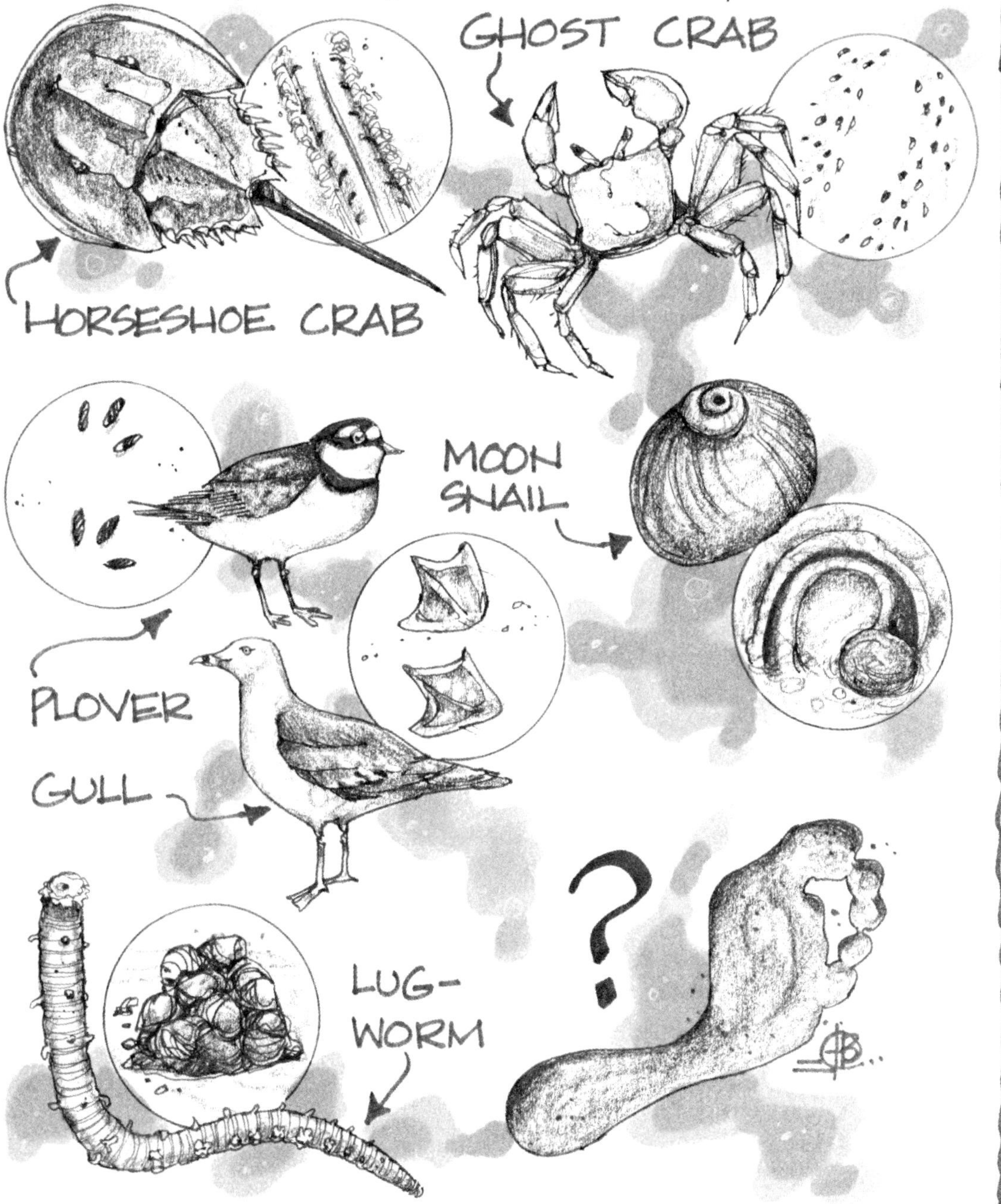

HORSESHOE CRAB

GHOST CRAB

PLOVER

GULL

MOON SNAIL

LUG-WORM

?

TO LAY AN EGG

The sea world is a deadly nursery for marine younglings. Predators devour 98% of eggs & storm tides maroon spawn ashore. To save their brood, parents create many odd shaped cases & capsules. Anchored to shells, stones or seaweed, these stiff egg shelters are quite unpalatable to scavengers. Here are some common cases, with their progenitors, beach-combers will discover.

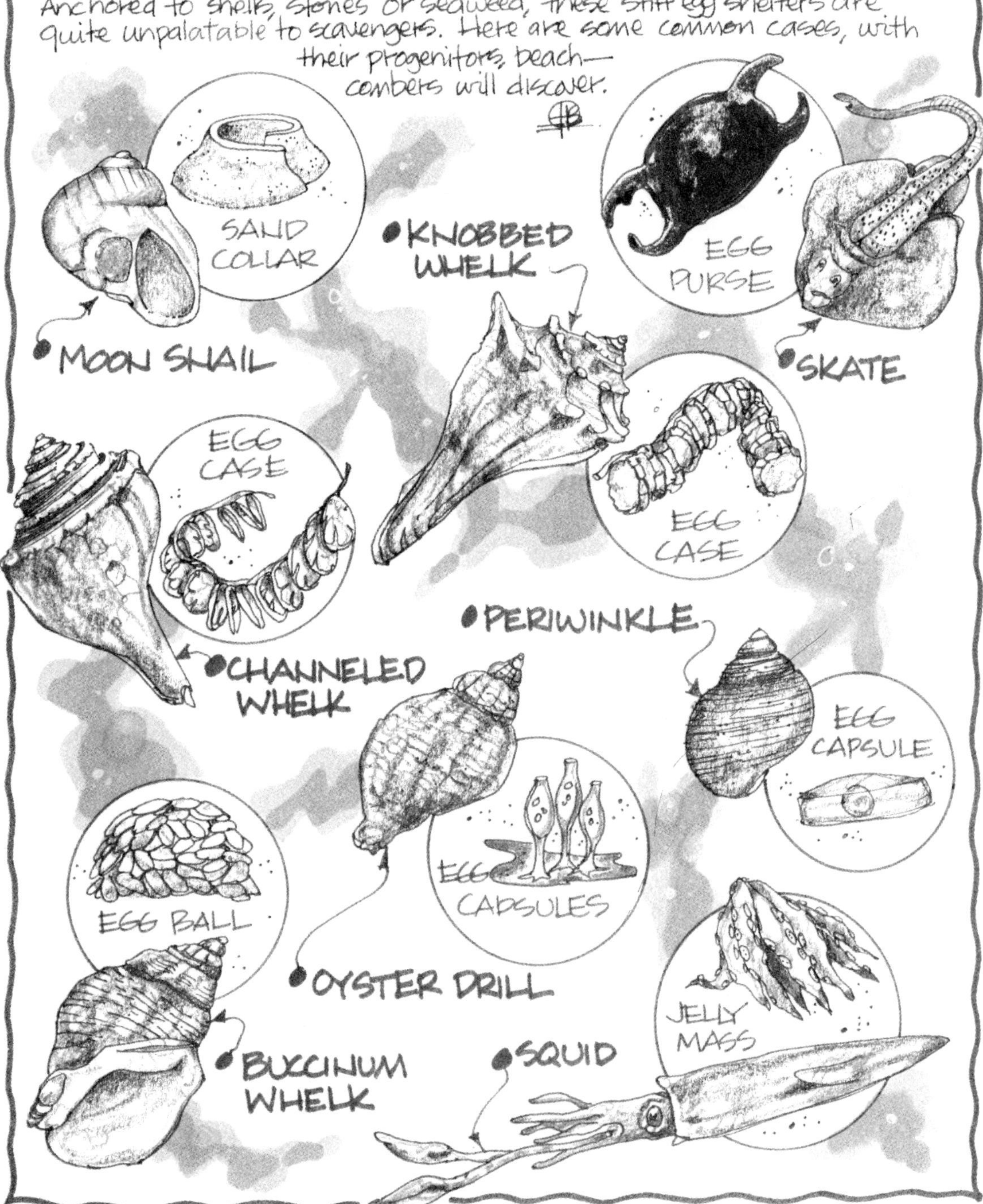

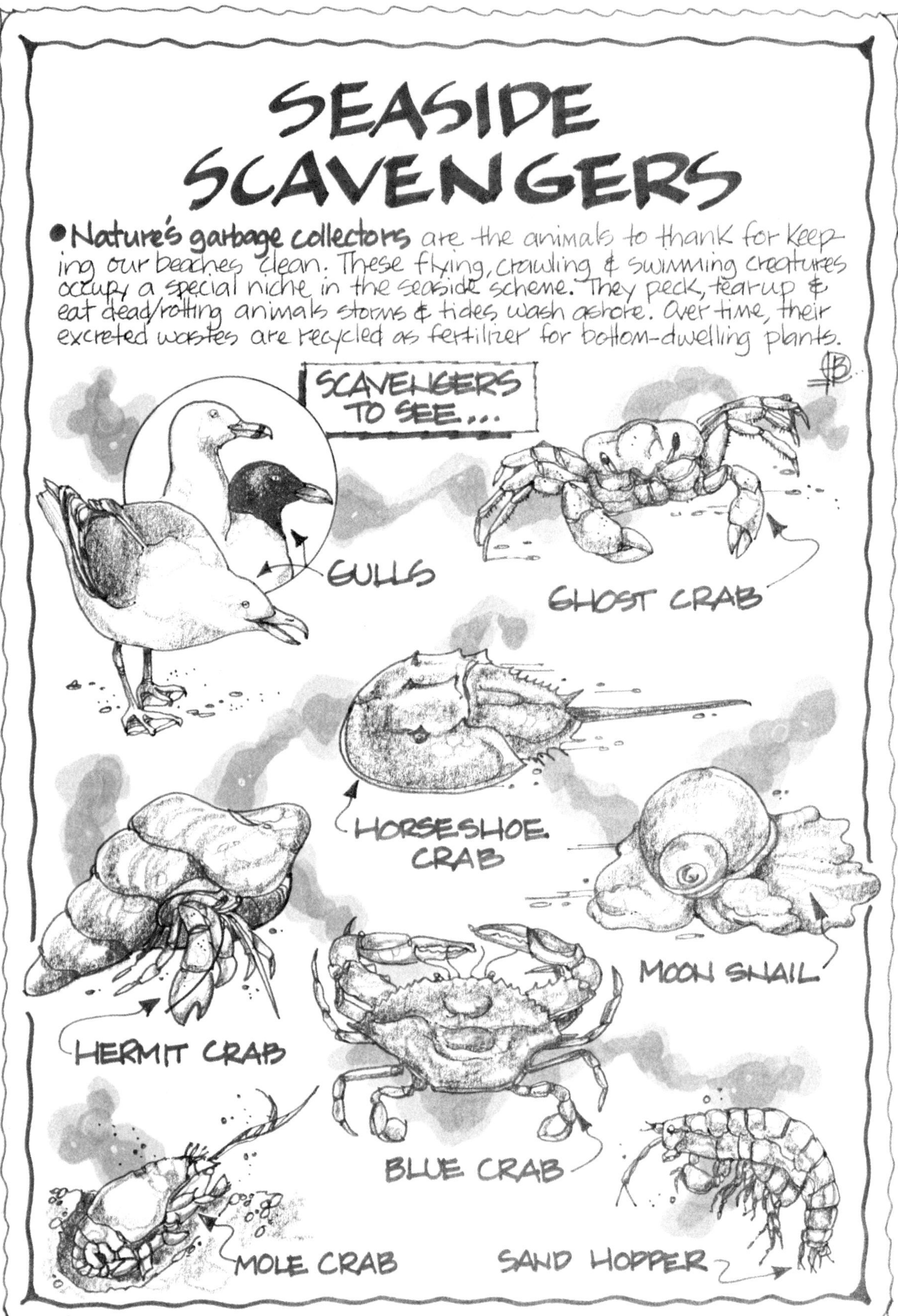
SEASIDE SCAVENGERS
• Nature's garbage collectors are the animals to thank for keep-
ing our beaches clean. These flying, crawling & swimming creatures
occupy a special niche in the seaside scheme. They peck, tear up &
eat dead/rotting animals storms & tides wash ashore. Over time, their
excreted wastes are recycled as fertilizer for bottom-dwelling plants.
SCAVENGERS TO SEE...
GULLS
GHOST CRAB
HORSESHOE CRAB
MOON SNAIL
HERMIT CRAB
BLUE CRAB
MOLE CRAB
SAND HOPPER

HIDDEN LIFE ON WHARF PILINGS

•A totem pole of tidal life abounds on underwater piles of docks, piers & wharves. Swashed by tidal flux, marine animals cleave to these man-made holdfasts, feeding on the sweep of mud & detritus, or each other. Creatures found here vary from high to low tide levels, survival dependent on ability to withstand air exposure.

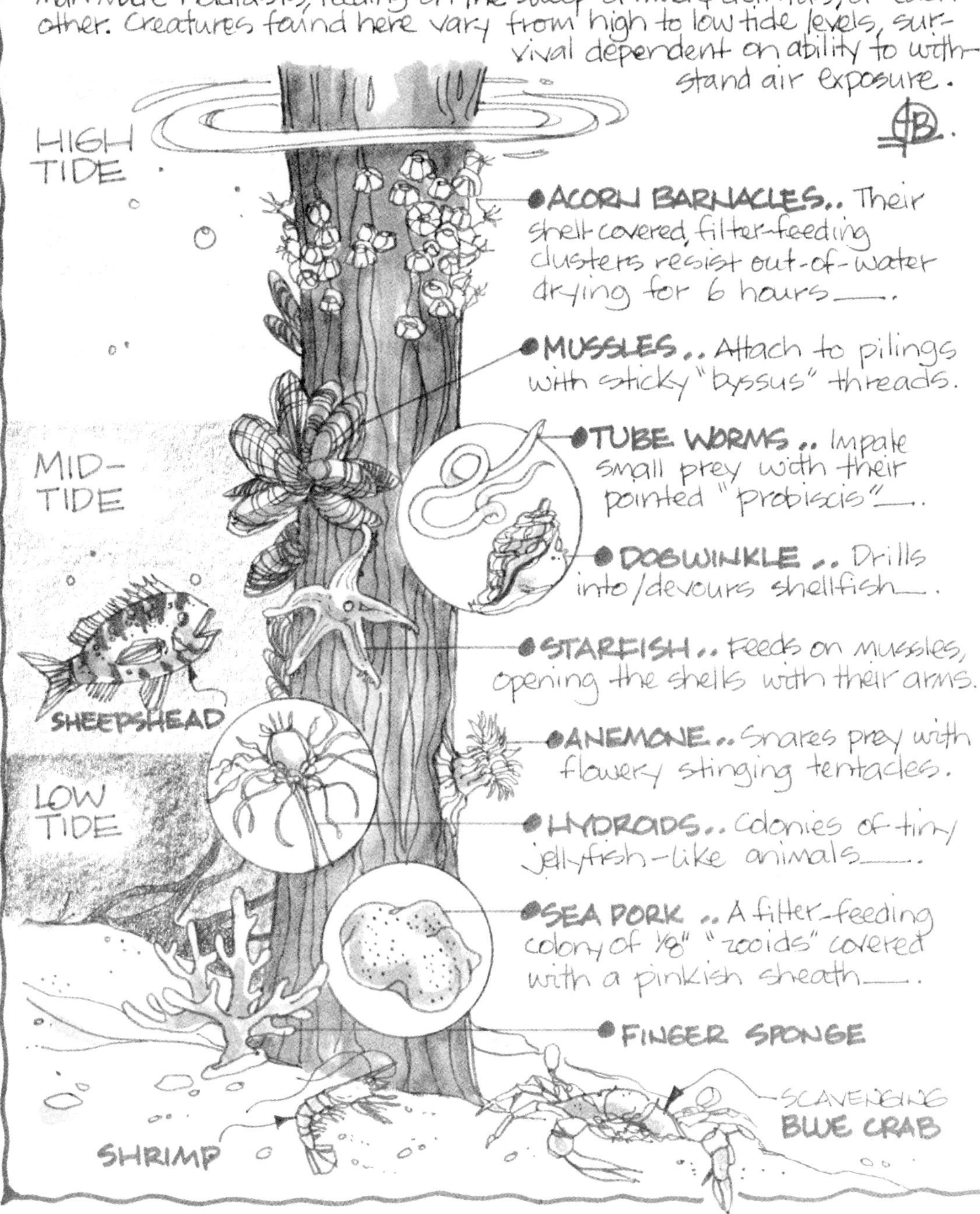

MARINE MINERS

Scores of saltwater animals spend their lives digging, boring and drilling into mud, wood, rock and each other. While they are common to our area, these sea world prospectors are secretive and well-entrenched. Learn about each creature by becoming familiar with the mysterious burrows it once excavated in the flotsam that washes ashore——.

SHELL

SHIPWORMS are not worms, but clams. Using their 2 sharp shells as rasps & rocking on their foot, they cut long, cylindrical holes in wood. Boring 3/4" daily, they can destroy untreated wharf pilings & hulls in less than a year!

FOOT

GRIBBLES are crustaceans that look more like small (3/16") insects. They bore 1/16" holes, with the grain, into submerged wood. They eat fungi living inside the timber, not the wood itself——.

OYSTER DRILLS are voracious carnivores which rasp pin holes into oyster shells & devour the defenseless mollusk inside. Other hole-drilling snails include whelks and moon snails.

BORING CLAMS include Martesia clams & angel wings. Martesia (right) tunnel into pilings, coral & even concrete harbor piles. By rocking on their muscular foot, they can twist their shells back & forth to abrade hard surfaces. Dug-away "tailings" are flushed with water from the siphons—.

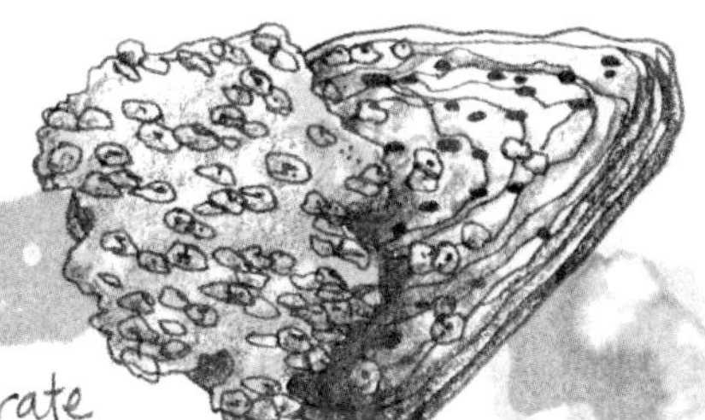

BORING SPONGES (lower right) penetrate clam & oyster shells, riddling them with tiny pits. They serve to disintegrate the shells into a rubble of calcium carbonate, comprising over 50% of our sand supply——.

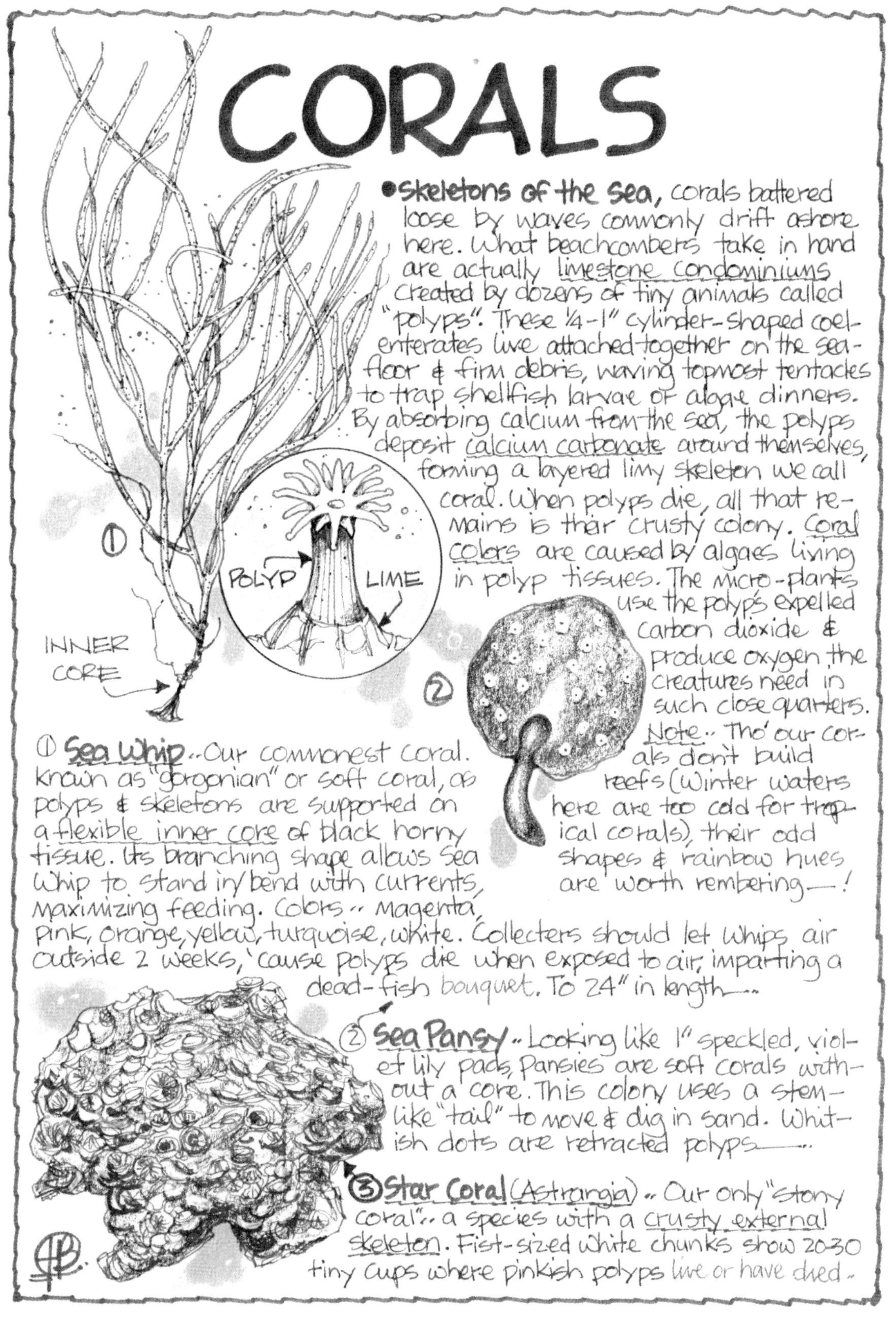
CORALS
•Skeletons of the Sea, corals battered loose by waves commonly drift ashore here. What beachcombers take in hand are actually limestone condominiums created by dozens of tiny animals called "polyps". These ¼–1" cylinder-shaped coelenterates live attached together on the sea-floor & firm debris, waving topmost tentacles to trap shellfish larvae or algae dinners. By absorbing calcium from the sea, the polyps deposit calcium carbonate around themselves, forming a layered limy skeleton we call coral. When polyps die, all that remains is their crusty colony. Coral colors are caused by algaes living in polyp tissues. The micro-plants use the polyp's expelled carbon dioxide & produce oxygen the creatures need in such close quarters. Note.. Tho' our corals don't build reefs (Winter waters here are too cold for tropical corals), their odd shapes & rainbow hues are worth rembering—!
①
POLYP
LIME
INNER CORE
②
① Sea Whip.. Our commonest coral. Known as "gorgonian" or soft coral, as polyps & skeletons are supported on a flexible inner core of black horny tissue. Its branching shape allows Sea Whip to stand in/bend with currents, maximizing feeding. Colors.. magenta, pink, orange, yellow, turquoise, white. Collecters should let whips air outside 2 weeks, 'cause polyps die when exposed to air, imparting a dead-fish bouquet. To 24" in length...
② Sea Pansy.. Looking like 1" speckled, violet lily pads, Pansies are soft corals without a core. This colony uses a stem-like "tail" to move & dig in sand. Whitish dots are retracted polyps—.
③ Star Coral (Astrangia).. Our only "stony coral".. a species with a crusty external skeleton. Fist-sized white chunks show 20-30 tiny cups where pinkish polyps live or have died..

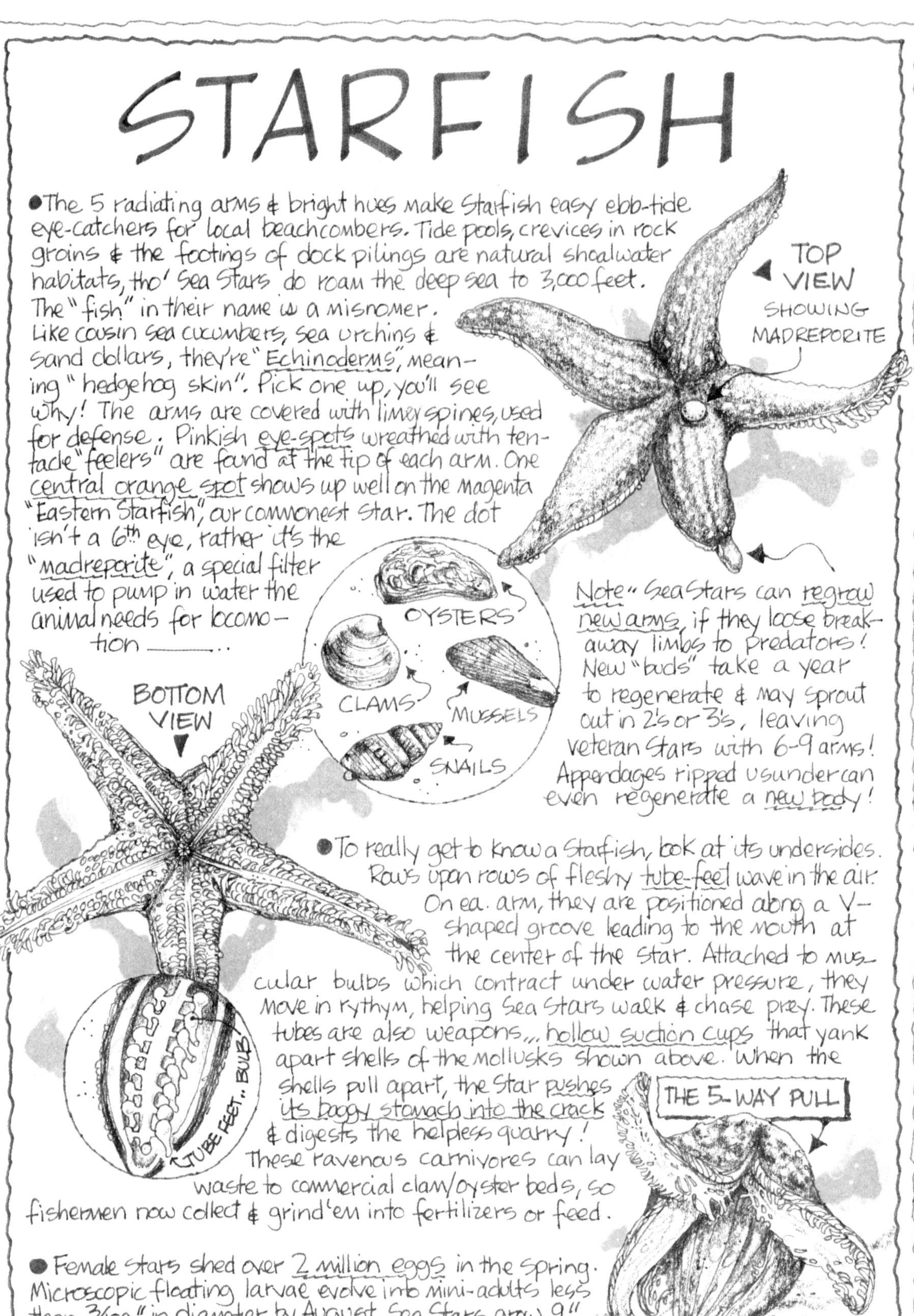
STARFISH
●The 5 radiating arms & bright hues make Starfish easy ebb-tide eye-catchers for local beachcombers. Tide pools, crevices in rock groins & the footings of dock pilings are natural shoalwater habitats, tho' Sea Stars do roam the deep sea to 3,000 feet. The "fish" in their name is a misnomer. Like cousin sea cucumbers, sea urchins & sand dollars, they're "Echinoderms", meaning "hedgehog skin". Pick one up, you'll see why! The arms are covered with limey spines, used for defense. Pinkish eye-spots wreathed with tentacle "feelers" are found at the tip of each arm. One central orange spot shows up well on the magenta "Eastern Starfish", our commonest star. The dot isn't a 6th eye, rather it's the "madreporite", a special filter used to pump in water the animal needs for locomotion ......
TOP VIEW SHOWING MADREPORITE
OYSTERS
CLAMS
MUSSELS
SNAILS
Note: Sea Stars can regrow new arms, if they loose break-away limbs to predators! New "buds" take a year to regenerate & may sprout out in 2's or 3's, leaving veteran Stars with 6-9 arms! Appendages ripped usunder can even regenerate a new body!
BOTTOM VIEW
●To really get to know a Starfish, look at its undersides. Rows upon rows of fleshy tube-feet wave in the air. On ea. arm, they are positioned along a V-shaped groove leading to the mouth at the center of the star. Attached to muscular bulbs which contract under water pressure, they move in rythym, helping Sea Stars walk & chase prey. These tubes are also weapons,,, hollow suction cups that yank apart shells of the mollusks shown above. When the shells pull apart, the Star pushes its baggy stomach into the crack & digests the helpless quarry! These ravenous carnivores can lay waste to commercial clam/oyster beds, so fishermen now collect & grind 'em into fertilizers or feed.
TUBE FEET.. BULB
THE 5-WAY PULL
●Female Stars shed over 2 million eggs in the spring. Microscopic floating larvae evolve into mini-adults less than 3/100" in diameter by August. Sea Stars grow 9" across, but will shrink & harden in winter's cold waves......

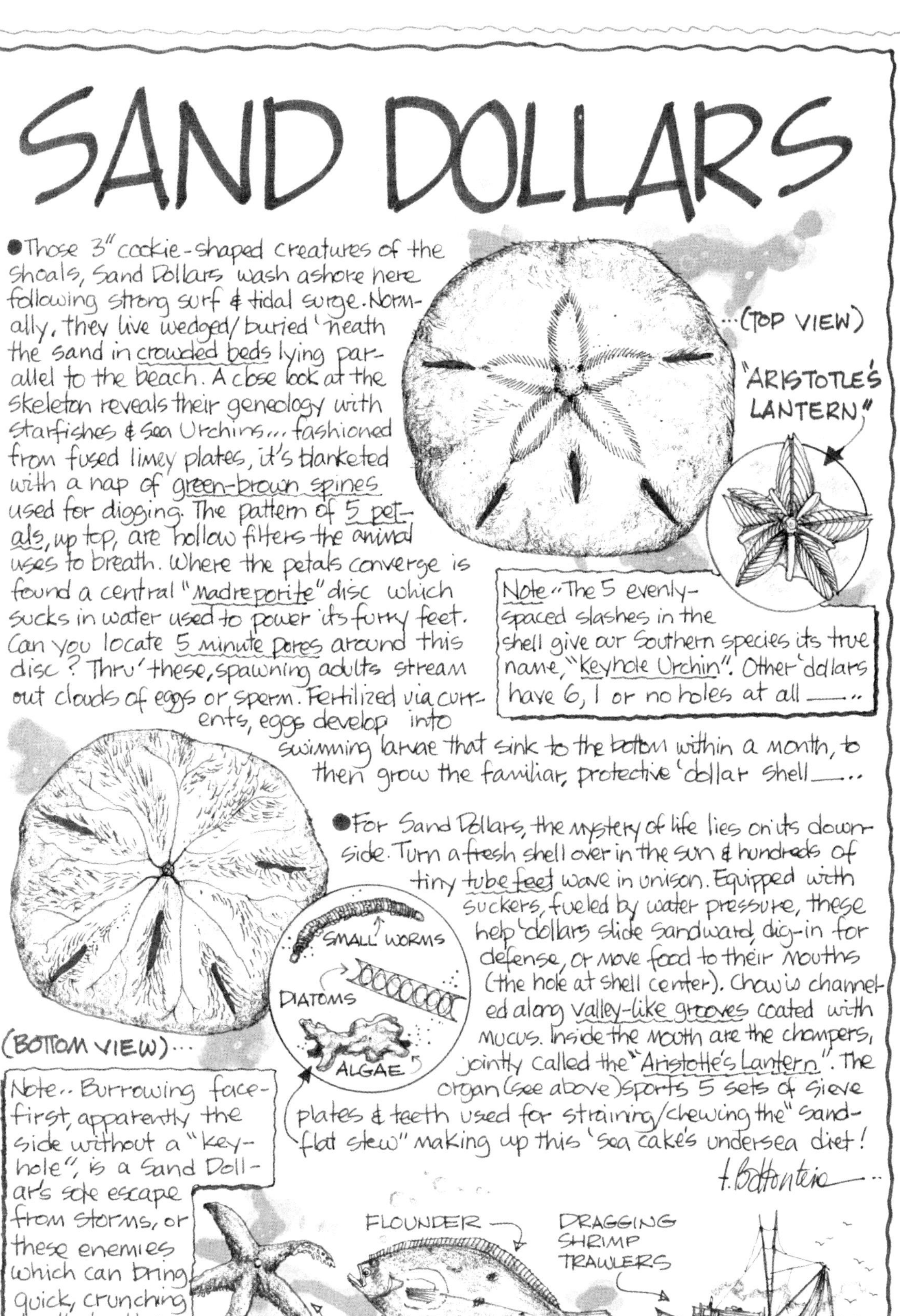
SAND DOLLARS
●Those 3" cookie-shaped creatures of the Shoals, Sand Dollars wash ashore here following strong surf & tidal surge. Normally, they live wedged/buried 'neath the sand in crowded beds lying parallel to the beach. A close look at the skeleton reveals their geneology with Starfishes & Sea Urchins... fashioned from fused limey plates, it's blanketed with a nap of green-brown spines used for digging. The pattern of 5 petals, up top, are hollow filters the animal uses to breath. Where the petals converge is found a central "Madreporite" disc which sucks in water used to power its furry feet. Can you locate 5 minute pores around this disc? Thru' these, spawning adults stream out clouds of eggs or sperm. Fertilized via currents, eggs develop into swimming larvae that sink to the botton within a month, to then grow the familiar, protective 'dollar shell.....
...(TOP VIEW)
"ARISTOTLE'S LANTERN"
Note.. The 5 evenly-spaced slashes in the shell give our Southern species its true name, "Keyhole Urchin". Other 'dollars have 6, 1 or no holes at all.....
●For Sand Dollars, the mystery of life lies on its down-side. Turn a fresh shell over in the sun & hundreds of tiny tube feet wave in unison. Equipped with suckers, fueled by water pressure, these help 'dollars slide sandward, dig-in for defense, or move food to their mouths (the hole at shell center). Chow is channeled along valley-like grooves coated with mucus. Inside the mouth are the chompers, jointly called the "Aristotle's Lantern". The organ (see above) sports 5 sets of sieve plates & teeth used for straining/chewing the "sand-flat stew" making up this 'sea cake's undersea diet!
SMALL WORMS
DIATOMS
ALGAE
(BOTTOM VIEW)...
Note.. Burrowing face-first, apparently the side without a "key-hole", is a Sand Dollar's sole escape from storms, or these enemies which can bring quick, crunching death to the colony!
STARFISH
FLOUNDER
DRAGGING SHRIMP TRAWLERS
F. Bottonteio...

HOW TO MAKE
SAND DOLLAR JEWELRY

• Our native Escamacu Indians were probably the pioneers in the art of Sand Dollar jewelry. They regularly styled sea shells into decorative amulets/ornaments. Today, this Low-Country craft is still alive & well, & one may choose medallions from sparkly displays in Island gift shops everywhere. But why pay out-the-nose for what you can make yourself? At low tide, search pools/flat sand beaches for 'dollars. They'll be strewn face up, just above the wave "splash," or buried 'neath a lump of sand the size of a sugar cookie. Use a spoon to dig under & excavate your treasure. Some folks even like to wade waist deep in the shoals, probing the soft bottom with their toes ___ !!

CONSERVATION NOTE ... Collect only dead 'dollars (those storm-kills or sun-bleached wash-ups). Take just what you need, leave the rest to eat, be eaten or crumble up into sand! I know of a case where visitors here gleaned 600 shells, then 2 days later chucked 'em all in the trash!

① GETTING THEM WHITE .. Soak 'dollars overnite in a solution of 1 part clorox to 3 parts water. Rinse-off & place shells on a paper towel, outside to dry. Let the strong S.C. sun do the real bleaching work!

② ADDING COLOR .. Brush on temperas or opaque water colors for bright tones. Dip 'dollars in ketchup to turn 'em pink, or mustard for lemon-yellow! For subtle, more natural dyes, soak shells in coffee (sepia tones) or herb teas (Sassafras makes a good orange) ___ ..

③ THE FINISH .. Protect your shell from moisture with 3-4 coatings of DaMar Spray Varnish, or Polyurethane diluted with laquer thinner. A safe recipe for kids is to use a mixture of Elmer's Glue-All & water, with powdered temperas mixed right-in. Using yarn or rawhide, string the shell thru' 2 of the 5 "keyholes" ___ ..

F. Bettontino ...

SEA CUCUMBER

●Resembling some globby-grey, washed-up Thuringer sausage rather than a marine creature, the Sea Cucumber rolls up on our low tide beaches April thru' November. It lives buried 'neath the muddy bottoms or rock jetties in Port Royal/Calibogue Sounds. Believe it-or-not, this 5" long, slug look-alike is kin to starfish & sand dollars, the symmetrical "echinoderms". Around its mouth are a cluster of branching tentacles, found in multiples of 5. Five double rows of feet help the animal crawl & burrow. Dinner is a simple slurped-up soup of decayed plants & plankton (like "diatoms") carried on the current. Shoveling up to 200 lbs. of grit thru' its baggy body ea. year, a "sea cuke" helps stir up sediments nearby shell fish filter as food themselves!

Note: The "crown of tentacles" is sticky to catch floating particles. Place a Sea Cucumber in the water, then watch the crown slowly emerge.

●Picking up a Sea Cucumber is an odd surprise. Ultra-sensitive to touch, the "hedgehog skin" contracts, turning the critter into a hard ball... a 1st line of defense against enemy crabs, urchins & starfish. As a last resort, desperate 'cucumbers turn inside-out, ejecting their sticky innards to stun, entangle & maybe gross-out predators! The organs, which regrow in 6 weeks, contain the chemical, "Holothurin". Scientists discovered it stimulates the heart as does Digitalis, and halts tumor growth in mice! In China & the East Indies, Sea Cucumbers are collected, dried & consummed as "Trepang", a gourmet's delight. The Japanese cook the animal in soy sauce & ginger. Hungry, anyone?

T. Ballantine

SPONGES

● **Aristotle's animals...** sponges are single or colonial creatures living on the sea floor, mud shoals, wharves & debris. The philosopher first discovered sponges actively jet water thru their bodies, tho' they do look more like marine plants. Absent are a head, mouth or internal organs. Sponges feed by pumping plankton-laden water & oxygen thru a network of internal water canals. Brown, gray, yellow or red, our sponges grow 3"–2 ft., range in shapes from branching to bushy to crusty. All species regrow new body parts... or the entire sponge if diced up! But wash-ups at So. Beach/Port Royal Sound are dead. Lay collected sponges in the sun a week to air out. Check spongy chambers for scads of sea animals (inset) hiding within...

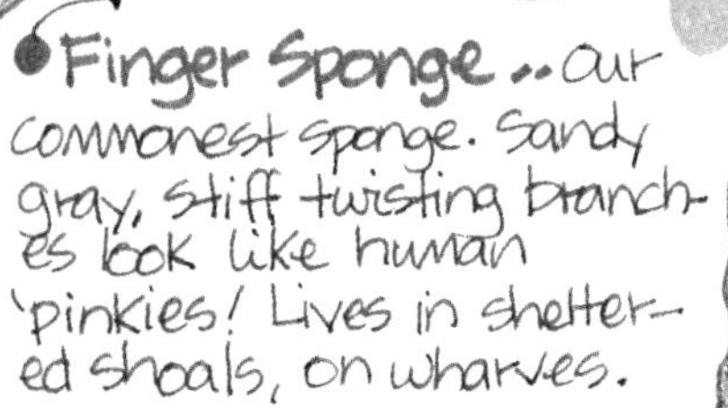

● **Finger Sponge..** Our commonest sponge. Sandy gray, stiff twisting branches look like human 'pinkies'! Lives in sheltered shoals, on wharves.

● **Velvet sponge..** A pale yellow, flattened cushion with fibers extending to blunt or sharp peaks. A rock groin sponge.

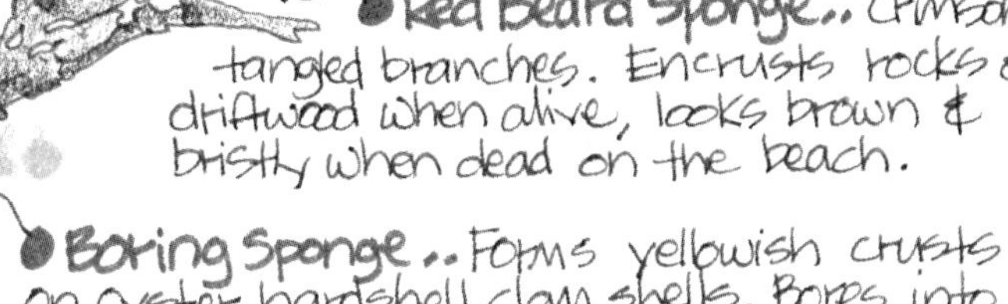

● **Red Beard Sponge..** Crimson tangled branches. Encrusts rocks & driftwood when alive, looks brown & bristly when dead on the beach.

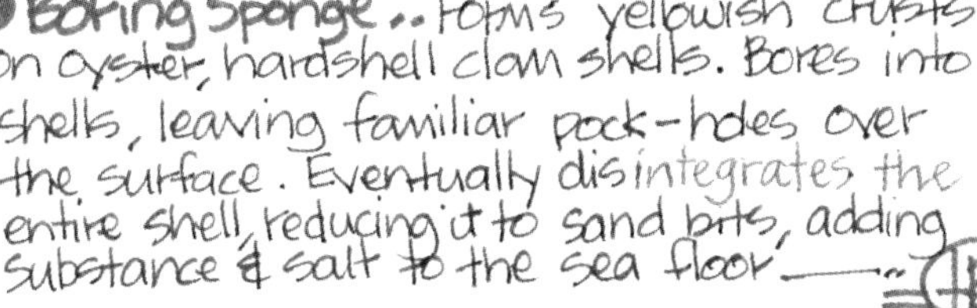

● **Boring Sponge..** Forms yellowish crusts on oyster, hardshell clam shells. Bores into shells, leaving familiar pock-holes over the surface. Eventually disintegrates the entire shell, reducing it to sand bits, adding substance & salt to the sea floor...

SEA PORK

● There is no creature more peculiar than that rubbery red, pink or gray blob known as Sea Pork which litters our low tide beaches. This dead-ringer for a brain or some puddy-like jellyfish is in fact a condominium of microscopic "zooid" animals living together in a leathery tunic made of cellulose. Less than 1/8" in size, each zooid works with its neighbors to pump streams of water & decayed plants into its sack-like body. It is usually easy to find the one encrusted, communal feeding "mouth" all the zooids share on the pork. Bottom dwelling Sea Pork grows attached to shoalwater rock jetties, wharves, corals & seaweeds. When storms 'n surf cast these colonies ashore, study the glistening globs. You'll see dozens of tiny white specks arranged in a stellar cluster. These are the zooids.

WATER (T) (P) (S)

Note: Using siphons near its 2 body openings, ea. zooid squirts in water past (T) strainer tentacles, (P) a pharynx & into (S) its stomach. Wastes are expelled through a hose-like intestine!

LARVAE

● Sea Pork zooids are both male & female, but only cross-fertilize their neighbors.' Eggs spawned into the sea hatch into swimming larvae that appear amazingly like frog-tadpoles! Their long tail is supported by a "notochord," a stiff rod of nerves that is also found in human embryos! To evolve into adulthood, larvae will sink to the sea bed & absorb their tails. Colonies form when grouped adults encase themselves with digested cellulose gleaned from the water.

● Sea Pork's protective sheath defends against crabs/snails, but is no match for these roving, big-toothed predators ➤

PART I .. THE STINGERS!

• For summertime swimmers, "Jaws" isn't the worst worry... "**Jellies**" are!! Jellyfish, lacking a backbone, heart, brain, blood or nervous system, are not true fish. Rather, they're a simple floating mouth & intestine housed in a see-thru' skeleton-muscle filled with a fluid called "mesoglea". Over 93% water, this jelly gives bouyancy & aids food storage. Weak swimming Jellies live at the mercy of wind, waves & tides. When Ocean currents wash up droves of warm-water Jellyfish, then we humans have a problem.

• The business-end of certain species is a trail of tentacles. Rooted there is a battery of cells with an exposed bristly trigger. Animal contact & chemical reaction causes the trigger to automatically uncoil a striking needle of stinging "nematocyst" cells, that explode with a painful toxin. The alkaloid poison paralyzes shrimps, fish, worms & other Jellies which are hoisted into the mouth and eaten!

ROOT
TRIGGER
NEEDLE
THE WEAPON!

① #1 **PORTUGESE MAN OF WAR**
Uncommon. Ranges near Gulf Stream. The 10" sky-blue bag is filled with gas! Winds nudge this colony of Jellies across the waves, so many "invade" at once.

Note: When the tentacles lash human flesh, the toxin causes burning welts. Treatment:
① Wash in soap & water.
② Apply alcohol, or meat tenderizer & vaseline.
③ Apply ice. Contact a Doctor for serious allergic reactions.

② #2 **SEA NETTLE**
Common in August, as young hatch in 80° waters. White "Medusa" (umbrella & tentacles) drapes back 3 ft! Wounds last weeks!

④ #4 **LION'S MANE**
The "Christmas Jelly" of cold waters. 6" reddish umbrellas drape hairy tentacle clusters below.

③ #3 **SEA WASP**.. Tentacles dangle from 4 corners of box-like body. These firm Jellies show up April–July.

BEWARE! THESE TENTACLES STING LONG AFTER THE JELLYFISH DIES!!

JELLYFISH

PART II .. THE SAFE!

• As long as the Sea's fertile waters embrace this Isle, we will know Jellyfish. 200 species bob the World's waves, but happily, most are harmless to humans. Instead of stinging prey, these pump gallons of water thru' their umbrella-bodies, slurping in larva, fry & plankton, & absorbing the sea's oxygen directly thru' their cell walls. Jellies may jam up shrimp nets or bother bathers, but on balance, they are a vital food for Sunfish, Sea Turtles, Squid, Frigate Birds & other Jellies. Orientals even pickle & steam'em as appetizers! Large Jellies shelter fish & grow algae edible for all in their big bells. Chemical agents used in combating cancer & bone disease have been derived from these current-side cast-offs!

• Note Life Cycle .. Wind, waves, water temp. & food supply determine ea. Jelly's season. Most ① parent Jellies cross-fertilize ② eggs in Spring. These .008" larval "planulas" float to the Ocean floor & grow into ③ vegetative "polyps". Polyps shed (A) "bud" sections that sprout more polyps, or (B) stack up in break-away saucers that ④ float seaward as ⑤ baby medusas. These forms grow into the bouncy bells closely encountered by swimmers —!

① MATING MEDUSAS

② LARVA

③ POLYP

A. BUD

B. ④ STACKING

⑤ BABY MEDUSA

MUSHROOM JELLY (below) .. Looks like some squishy, clear Jellyball that dangles long fleshy fingers. Bell is 1½ ft. across! Appears Mar.-June. This is that 'famous' edible Jelly.

COMB JELLIES .. Are not true Jellyfish. 8 rows of cilia, not tentacles, "comb" in plankton "soup". These are winter wash-ups.

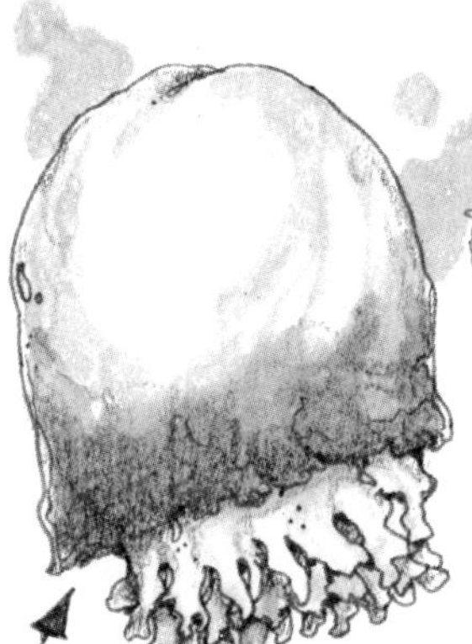

JELLYBALL .. Big as a head of cabbage, about 10" in diameter. A reddish-purple band marks the bell. Litters our Easter beaches. Its tough hide takes days to decompose — ...

MOON JELLY .. Roundish & flat like a pancake. Over a foot wide! A magenta sunburst surrounds central "U" shaped organs. An Autumn thru' Spring beach blob —.

F. Boltontine ...

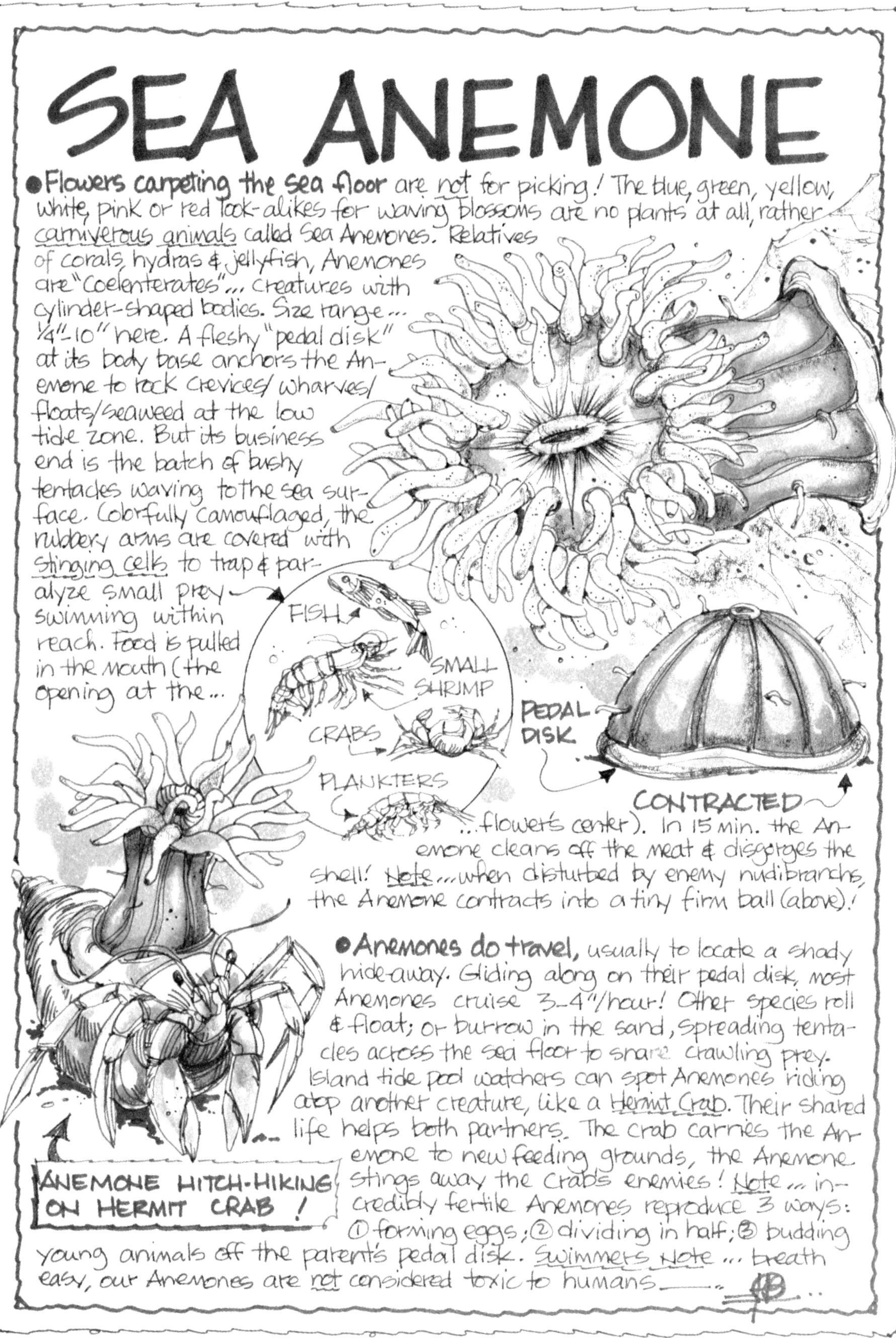
SEA ANEMONE
●Flowers carpeting the sea floor are not for picking! The blue, green, yellow, white, pink or red look-alikes for waving blossoms are no plants at all, rather carniverous animals called Sea Anemones. Relatives of corals, hydras & jellyfish, Anemones are "Coelenterates"... creatures with cylinder-shaped bodies. Size range... 1/4"-10" here. A fleshy "pedal disk" at its body base anchors the Anemone to rock crevices/wharves/floats/seaweed at the low tide zone. But its business end is the batch of bushy tentacles waving to the sea surface. Colorfully camouflaged, the rubbery arms are covered with stinging cells to trap & paralyze small prey swimming within reach. Food is pulled in the mouth (the opening at the...
FISH
SMALL SHRIMP
CRABS
PLANKTERS
PEDAL DISK
CONTRACTED
...flower's center). In 15 min. the Anemone cleans off the meat & disgorges the shell! Note... when disturbed by enemy nudibranchs, the Anemone contracts into a tiny firm ball (above)!
●Anemones do travel, usually to locate a shady hide-away. Gliding along on their pedal disk, most Anemones cruise 3-4"/hour! Other species roll & float; or burrow in the sand, spreading tentacles across the sea floor to snare crawling prey. Island tide pool watchers can spot Anemones riding atop another creature, like a Hermit Crab. Their shared life helps both partners. The crab carries the Anemone to new feeding grounds, the Anemone stings away the crab's enemies! Note... incredibly fertile Anemones reproduce 3 ways: ① forming eggs; ② dividing in half; ③ budding young animals off the parent's pedal disk. Swimmers Note... breath easy, our Anemones are not considered toxic to humans...
ANEMONE HITCH-HIKING ON HERMIT CRAB!

CLAM WORM

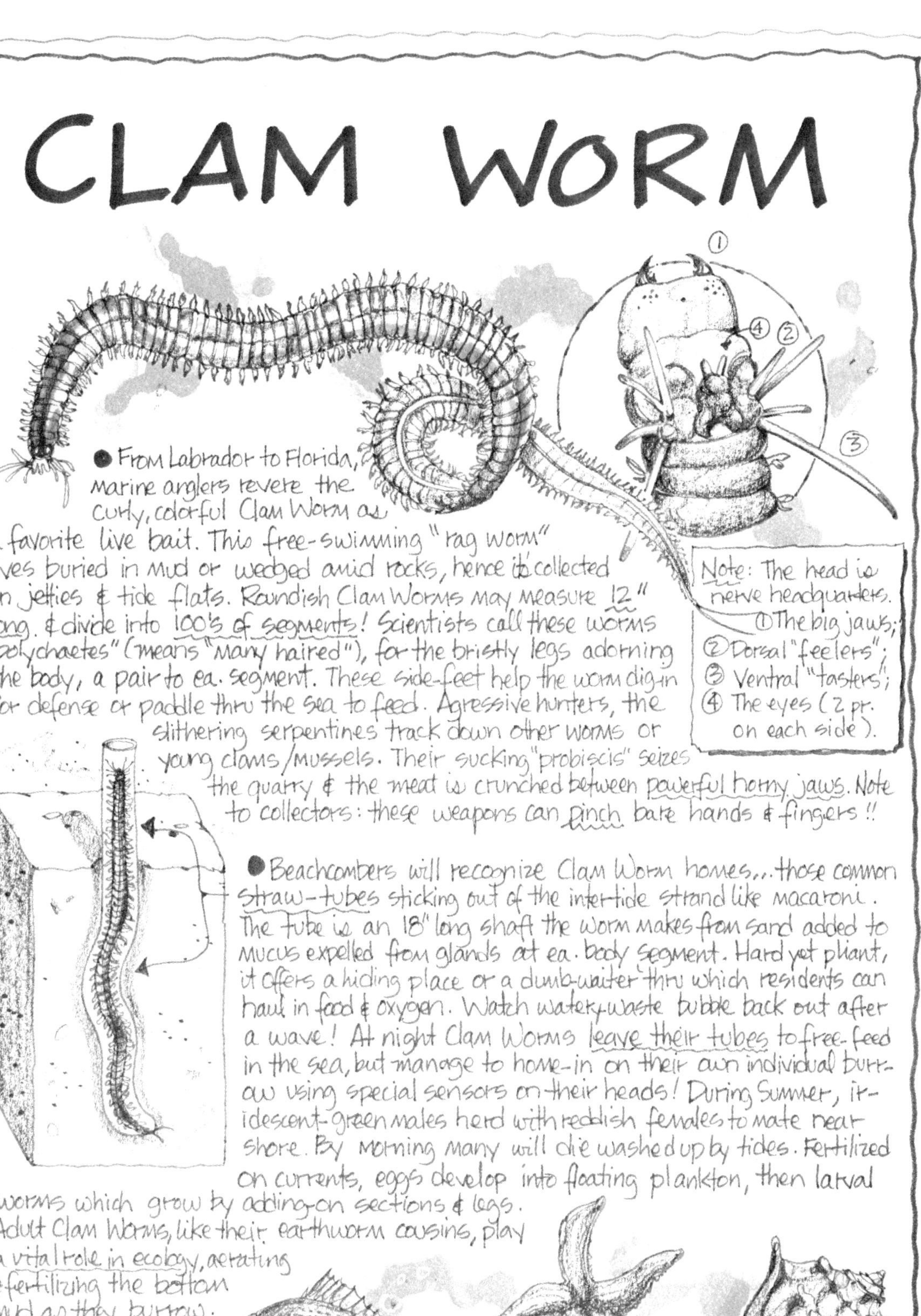

● From Labrador to Florida, marine anglers revere the curly, colorful Clam Worm as a favorite live bait. This free-swimming "rag worm" lives buried in mud or wedged amid rocks, hence it's collected on jetties & tide flats. Roundish Clam Worms may measure 12" long & divide into 100's of segments! Scientists call these worms "polychaetes" (means "many haired"), for the bristly legs adorning the body, a pair to ea. segment. These side-feet help the worm dig in for defense or paddle thru the sea to feed. Agressive hunters, the slithering serpentines track down other worms or young clams/mussels. Their sucking "probiscis" seizes the quarry & the meat is crunched between powerful horny jaws. Note to collectors: these weapons can pinch bare hands & fingers!!

Note: The head is nerve headquarters.
① The big jaws;
② Dorsal "feelers";
③ Ventral "tasters";
④ The eyes (2 pr. on each side).

● Beachcombers will recognize Clam Worm homes... those common straw-tubes sticking out of the intertide strand like macaroni. The tube is an 18" long shaft the worm makes from sand added to mucus expelled from glands at ea. body segment. Hard yet pliant, it offers a hiding place or a dumb-waiter thru which residents can haul in food & oxygen. Watch watery waste bubble back out after a wave! At night Clam Worms leave their tubes to free-feed in the sea, but manage to home-in on their own individual burrow using special sensors on their heads! During Summer, iridescent-green males herd with reddish females to mate near shore. By morning many will die washed up by tides. Fertilized on currents, eggs develop into floating plankton, then larval worms which grow by adding-on sections & legs. Adult Clam Worms, like their earthworm cousins, play a vital role in ecology, aerating & fertilizing the bottom mud as they burrow.

Note: The Clam Worms big enemies are these bottom dwellers.

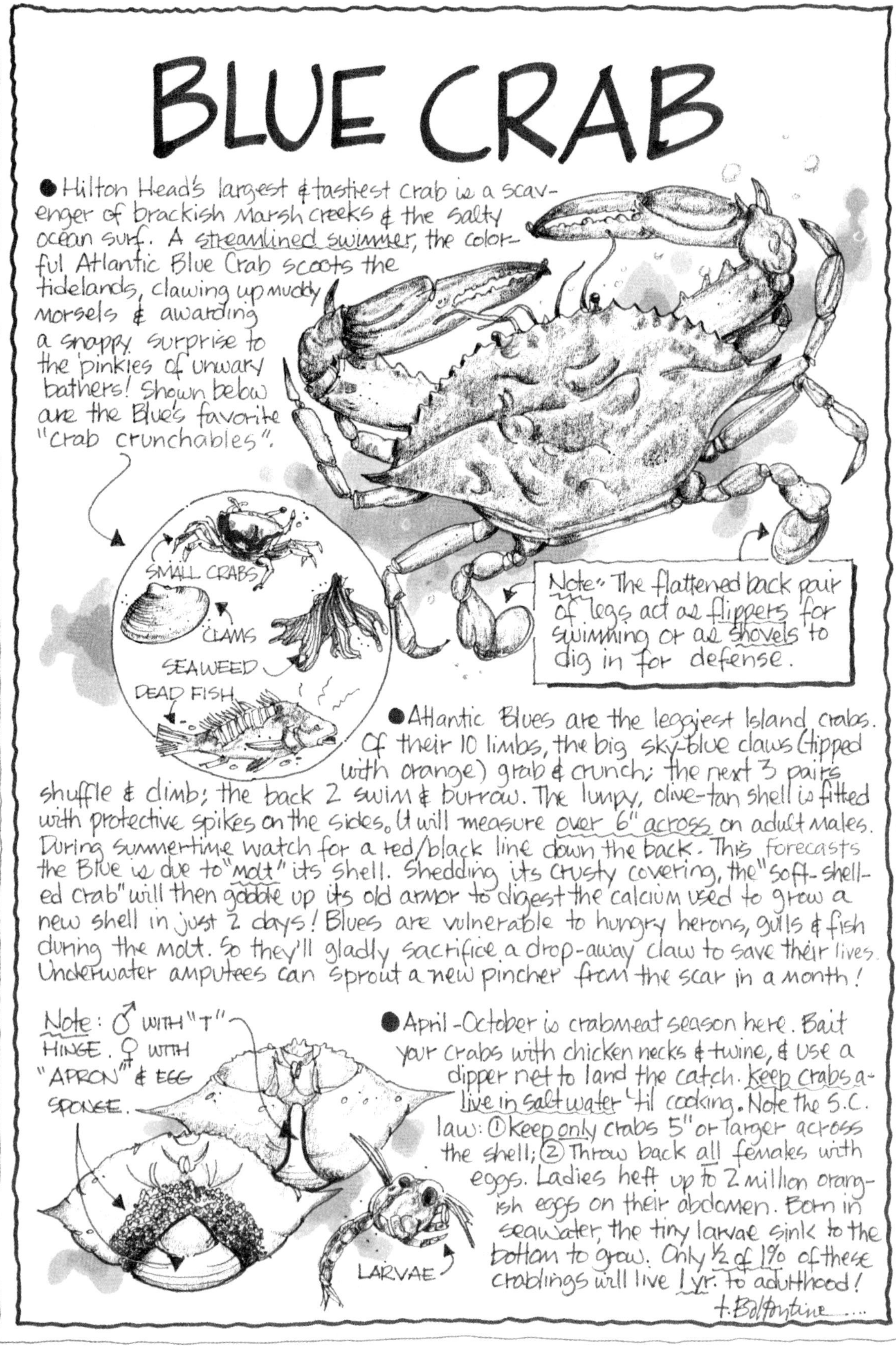
BLUE CRAB
●Hilton Head's largest & tastiest crab is a scavenger of brackish marsh creeks & the salty ocean surf. A streamlined swimmer, the colorful Atlantic Blue Crab scoots the tidelands, clawing up muddy morsels & awarding a snappy surprise to the pinkies of unwary bathers! Shown below are the Blue's favorite "crab crunchables".
SMALL CRABS
CLAMS
SEAWEED
DEAD FISH
Note: The flattened back pair of legs act as flippers for swimming or as shovels to dig in for defense.
●Atlantic Blues are the leggiest Island crabs. Of their 10 limbs, the big sky-blue claws (tipped with orange) grab & crunch; the next 3 pairs shuffle & climb; the back 2 swim & burrow. The lumpy, olive-tan shell is fitted with protective spikes on the sides. It will measure over 6" across on adult males. During summertime watch for a red/black line down the back. This forecasts the Blue is due to "molt" its shell. Shedding its crusty covering, the "soft-shelled crab" will then gobble up its old armor to digest the calcium used to grow a new shell in just 2 days! Blues are vulnerable to hungry herons, gulls & fish during the molt. So they'll gladly sacrifice a drop-away claw to save their lives. Underwater amputees can sprout a new pincher from the scar in a month!
Note: ♂ WITH "T" HINGE. ♀ WITH "APRON" & EGG SPONGE.
●April-October is crabmeat season here. Bait your crabs with chicken necks & twine, & use a dipper net to land the catch. Keep crabs alive in salt water 'til cooking. Note the S.C. law: ① keep only crabs 5" or larger across the shell; ② Throw back all females with eggs. Ladies heft up to 2 million orangish eggs on their abdomen. Born in seawater, the tiny larvae sink to the bottom to grow. Only ½ of 1% of these crablings will live 1 yr. to adulthood!
LARVAE
T. Ballantine

HERMIT CRAB

● **Look inside that seashell** before you hold it to your ear to "hear the ocean". You may get a rude ear-ring ... a pinch from a Hermit Crab!

This soft-bellied marine crab has no shell of its own, so to hide from predators it seeks shelter in empty snail shells. When they outgrow their old "pad", these restless renters probe the linings of new, larger shells with their long tentacles (T), frisking out debris, worms & even other Hermits, which they eat! Hermits move in by withdrawing their abdomens from the old shells & darting into the new. If the next abode proves too heavy, they will pull out & resume their "tour of homes". Watch for barnacles, limpets & especially stinging Sea Anemones riding atop a Hermit's shell. They feed on bits 'n pieces the crab leaves as it scavenges tide pools/rock piles. When Hermits switch houses, they pull Anemones loose & stick 'em on their new shell. The growing Anemone will eventually dissolve the snail, enveloping & protecting the Hermit in its stretchy body, sparing the crab forever from the ordeal of house hunting —!

● The crab's 1-2" body is a tapered spiral to match the inner columns of these snail shells: Rear claws (R) hook Hermits into their homes. These secure the crabs so well that you can't dig the critters out if you want the shells! Soak in fresh water & clorox ... it'll come out! Large claws (C) tear apart food & close off the shell's "front door" opening when Hermits pull in to hide. 2 pair of walking feet (W) help Hermits drag around shells 5 times the size of their bodies —!

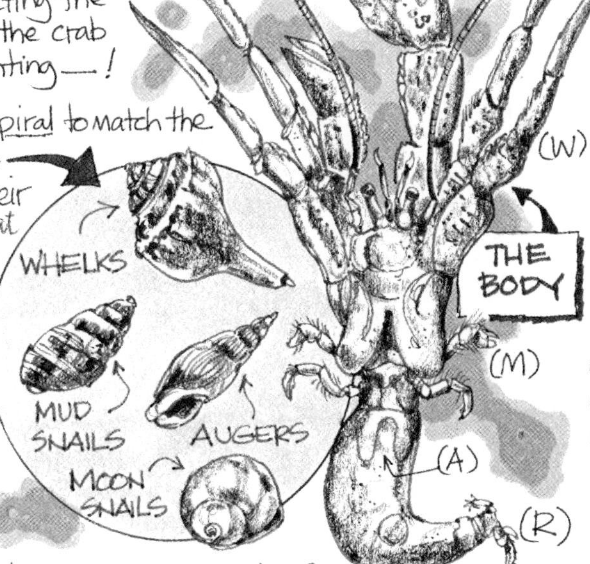

● Spring finds the bigger male Hermit dragging around a female, waiting for her to shed her shell. He deposits sperm on her abdomen (A) & here she'll carry fertilized eggs with 4 hairy middle claws (M). Ma' aerates & cleans the clutch by waving her tail in sea water. 1/10" hatchlings are brushed off her body, to settle on the bottom & begin the search for shells in the menagerie of cast-off calcium apartments there —!!

J. Ballantine ..

GHOST CRAB

• **Like flitting phantoms of the night,** Ghost Crabs prowl our beaches between sundown & dawn. Sometime after dinner, in the Summer, take your flashlight down to the evening beach. Your beacon will spotlight dozens of 2" square-shelled, long-legged crabs whose beige bodies camouflage with the nearby sand, so that they seem to vanish right before your eyes! Hence, the name "Ghost" Crab! Their Latin label, Ocypoda, means "swift-footed"... & they are. Scuttling around on tiptoes at 10 mph, the waterside wraiths run sideways & make quick directional changes to escape predators. 2 black eyes stick up like periscopes with 360° all-sides-at-once vision. Ghost Crabs see so well they'll snatch up flying insects in midair. But they can't see straight up, so to hide from hungry birds, they dig.

• Those 1-2" golf-ball sized holes in the dry sand beachcombers see are the doors to Ghost Crab burrows. The creatures may tunnel down 4 ft. at 45° 'til they make a turn-around chamber in wet grains that won't collapse. Come nightfall, when shorebirds fly to roost, the crabs emerge & run to the sea to get oxygen from the water washing over their gills. They'll scavenge the strand for food (at right) & drag chow back into their caves by daybreak!

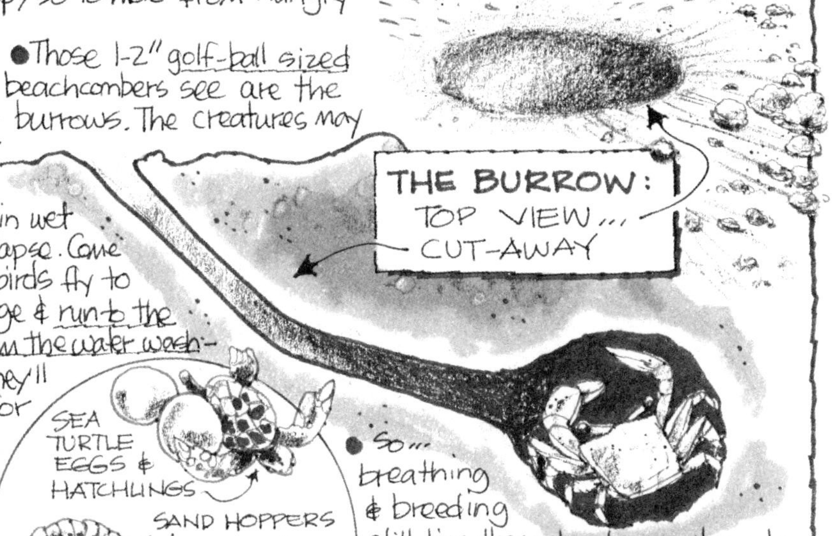

THE BURROW:
TOP VIEW...
CUT-AWAY

SEA TURTLE EGGS & HATCHLINGS
SAND HOPPERS
MOLE CRABS
COQUINAS

• So... breathing & breeding still ties these land-crawlers to the sea. Females carry eggs under their tails & lay 'em in salt water by June. At first the larvae hide away below the waves. But as their shells harden & grow, Ghostlings burrow farther up into hard sand. Thus the holes get bigger & deeper the closer they are to the dunes! Ghost Crabs hibernate over winter there, "holding their breath" 6 weeks by storing oxygen in special sacs near the gills!

STONE CRAB

● **Black fingers** or the Stone Crab is a chunky member of the mud crab family. It is identified by the dark tips on both big claws. Colored the hue of muddy sand, the oval carapace (top shell) is about 3"x4" & the body nearly 2" thick. Beachcombers may discover the hollow carcass of a dead stoney awash at South Beach, Port Royal or Dolphin Head. As shellfishermen know, this crustacean dwells abundantly in oyster beds, crevices of rock sea walls (the origin of the name, "Stone" crab) & deep mud burrows in salt marsh creek banks. Mats of sponges & bryzoans growing under floating docks are another habitat the crab haunts.

● **Stone Crabs stalk shellfish beds.** Here they prey on oysters, clams & barnacles. Their stout chelae (claws) can crack right through the ½" shells of young bivalves! Harder adult shells are chiseled away. Leading a secretive, subtidal life amid holes, cracks & shadows, to depths of 20 ft., Stone Crabs may live 8-10 years ... although they are preyed upon themselves by large fish, like drum.

THE SWEET MEAT... ...IS FORKED OUT.

● **Stone Crabs are edible.** The claw-meat is considered a real delicacy along both the East & West Coasts. Fishermen either trap the crabs, or yank 'em out of their digs with a hooked iron tool (not with bare hands!). They twist off the claws, then throw the animal back. New chelae regrow in 18 months... but these "retreads" are never quite as large again. The meat in the knuckles is sweetest & is served hot or cold, garnished with melted butter or a spicy mustard.

SPIDER CRAB

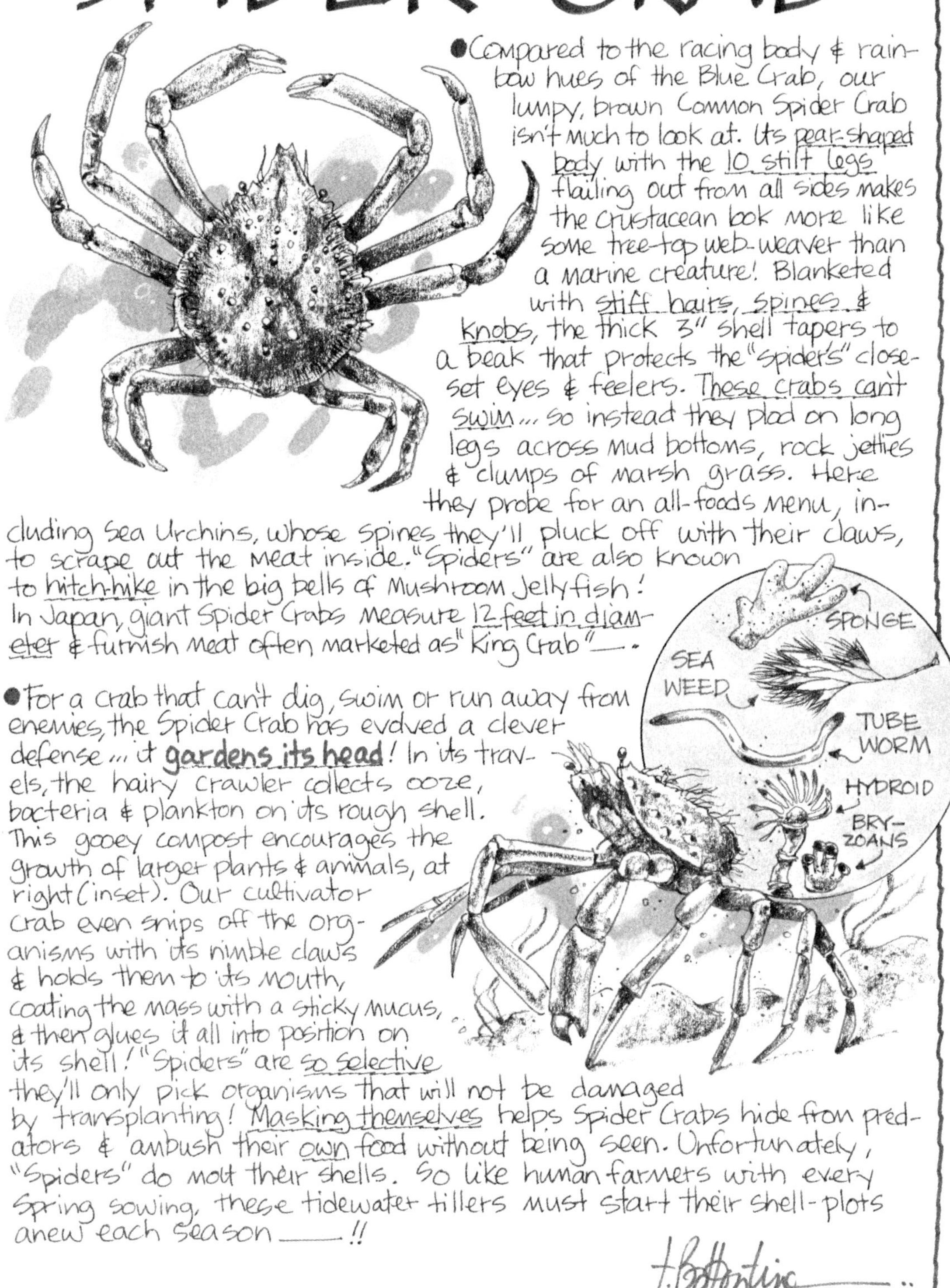

● Compared to the racing body & rainbow hues of the Blue Crab, our lumpy, brown Common Spider Crab isn't much to look at. Its pear-shaped body with the 10 stilt legs flailing out from all sides makes the crustacean look more like some tree-top web-weaver than a marine creature! Blanketed with stiff hairs, spines & knobs, the thick 3" shell tapers to a beak that protects the "spider's" close-set eyes & feelers. These crabs can't swim... so instead they plod on long legs across mud bottoms, rock jetties & clumps of marsh grass. Here they probe for an all-foods menu, including Sea Urchins, whose spines they'll pluck off with their claws, to scrape out the meat inside. "Spiders" are also known to hitch-hike in the big bells of Mushroom Jellyfish! In Japan, giant Spider Crabs measure 12 feet in diameter & furnish meat often marketed as "King Crab"——.

● For a crab that can't dig, swim or run away from enemies, the Spider Crab has evolved a clever defense... it **gardens its head**! In its travels, the hairy crawler collects ooze, bacteria & plankton on its rough shell. This gooey compost encourages the growth of larger plants & animals, at right (inset). Our cultivator crab even snips off the organisms with its nimble claws & holds them to its mouth, coating the mass with a sticky mucus, & then glues it all into position on its shell! "Spiders" are so selective they'll only pick organisms that will not be damaged by transplanting! Masking themselves helps Spider Crabs hide from predators & ambush their own food without being seen. Unfortunately, "Spiders" do molt their shells. So like human farmers with every Spring sowing, these tidewater tillers must start their shell-plots anew each season——!!

T. Ballantine

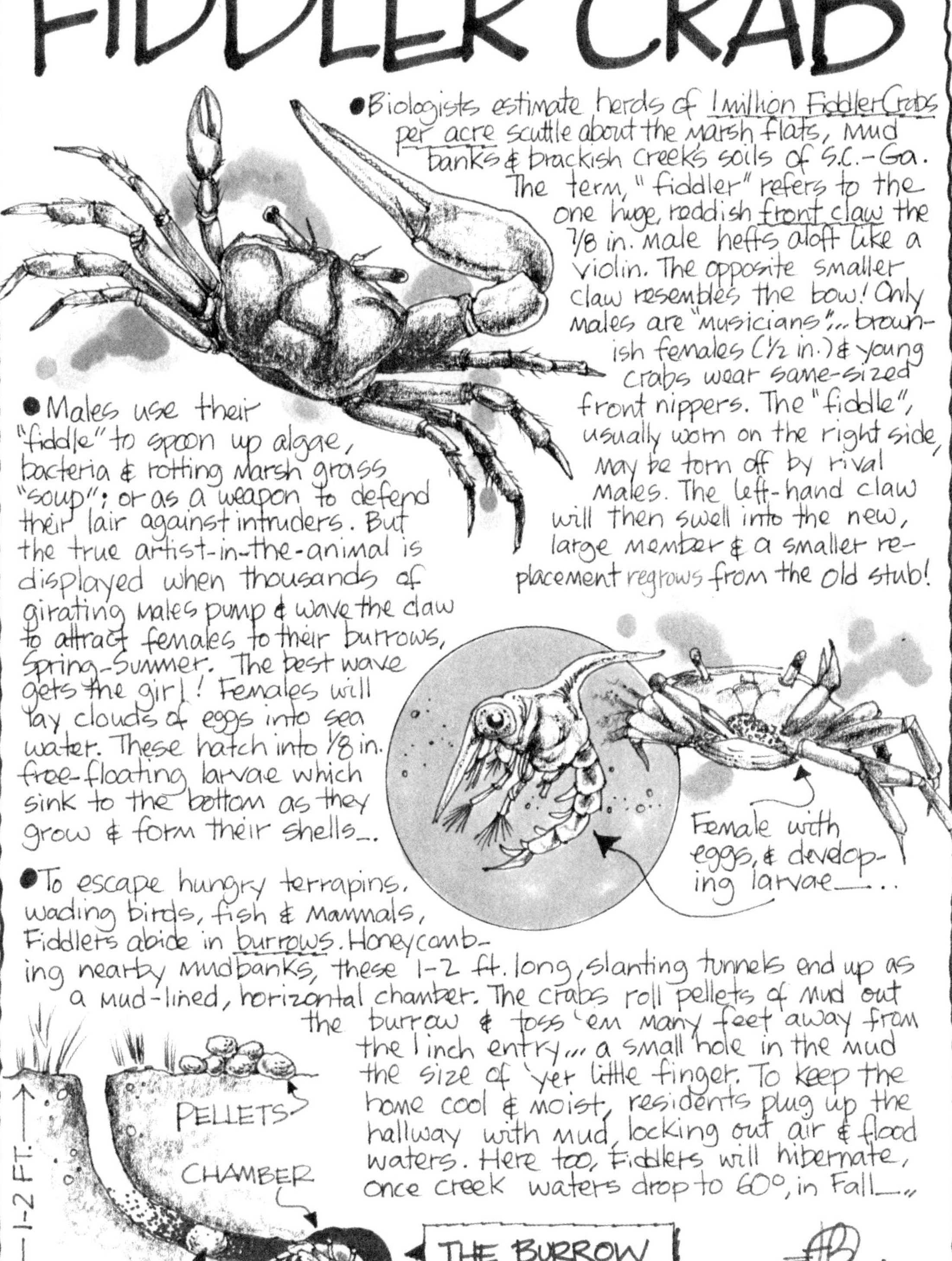

FIDDLER CRAB

• Biologists estimate herds of 1 million Fiddler Crabs per acre scuttle about the marsh flats, mud banks & brackish creek's soils of S.C.-Ga. The term, "fiddler" refers to the one huge, reddish front claw the 7/8 in. male hefts aloft like a violin. The opposite smaller claw resembles the bow! Only males are "musicians"... brownish females (1/2 in.) & young crabs wear same-sized front nippers. The "fiddle", usually worn on the right side, may be torn off by rival males. The left-hand claw will then swell into the new, large member & a smaller replacement regrows from the old stub!

• Males use their "fiddle" to spoon up algae, bacteria & rotting marsh grass "soup"; or as a weapon to defend their lair against intruders. But the true artist-in-the-animal is displayed when thousands of girating males pump & wave the claw to attract females to their burrows, Spring-Summer. The best wave gets the girl! Females will lay clouds of eggs into sea water. These hatch into 1/8 in. free-floating larvae which sink to the bottom as they grow & form their shells...

• To escape hungry terrapins, wading birds, fish & mammals, Fiddlers abide in burrows. Honeycombing nearby mudbanks, these 1-2 ft. long, slanting tunnels end up as a mud-lined, horizontal chamber. The crabs roll pellets of mud out the burrow & toss 'em many feet away from the 1 inch entry... a small hole in the mud the size of 'yer little finger. To keep the home cool & moist, residents plug up the hallway with mud, locking out air & flood waters. Here too, Fiddlers will hibernate, once creek waters drop to 60°, in Fall...

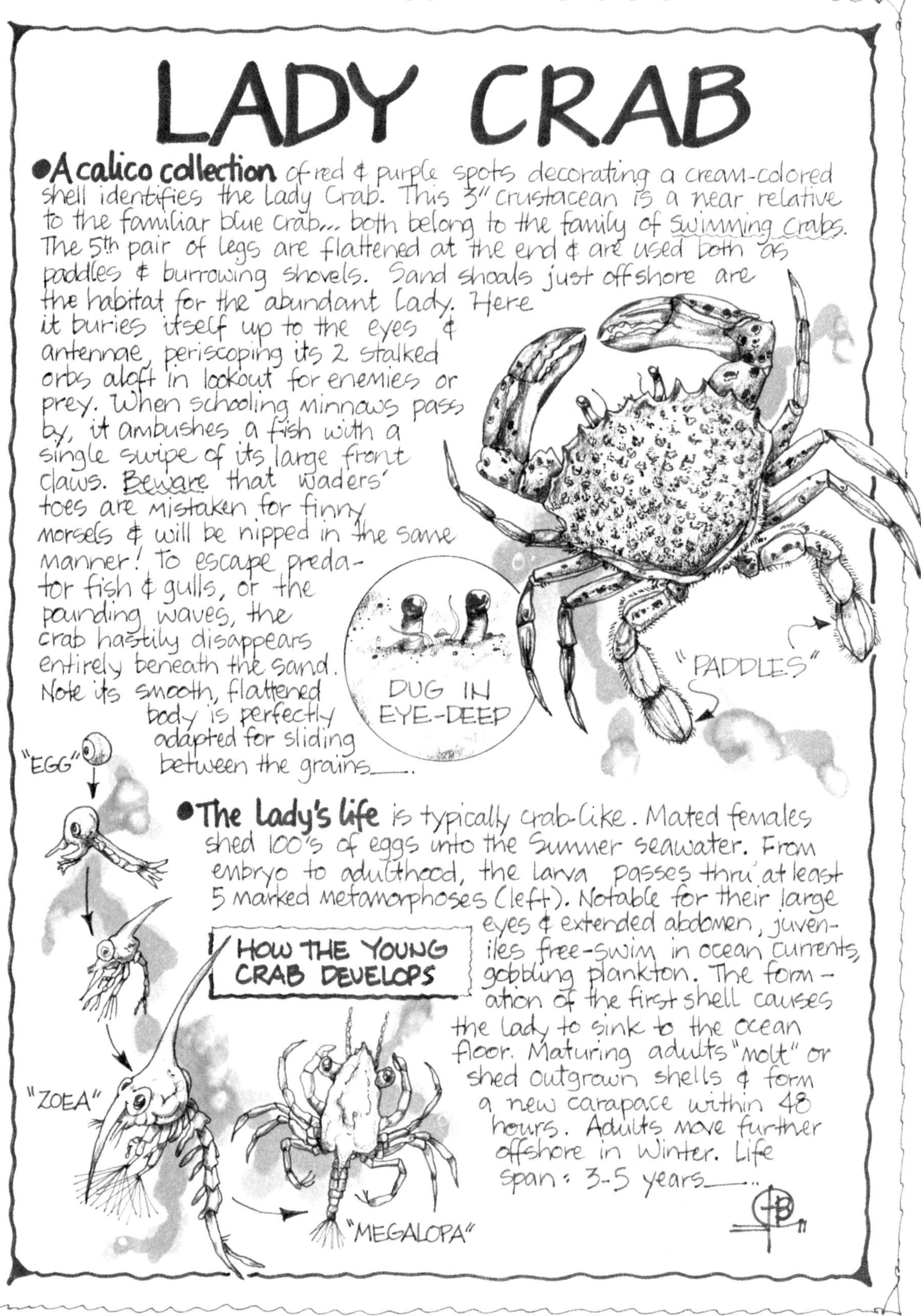

LADY CRAB

•A calico collection of red & purple spots decorating a cream-colored shell identifies the Lady Crab. This 3" crustacean is a near relative to the familiar blue crab... both belong to the family of swimming crabs. The 5th pair of legs are flattened at the end & are used both as paddles & burrowing shovels. Sand shoals just offshore are the habitat for the abundant Lady. Here it buries itself up to the eyes & antennae, periscoping its 2 stalked orbs aloft in lookout for enemies or prey. When schooling minnows pass by, it ambushes a fish with a single swipe of its large front claws. Beware that waders' toes are mistaken for finny morsels & will be nipped in the same manner! To escape predator fish & gulls, or the pounding waves, the crab hastily disappears entirely beneath the sand. Note its smooth, flattened body is perfectly adapted for sliding between the grains___.

•The lady's life is typically crab-like. Mated females shed 100's of eggs into the Summer seawater. From embryo to adulthood, the larva passes thru at least 5 marked metamorphoses (left). Notable for their large eyes & extended abdomen, juveniles free-swim in ocean currents, gobbling plankton. The formation of the first shell causes the lady to sink to the ocean floor. Maturing adults "molt" or shed outgrown shells & form a new carapace within 48 hours. Adults move further offshore in Winter. Life span: 3-5 years___.

OYSTER CRAB

Commensile crabs are bantam-sized crustaceans which live inside another animal or animal habitat. Their life is sustained by what the host provides, meanwhile they may assist the creature they cohabit in some way. Most familiar is the Oyster Crab. The female (right) dwells in the gill cavity of an oyster. Here she feeds on plankton & detritus the bivalve filters. In return for free room & board... shelter, food & oxygen... the crab serves to "degunk" the debris from the oyster's gill filaments. Oyster crabs are called "pea crabs" for their diminutive size. Males (3/16") are smaller than the females (5/8" to 1"), for good romantic reason (see below). The thin shell is roundish & white, without markings. The legs are small & lack hairs.

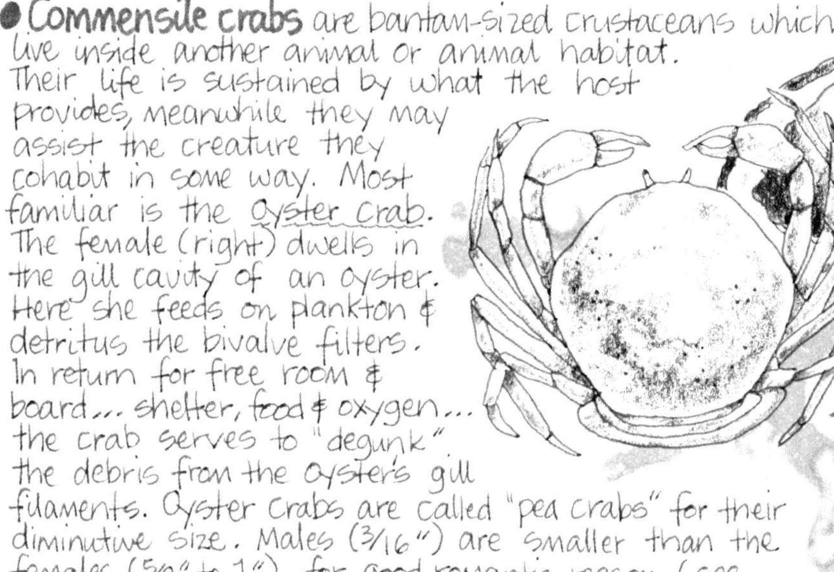

Note: Oyster crabs typically turn up as extra-meaty surprises at oyster roasts!

Home is a world inside a world for commensile crabs. Here are various marine animals which host these crustacean messmates...

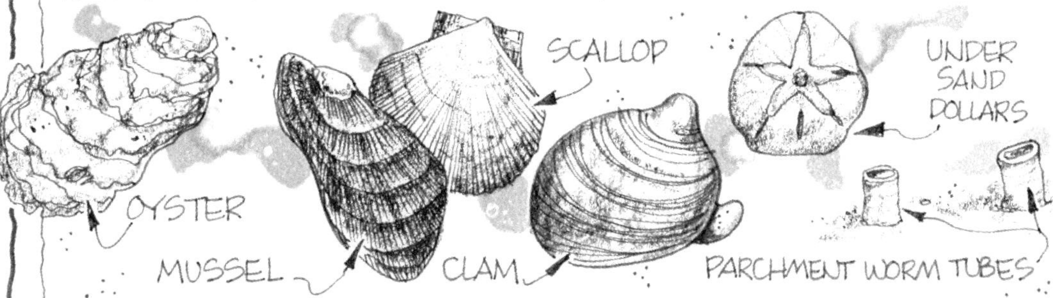

Freeloading or bondage? Tracing the Oyster Crab's life cycle reveals its inside ways may be more a problem of size than choice. Free-swimming males are tiny enough to squeeze thru' the ½" gap Oysters make to filter-feed. They navigate in to mate the females, then swim out to die. Females stay "oyster cloistered" & grow too plump to leave the host! Thus imprisoned in their own kitchen, their body degenerates for lack of predators. Their eyes shrink, the shell softens. Limbs weaken. By Summer, 100's of hatchling "peas" will swim out as larvae. The following year, females of the lot will enter the oysters' water-filtering system. Life span: 2-3 years.

LESSER CRABS

OF THE COASTAL SHORE

• **A beachcomber's secret** is that whole hosts of colorful & interesting crabs live underfoot & 'neath nearby waves. Search jetties, driftwood wreckage, tide pools & swash lines for cast-off shells, or live specimens of these 4 common Carolina crustaceans—.

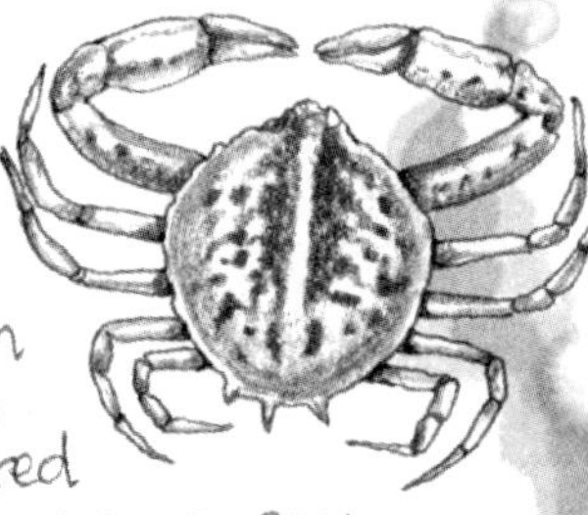

• **PURSE CRAB** (2"): Its globe-shaped shell is beige, with a smattering of wine-colored patterns. Its name compares its shape to a child's pocket penny purse. These crabs live just offshore to depths of about 10 feet.

• **SPECKLED CRAB** (4½"), below: White spots decorate the brown back & legs. Like its cousin Blue Crab, its carapace is pointed at the ends & the 5th pair of legs are flattened for swimming & digging. Speckled crabs favor rock-pile bound tide pools, as are found in North Forest beach.

• **FEMALE FIDDLER CRABS** (1"): Their olive-brown color camouflages to the wood bits, dead animals & seaweed hideouts they keep. When debris are overturned, they scamper in every direction. The shell is squarish & unmarked. Unlike the male Fiddlers, the females show small claws of equal size. They will be most common at South Beach & along the Port Royal Sound area.

• **MOLE CRAB** (1"): This beach-colored, egg-shaped "Sandbug" burrows in the wet beach below the splashing waves. Here it gulps seawater & extracts plankton & algae as food. Its diminished legs, usually folded under the body, are adapted for tunneling downward & backward. Feathery antenna serve to clean body parts. Mole crabs are favored prey for willets & gulls—.

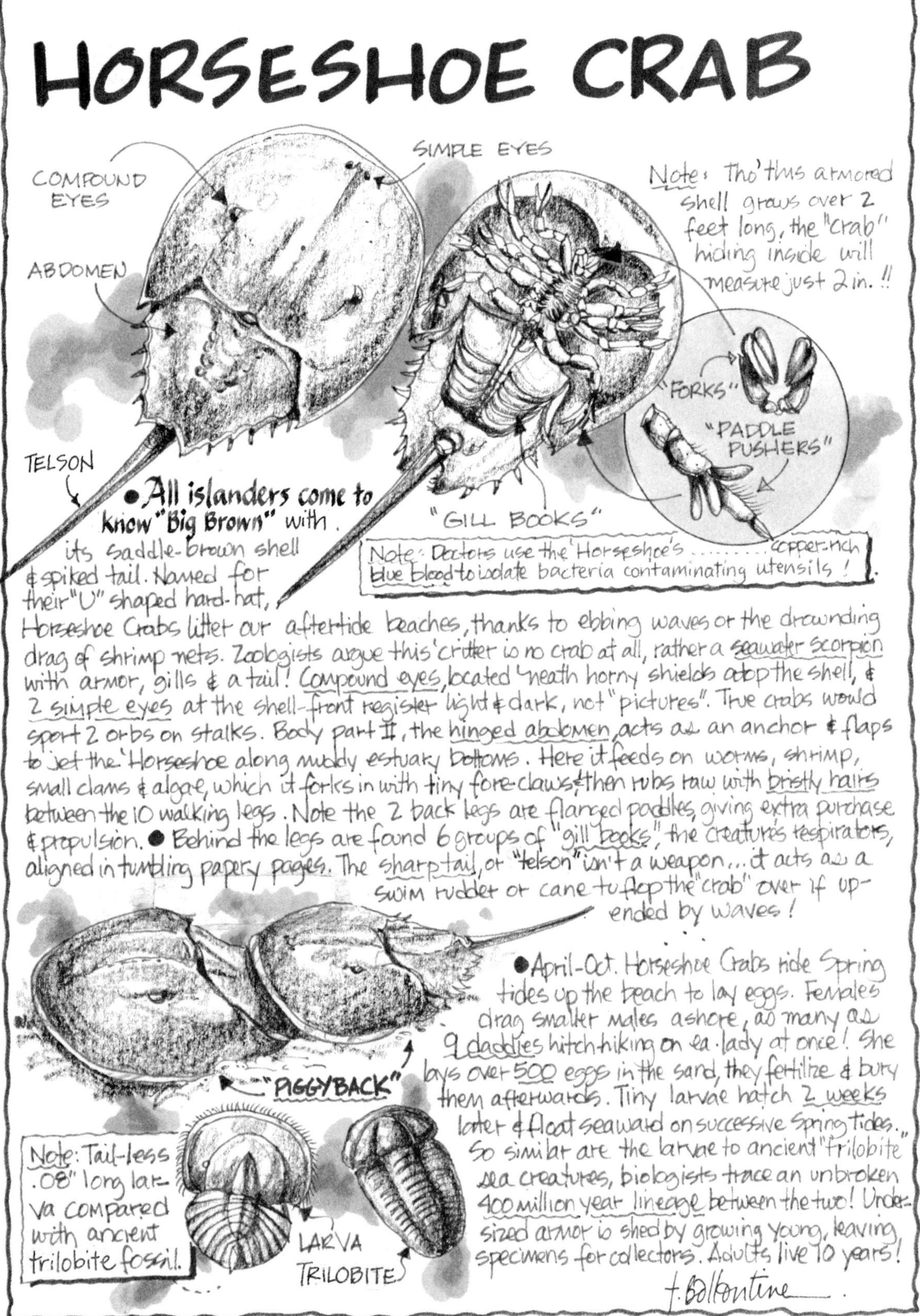
HORSESHOE CRAB
COMPOUND EYES
SIMPLE EYES
ABDOMEN
TELSON
Note: Tho' this armored shell grows over 2 feet long, the "crab" hiding inside will measure just 2 in. !!
"FORKS"
"PADDLE PUSHERS"
"GILL BOOKS"
Note: Doctors use the 'Horseshoe's .... copper-rich blue blood to isolate bacteria contaminating utensils!
●All islanders come to know "Big Brown" with its saddle-brown shell & spiked tail. Named for their "U" shaped hard-hat, Horseshoe Crabs litter our aftertide beaches, thanks to ebbing waves or the drownding drag of shrimp nets. Zoologists argue this 'critter is no crab at all, rather a seawater scorpion with armor, gills & a tail! Compound eyes, located 'neath horny shields atop the shell, & 2 simple eyes at the shell-front register light & dark, not "pictures". True crabs would sport 2 orbs on stalks. Body part II, the hinged abdomen, acts as an anchor & flaps to jet the 'Horseshoe along muddy estuary bottoms. Here it feeds on worms, shrimp, small clams & algae, which it forks in with tiny fore-claws & then rubs raw with bristly hairs between the 10 walking legs. Note the 2 back legs are flanged paddles, giving extra purchase & propulsion. ● Behind the legs are found 6 groups of "gill books", the creature's respirators, aligned in tumbling papery pages. The sharp tail, or "telson" isn't a weapon... it acts as a swim rudder or cane to flop the "crab" over if up-ended by waves!
"PIGGYBACK"
●April-Oct. Horseshoe Crabs ride Spring tides up the beach to lay eggs. Females drag smaller males ashore, as many as 9 daddies hitch-hiking on ea. lady at once! She lays over 500 eggs in the sand, they fertilize & bury them afterwards. Tiny larvae hatch 2 weeks later & float seaward on successive Spring tides.. So similar are the larvae to ancient "trilobite" sea creatures, biologists trace an unbroken 400 million year lineage between the two! Undersized armor is shed by growing young, leaving specimens for collectors. Adults live 10 years!
Note: Tail-less .08" long larva compared with ancient trilobite fossil.
LARVA
TRILOBITE

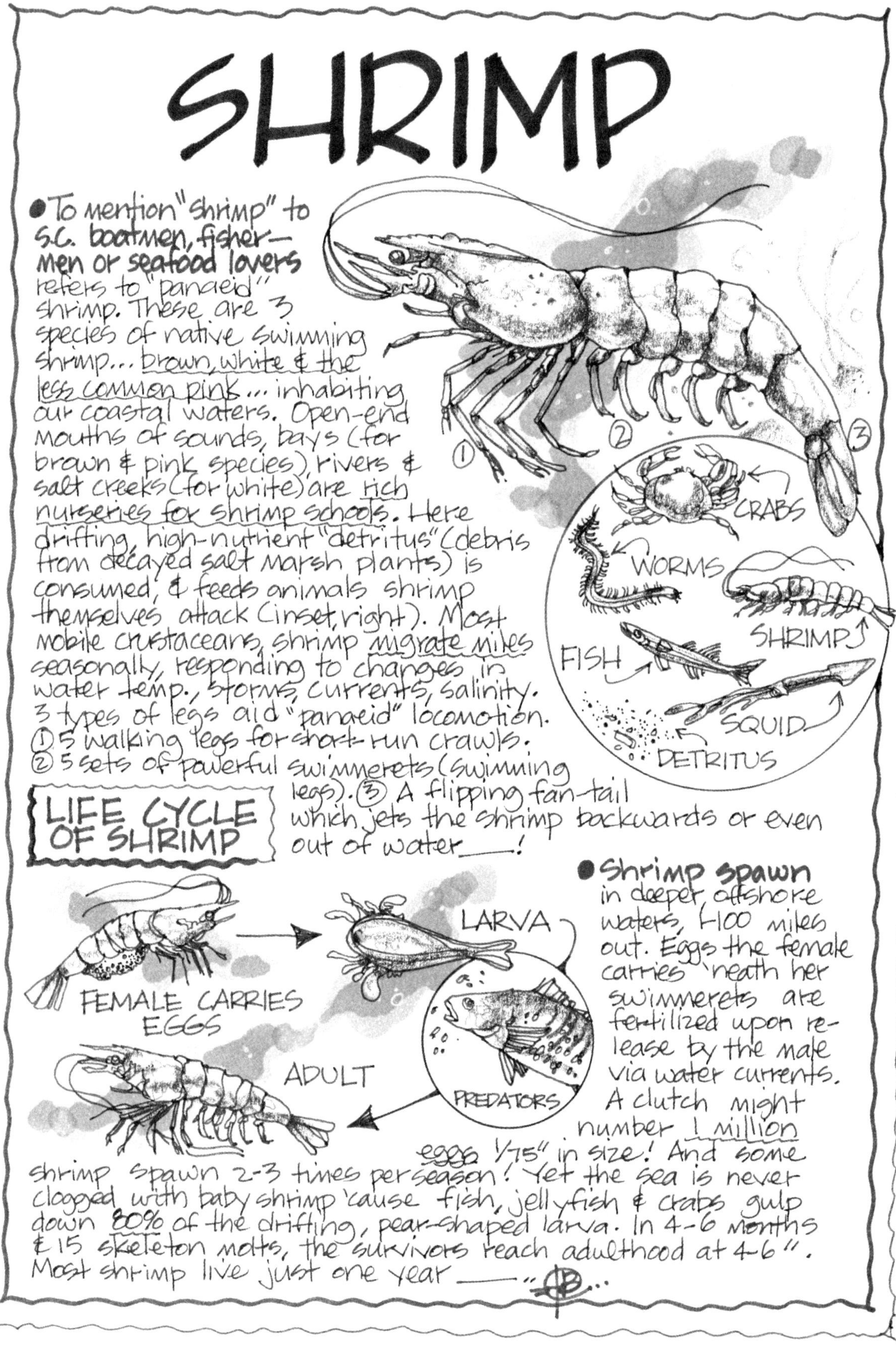
SHRIMP
●To mention "shrimp" to S.C. boatmen, fishermen or seafood lovers refers to "panaeid" shrimp. These are 3 species of native swimming shrimp... brown, white & the less common pink... inhabiting our coastal waters. Open-end mouths of sounds, bays (for brown & pink species), rivers & salt creeks (for white) are rich nurseries for shrimp schools. Here drifting, high-nutrient "detritus" (debris from decayed salt marsh plants) is consumed, & feeds animals shrimp themselves attack (inset, right). Most mobile crustaceans, shrimp migrate miles seasonally, responding to changes in water temp., storms, currents, salinity. 3 types of legs aid "panaeid" locomotion. ① 5 walking legs for short-run crawls. ② 5 sets of powerful swimmerets (swimming legs). ③ A flipping fan-tail which jets the shrimp backwards or even out of water——!
①
②
③
CRABS
WORMS
SHRIMP
FISH
SQUID
DETRITUS
LIFE CYCLE OF SHRIMP
FEMALE CARRIES EGGS
LARVA
PREDATORS
ADULT
●Shrimp spawn in deeper, offshore waters, †100 miles out. Eggs the female carries 'neath her swimmerets are fertilized upon release by the male via water currents. A clutch might number 1 million eggs 1/75" in size! And some shrimp spawn 2-3 times per season! Yet the sea is never clogged with baby shrimp 'cause fish, jellyfish & crabs gulp down 80% of the drifting, pear-shaped larva. In 4-6 months & 15 skeleton molts, the survivors reach adulthood at 4-6". Most shrimp live just one year——"

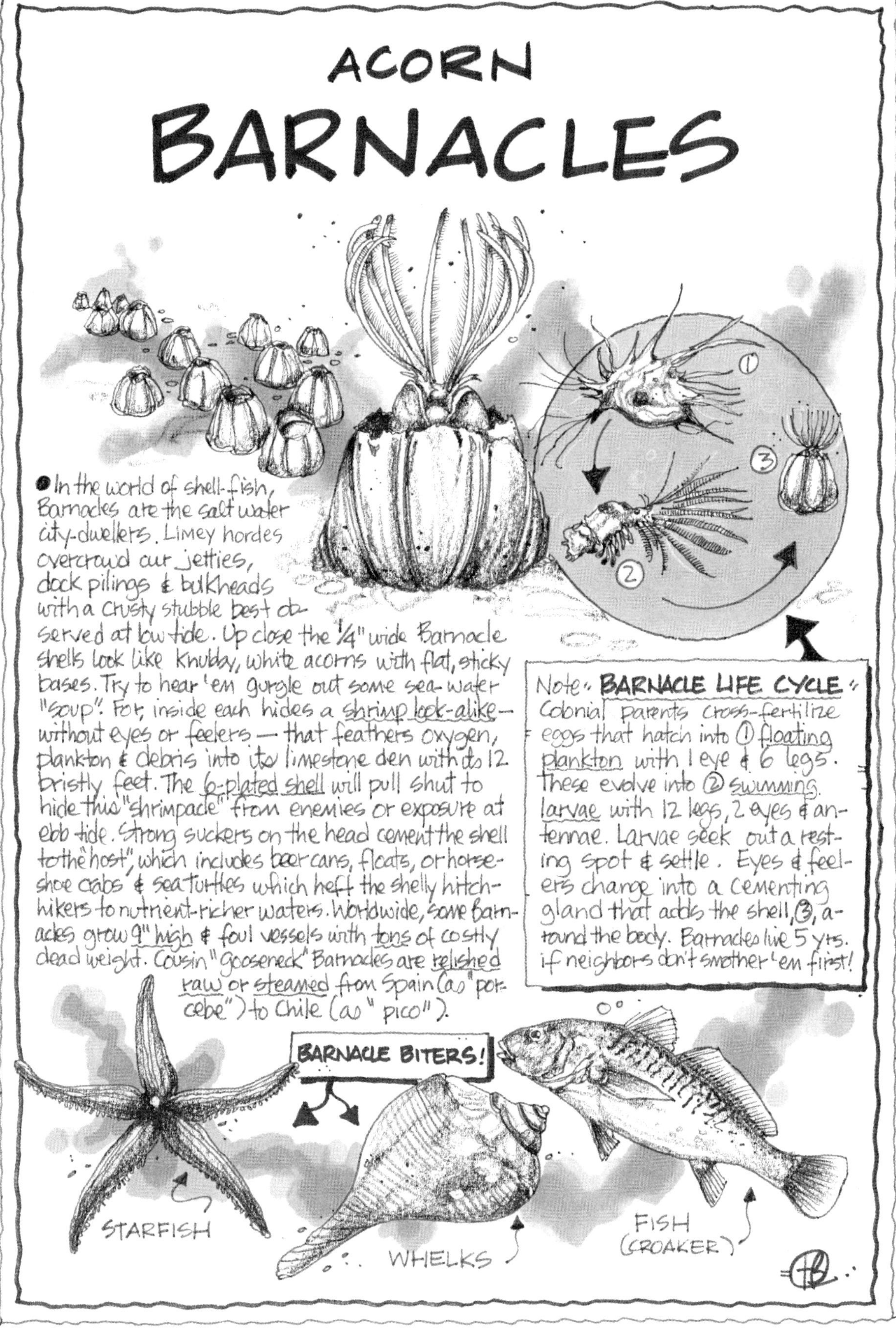
ACORN
BARNACLES
In the world of shell-fish,
Barnacles are the salt water
city-dwellers. Limey hordes
overcrowd our jetties,
dock pilings & bulkheads
with a crusty stubble best ob-
served at low tide. Up close the 1/4" wide Barnacle
shells look like knubby, white acorns with flat, sticky
bases. Try to hear 'em gurgle out some sea-water
"soup". For, inside each hides a shrimp look-alike—
without eyes or feelers — that feathers oxygen,
plankton & debris into its limestone den with its 12
bristly feet. The 6-plated shell will pull shut to
hide this "shrimpacle" from enemies or exposure at
ebb tide. Strong suckers on the head cement the shell
to the "host", which includes beer cans, floats, or horseshoe crabs & sea turtles which heft the shelly hitch-
hikers to nutrient-richer waters. Worldwide, some Barnacles grow 9" high & foul vessels with tons of costly
dead weight. Cousin "gooseneck" Barnacles are relished
raw or steamed from Spain (as "per-
cebe") to Chile (as "pico").
1
2
3
Note: BARNACLE LIFE CYCLE:
Colonial parents cross-fertilize
eggs that hatch into 1 floating
plankton with 1 eye & 6 legs.
These evolve into 2 swimming
larvae with 12 legs, 2 eyes & antennae. Larvae seek out a resting spot & settle. Eyes & feelers change into a cementing
gland that adds the shell, 3, a-
round the body. Barnacles live 5 yrs.
if neighbors don't smother 'em first!
BARNACLE BITERS!
STARFISH
WHELKS
FISH
(CROAKER)

● **Bigfoot of the snail world** stalks Hilton Head's tide flats & estuaries. Close cousins to Florida's colorful Conchs, the 5-9" long Knobbed Whelks are named for their trademark pointy peaks atop their amber shells, painted with purplish/brown streaks. Look for Whelk shells soon after Atlantic storms or after high spring tides, along Calibogue Sound, Skull Creek and the Dolphin Head strand.

Note: Egg Case (up to 2 ft. long); & "trap door" foot used to protect, dig, stomp 'n slide.

● 'Though shore-stranded shells... the ones you hold to your ear to hear the ocean... are usually vacant, 'neath the brine this concrete cavern is home for No. America's largest salt water snail. It measures 6" long & shows 2 erect, stalky eyes & a tapered trunk-like "probiscis". Hungry Whelks plow thru' the mud with their 3" muscular foot to hunt shellfish. Stomping on their limy quarry, they'll pulverize the victim with repeated bludgeonings from their heavy shell, then insert their hollow probiscis like a straw, & suck out the meat! But this fleshy tube is favored bait for enemy bass 'n crabs... so Whelks under attack will use their foot to either burrow backwards, lay down a slimy escape route or squeeze up into the shell, closing the gap with a hard, bony door!

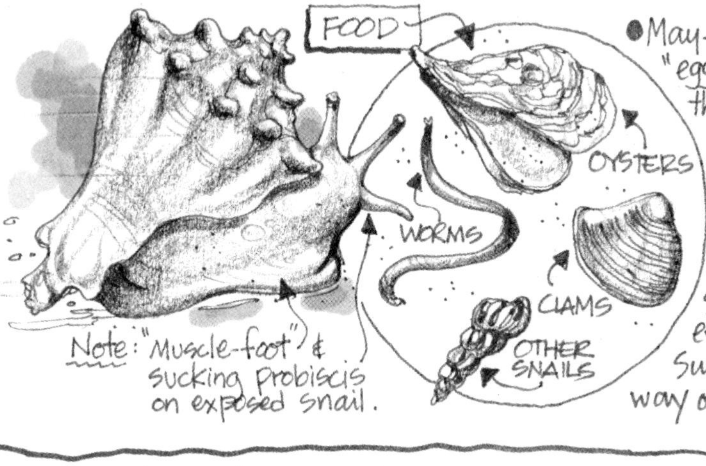

FOOD

OYSTERS

WORMS

CLAMS

OTHER SNAILS

Note: "Muscle-foot" & sucking probiscis on exposed snail.

● May-Oct. watch the beach for Whelk "egg cases". Female snails create these 2' long, "umbilical cords" with papery incubation chambers attached. Each capsule holds 10-15 eggs that grow to miniature Whelks, feeding on stored plankton & oxygen inside. To see the young, hold the case at eye level so it's back lit by the Sun. At 2 wks., young chew their way out of a hole atop ea. capsule.

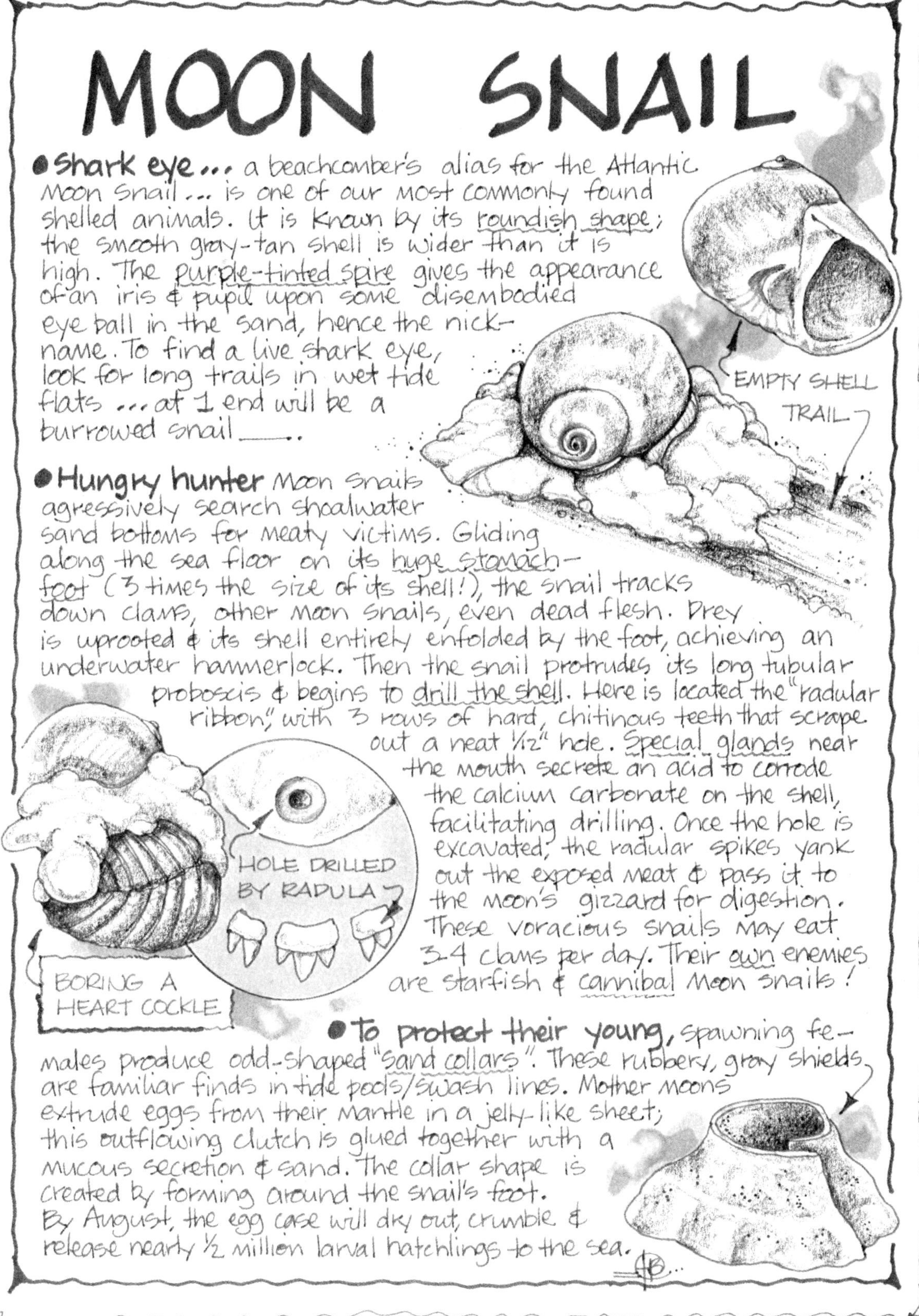
MOON SNAIL
● Shark eye... a beachcomber's alias for the Atlantic Moon Snail... is one of our most commonly found shelled animals. It is known by its roundish shape; the smooth gray-tan shell is wider than it is high. The purple-tinted spire gives the appearance of an iris & pupil upon some disembodied eye ball in the sand, hence the nickname. To find a live shark eye, look for long trails in wet tide flats ... at 1 end will be a burrowed snail ——.
EMPTY SHELL
TRAIL
● Hungry hunter Moon snails agressively search shoalwater sand bottoms for meaty victims. Gliding along the sea floor on its huge stomach-foot (3 times the size of its shell!), the snail tracks down clams, other moon snails, even dead flesh. Prey is uprooted & its shell entirely enfolded by the foot, achieving an underwater hammerlock. Then the snail protrudes its long tubular proboscis & begins to drill the shell. Here is located the "radular ribbon," with 3 rows of hard, chitinous teeth that scrape out a neat 1/12" hole. Special glands near the mouth secrete an acid to corrode the calcium carbonate on the shell, facilitating drilling. Once the hole is excavated, the radular spikes yank out the exposed meat & pass it to the moon's gizzard for digestion. These voracious snails may eat 3-4 clams per day. Their own enemies are starfish & cannibal moon snails!
HOLE DRILLED BY RADULA
BORING A HEART COCKLE
● To protect their young, spawning females produce odd-shaped "sand collars". These rubbery, gray shields are familiar finds in tide pools/swash lines. Mother moons extrude eggs from their mantle in a jelly-like sheet; this outflowing clutch is glued together with a mucous secretion & sand. The collar shape is created by forming around the snail's foot. By August, the egg case will dry out, crumble & release nearly 1/2 million larval hatchlings to the sea.

SALTMARSH SNAILS

●Scads of snails roam the cordgrass root clumps & murky pools of our salt marshes. Most of these mudbank mollusks adapt to the quixotic tides & temperatures there by closing off their shell openings against drying winds/sun with a horny, flat "operculum" trap door. Slithering across the slippery muck is made easy with their big walking foot. Feather-like gills comb oxygen from the soiled, swirling waters. Locating lunch with 2 sensitive tentacles & eyes, snails crunch up algae, rotting grass & even kindred shellfish with a mean set of jaws & a rasping "radula" tongue. Note the habits & homes of these familiar four... as identifying the blackened, mud-stained inch-longs may be a tall order —!!

HB

SALTMARSH SNAIL

●½ inch... the one snail with a lung & no operculum. Climbs grass stems to breath air at high tide, but can "hold its breath" one hour when water-washed at Spring Tide. A favored food of wild ducks —..

PERIWINKLE

●1 inch... grayish-black. Ranges from marsh to beach tide pools. The famous edible (roasted) snail of Europe. Emmigrated to America on the hulls of steamers 'round 1900. Food for Gulls & Sandpipers, Periwinkles are the Island's commonest small snail of the tidelands —...

OYSTER DRILL

●1 inch... a whitish whelk. Found in oyster beds, where it clambers atop oysters & clams & drills a neat pinhole in the shell with its radula. Next it sucks out the meat & moves on to the next shell —!

MUD SNAIL

●1 inch... darkish & sculptured. It is found in pools near marsh grasses & sand flats. Feeds on dead fish. Like Oyster Drills, the Mud Snail is devoured in droves by Egrets & Herons. Stranded high & dry, all saltmarsh snails make a free dinner for these waders whose able eyes & large feet help locate morsels in the mud —..

● **Beauty on the blob** is the marine manner of the secretive little Nudibranch. This is a colorful sea slug, a jelly-bodied snail without a shell. The name, Nudibranch translates as, "naked gills," referring to the slug's unique respiratory system. It breathes through a noticeable branchial plume (B) on its back rather than using gills. 3 sets of tentacles protrude: cereta (CR), brightly colored stalks that camouflage the slug with ambient corals & sponges; cephalic tentacles (CPH), which are sensitive to touch, taste or smell; club-shaped rhinophores (R) to detect odors ___.

● **Humm's Polycera** (right ▸) is our native Nudibranch. Under 1/2" long, it wears speckles on a cloudy gray back. Exquisite bands of turquoise & yellow decorate the tentacles. Its home is the shoals, where it awkwardly swims foot upward, or hugs grass & clumped sponge-coral colonies. Here it feeds upon the sponges themselves & countless bryzoans, sea anemones & hydroids coexisting in the growth (see inset). One might think this creep-along slug lacking a shell would make easy pickins' for enemy crabs & starfish. But it employs 3 effective defenses: tentacle camouflage; "stink"... the slug releases a pungent, rotten smell when handled; poison... when it eats hydroids & anemones it ingests their stinging cells. Unaffected by the venom, it "discharges the charge" via the cereta upon predators when touched ___!

● **Nudibranchs are hermaphrodites.** Each slug has both sperm & eggs itself, but must exchange sperm with another to achieve fertilization... a kind of trade-off mating. The egg-strings are covered with mucous mixed with sea water. A special chemical coats the clutch, rendering it foul-tasting to predators. Soon after hatching, microscopic young forever shed their snail shells.

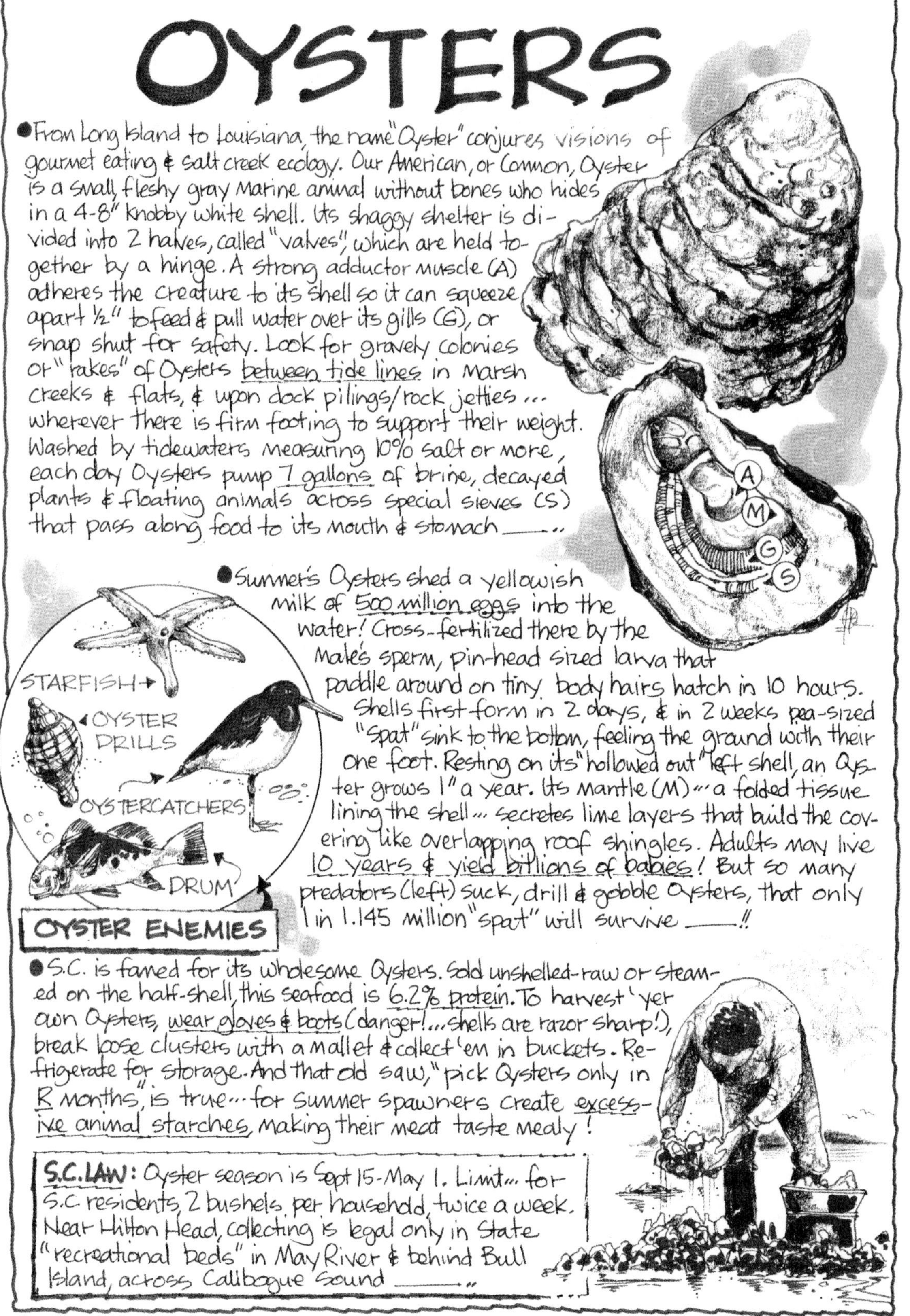

OYSTERS

• From Long Island to Louisiana, the name "Oyster" conjures visions of gourmet eating & salt creek ecology. Our American, or Common, Oyster is a small, fleshy gray marine animal without bones who hides in a 4-8" knobby white shell. Its shaggy shelter is divided into 2 halves, called "valves", which are held together by a hinge. A strong adductor muscle (A) adheres the creature to its shell so it can squeeze apart ½" to feed & pull water over its gills (G), or snap shut for safety. Look for gravely colonies or "rakes" of Oysters between tide lines in marsh creeks & flats, & upon dock pilings/rock jetties ... wherever there is firm footing to support their weight. Washed by tidewaters measuring 10% salt or more, each day Oysters pump 7 gallons of brine, decayed plants & floating animals across special sieves (S) that pass along food to its mouth & stomach ——..

• Summer's Oysters shed a yellowish milk of 500 million eggs into the water! Cross-fertilized there by the male's sperm, pin-head sized larva that paddle around on tiny body hairs hatch in 10 hours. Shells first form in 2 days, & in 2 weeks pea-sized "spat" sink to the bottom, feeling the ground with their one foot. Resting on its "hollowed out" left shell, an Oyster grows 1" a year. Its mantle (M) ... a folded tissue lining the shell ... secretes lime layers that build the covering like overlapping roof shingles. Adults may live 10 years & yield billions of babies! But so many predators (left) suck, drill & gobble Oysters, that only 1 in 1.145 million "spat" will survive ——!!

• S.C. is famed for its wholesome Oysters. Sold unshelled-raw or steamed on the half-shell, this seafood is 6.2% protein. To harvest 'yer own Oysters, wear gloves & boots (danger! ... shells are razor sharp!), break loose clusters with a mallet & collect 'em in buckets. Refrigerate for storage. And that old saw, "pick Oysters only in R months," is true ... for summer spawners create excessive animal starches, making their meat taste mealy!

S.C. LAW: Oyster season is Sept 15-May 1. Limit ... for S.C. residents, 2 bushels per household, twice a week. Near Hilton Head, collecting is legal only in State "recreational beds" in May River & behind Bull Island, across Calibogue Sound ——..

ECOLOGY OF AN
OYSTER BED

● **Clustered colonies** of oyster shells combine to form one of the marshland's richest animal communities, called a bed or "rake". A mild tidal flow, laden with plankton & detritus decay supplies food & oxygen to the filter-feeding bivalves. Easily observed at the mid-tide zone in salt creeks & flats, together these oysters are a center hub in a wetland wheel of life & death___.

PHYTOPLANKTON... Microscopic plants drawn in with water currents feed oysters.

RAYS, DRUM & SHEEPSHEAD... Easily crush the shells with their strong beaks or jaws___.

OYSTER DRILLS... Small (7/10") snails rasp holes in oyster shells, suck out the helpless mollusk inside. Drills take up to 3 weeks to eat 1 oyster.

LIFE IN THE SHELL... Slipper snails & pea crabs rob food strained through gills. Parasitic fungi kill many young oysters.

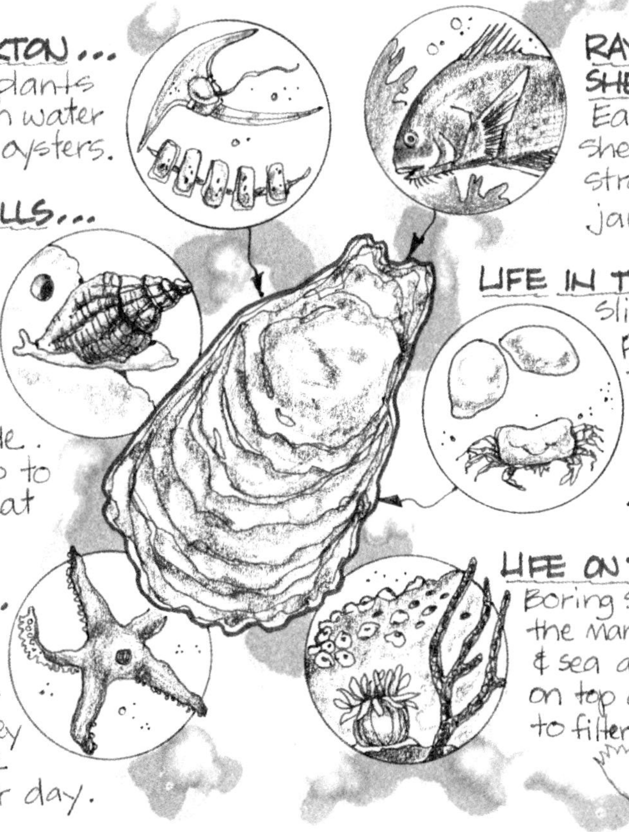

STARFISH... Prey upon oysters by pulling apart the shells. They may consume 6 oysters per day.

LIFE ON THE SHELL... Boring sponges riddle the mantle. Sea whips & sea anemones perch on top of the oyster to filter-feed too.

OYSTER BARS... The pile-up of dead shells makes hard banks where young "spat" oysters settle & grow. So these beds continually enlarge. Current-borne organic matter nurtures grasses, herbs & shrubs. These shell breakwaters collect tide pools teeming with crabs, snails, worms & hungry wading birds___..

MUSSELS

● **Atlantic Ribbed Mussels** are the variety of mussel most common to the Carolina coastal zones. Typically, they are found entrenched ½ way in mud flats & marsh grass clumps, or clustered amongst the jagged jumble of oysters clumping dock pilings. Closely akin to clams & oysters, these bivalves are 3-4" long. Outside, their strong, thin shells are dingy, yellowish-green (young) to gray (mature) ... quite a contrast to the blue-white iridescence glazing the interior. The numerous raised ribs radiating from the hinge on both valves (shells) give the animal its surname____.

● **Spiders of the sea,** mussels are renowned for making a "web" of sorts. Near the small foot is a well-developed byssogenous gland. It secretes sticky byssus, a protein substance which forms incredibly tough fibery strands when it hardens in salty water. These yellow threads help the mussel anchor itself to nearby objects. Moored strongly enough to withstand the force of currents, the shellfish can inhabit wave-washed zones often too harsh for enemy starfish. But a mussel does move ... usually to avoid colonial smothering. Here it snaps its own byssal fibers & sends out new ones in another direction 'til they adhere to roots, shells, etc. By contracting its muscles, it hauls itself forward along its homemade guy lines in small circles____.

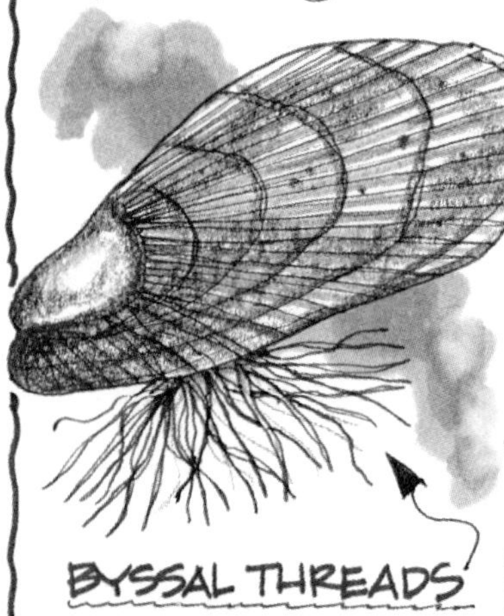

BYSSAL THREADS

● **How Mussels breath & eat.** Their gills filter brackish tidal water, separating out detritus & oxygen. Up to 9 gal./hr. is circulated! Special hairs wave the captured organic matter into a gluey mass & down the fibrous gills toward the mouth. Remarkably, a tiny crustacean, the ½" pea crab, may dwell right in the gills to scrape away "gunk" clogging filaments. Nature always provides____.

Note: 'Tho it is not well known, Ribbed Mussels are edible. Best to cook 'em in with oysters. To avoid contamination from human pollutants, harvest these mussels in public oyster beds only.

COASTAL CLAMS

SIPHONS

FOOT

●**Crowds of Clamshells** which wash ashore here are especially abundant following Fall/Winter storms. Clams are animals normally living 'neath surface sand/mud along seacoast/salt marsh creeks. When popped loose by surf or ravished by carnivorous snails, starfish & crabs, the creatures die & their hard shells remain! These mollusks (soft-bodied "shellfish") differ from Oysters chiefly for their foot. Sticking out between the 2 shells (called "bivalves"), the muscle helps the Clam burrow for defense or scoot sidewards. 2 tube-like siphons protrude from the opposite end to the surface & suck in murky shoalwater, a perfect soupmix of plankton for the stomach & oxygen for the gills (located by the foot). Note.. You can tell the age of most clams by counting "rings" on their shells. The radiating ridges bunched in close lines represent slow Winter shell-growth. Count bunches to determine a Clam's age!

Common Clams:

●**So. Quahog** (Hard-Shell Clam).. 5"; grayish, thick as a china plate! Inner portion of the white/purple shell was broken, drilled & punched into 1/4" "Wampum" beads by local Indians (see inset). A mudflat clam.

●**Jackknife Clam**.. 5-6"; fragile, thin as a Gillette straight-edge razor! Fastest digging clam, burrows under sandy mud flats in seconds!

●**Surf Clam**.. 6"; smooth, creamy, oval clam of sand bottoms, from surf zone to 100 ft. depths.

●**Coquinas**.. 3/4"; overcrowded colonies abound in sand, are swept ashore in piles. Colors: gray-amber-lavender.

●**Channeled Duck Clam**.. 2-3"; deep concentric rings show on thin white shell. So brittle, pieces break off in yer' hand! Lives in sandy mud.

●**Cockles**.. 2-6"; heart-shaped, thick amber shell. Ribs extend the length of shell, not in concentric rings. Lives on the sea floor.

●**Soft-Shell Clam**.. 3"; elliptical & flat, darkish-brown splotches on edge of amber top shell. 'Holes up in sandy mud, has especially "long neck" (siphons).

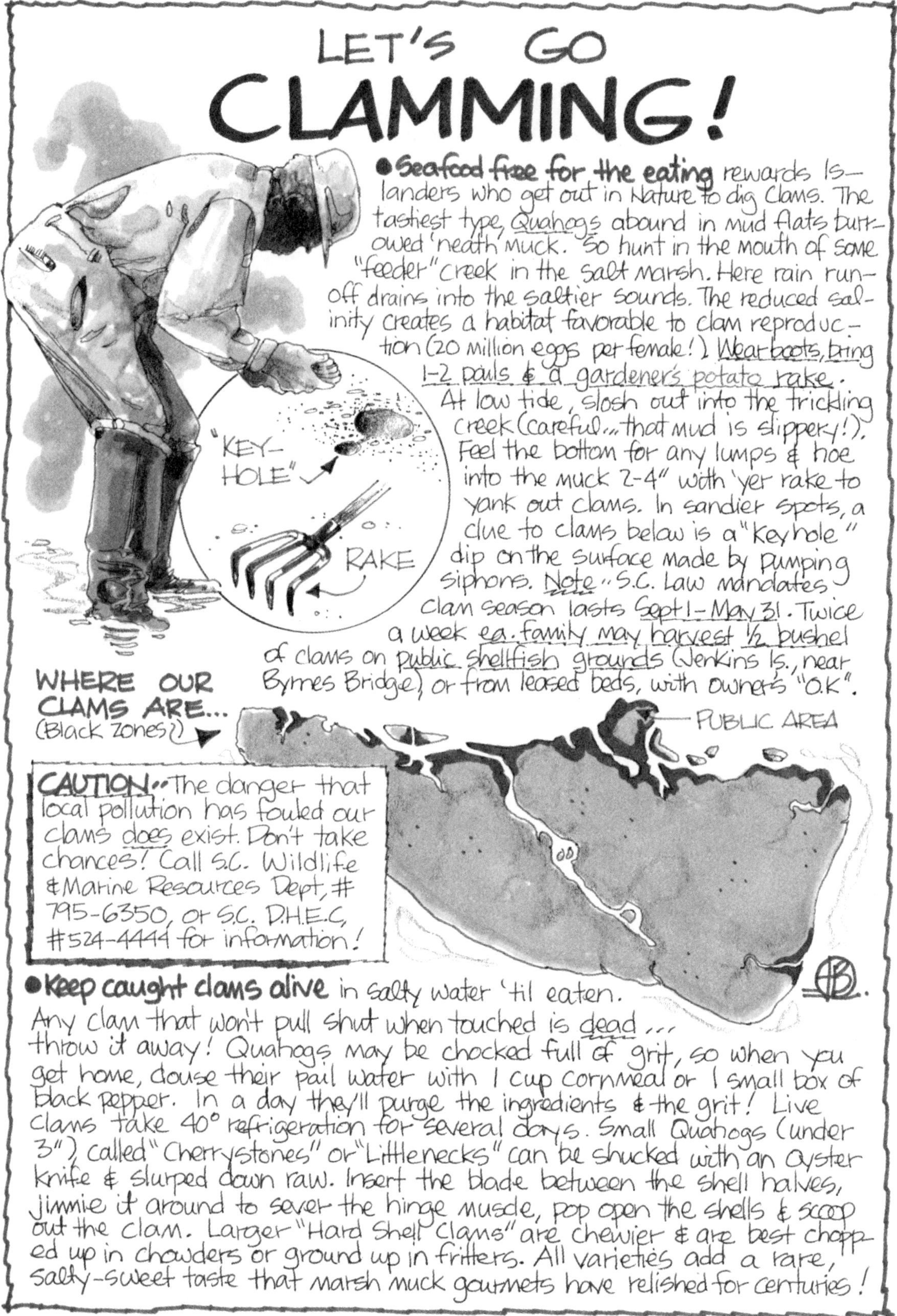
LET'S GO CLAMMING!
● Seafood free for the eating rewards Islanders who get out in Nature to dig Clams. The tastiest type, Quahogs abound in mud flats burrowed 'neath muck. So hunt in the mouth of some "feeder" creek in the salt marsh. Here rain run-off drains into the saltier sounds. The reduced salinity creates a habitat favorable to clam reproduction (20 million eggs per female!) Wear boots, bring 1-2 pails & a gardener's potato rake. At low tide, slosh out into the trickling creek (careful... that mud is slippery!). Feel the bottom for any lumps & hoe into the muck 2-4" with 'yer rake to yank out clams. In sandier spots, a clue to clams below is a "Keyhole" dip on the surface made by pumping siphons. Note.. S.C. Law mandates clam season lasts Sept 1 - May 31. Twice a week ea. family may harvest ½ bushel of clams on public shellfish grounds (Jenkins Is., near Byrnes Bridge), or from leased beds, with owner's "O.K".
"KEY-HOLE"
RAKE
WHERE OUR CLAMS ARE... (Black Zones?)
PUBLIC AREA
CAUTION.. The danger that local pollution has fouled our clams does exist. Don't take chances! Call S.C. Wildlife & Marine Resources Dept, # 795-6350, or S.C. D.H.E.C, #524-4444 for information!
● Keep caught clams alive in salty water 'til eaten. Any clam that won't pull shut when touched is dead... throw it away! Quahogs may be chocked full of grit, so when you get home, douse their pail water with 1 cup cornmeal or 1 small box of black pepper. In a day they'll purge the ingredients & the grit! Live clams take 40° refrigeration for several days. Small Quahogs (under 3"), called "Cherrystones" or "Littlenecks" can be shucked with an Oyster knife & slurped down raw. Insert the blade between the shell halves, jimmie it around to sever the hinge muscle, pop open the shells & scoop out the clam. Larger "Hard Shell Clams" are chewier & are best chopped up in chowders or ground up in fritters. All varieties add a rare, salty-sweet taste that marsh muck gourmets have relished for centuries!

ELEGANCE
ON THE ESTUARY

ANGEL WINGS...

● Blessed is the beachcomber that happens upon a pair of 2 "unfolded wings" of this equisitely sculptured Mollusk. Named for its arcing, elliptical shape & snow-white color, the shell shows 26 knobby ribs which ray-out across the top. The animal-owner, of course, was once a clam which normally lived 1-3 ft. below mud/sand. Angel Wings are famous borers. Anchoring itself with its sturdy foot, the creature rocks back & forth to scrape out a hole in mud, wood & even rock with the long, sharp end of its shell! The clam burrows in & enlarges its hideway home as it grows. Only the siphons will poke out, pumping algae dinners in/out with the tides. Roving crabs, starfish & worms are the Angel's enemies, which along with storms kill & unearth the beautiful shells. In such cases, Mussels may take over the vacant burrows.

5-7"

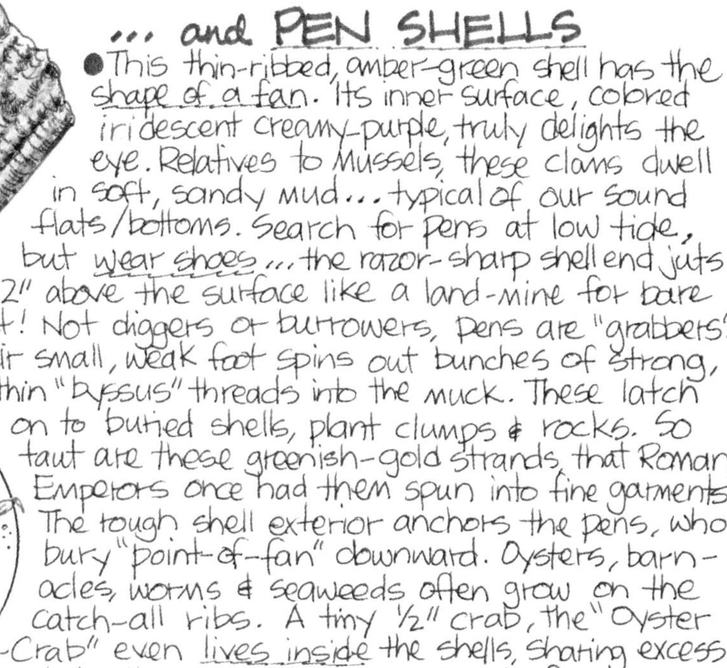

6-8"

... and PEN SHELLS

● This thin-ribbed, amber-green shell has the shape of a fan. Its inner surface, colored iridescent creamy-purple, truly delights the eye. Relatives to Mussels, these clams dwell in soft, sandy mud... typical of our sound flats/bottoms. Search for pens at low tide, but wear shoes ... the razor-sharp shell end juts 2" above the surface like a land-mine for bare feet! Not diggers or burrowers, pens are "grabbers"! Their small, weak foot spins out bunches of strong, thin "byssus" threads into the muck. These latch on to buried shells, plant clumps & rocks. So taut are these greenish-gold strands that Roman Emperors once had them spun into fine garments! The tough shell exterior anchors the pens, who bury "point-of-fan" downward. Oysters, barnacles, worms & seaweeds often grow on the catch-all ribs. A tiny ½" crab, the "Oyster Crab" even lives inside the shells, sharing excess debris the host pumps in when it feeds ___!!

SQUID

● **Memories of monsters** such as the tentacled terror from "20,000 Leagues Under the Sea" may be conjured when one thinks of squid. In truth, common squid, a mere 8-20", abound in inshore & offshore waters here. These missle-shaped cousins to the octopus belong to a group of animals called Cephalapods, meaning "head footed." From the jumble of tentacles & 2 big eyes, their elongated, cylindrical shape flattens & tapers to a point, at the hind end. Squid show 10 arms... 2 longer for capturing food & mating; 8 shorter for handling prey. They do not have a shell, rather are covered with a muscular "mantle" which acts like a light-weight supporting reg, allowing buoyancy. This jelly-white sheath is speckled with brownish spottings. When you handle the squid, these dots pulsate... first enlarging, then contracting, seeming to vanish right before your eyes! The creature's color-changing reveals its gift of camouflage. Its hue can be darkened (more spots) to match the sea floor, or paled (less spots) when swimming near the surface, at night.

● **Backward jet-propulsion** is the squid's swimming style. By drawing water into its wide mantle opening & pumping out a stream thru' a funnel (near the eye), it darts to the rear in quick spurts. To defend against predators (dolphin, fish), squids produce ink. When ejected, this purplish dye makes a smoke screen which confuses the sight, smell & taste of the enemy while the squid escapes. Common squid themselves eat small schooling fish. Prey is encircled with tentacles, held fast with rows of strong suction cups. Sea meat is pushed to the mouth where it is torn into chunks by a strong beak. Tentacles will regrow if yanked off by enemies!

SWIMMING DIRECTION

● **Stringy egg masses** are spawned by bred females in the spring. These sticky fingers adhere to hard surfaces. Each strand containing about 100 eggs may be clumped with masses from other squids, blanketing bottoms of creeks/sounds. But the clusters are seldom attacked. Apparently, their flavor is vile to starfish, urchins & other egg-eatin' sea life!

EGG MASS

• **A searing Southern sun** bakes the sand hills by the sea into a hot, harsh clime for insects. Surface temperatures can reach 120°! In this heat, a "bug's" body juices cook, coagulating internally. Still, 6-leggers do inhabit the dunes. Appearing at night, dawn or dusk, keeping on the wing, these 6 insects have mastered survival in the sand.

Grasshoppers perch on tall grasses like sea oats, staying wind-cooled.

Deerflies strafe the dune zone, hunting warm-blooded prey.

Robberflies capture insects in midair & suck out their bodily fluids.

Digger Wasps burrow into cooler, deeper sand & rise in the air to cool off.

Velvet Ants, actually wasps, have a dense fur which provides insulating airspace around the body.

Tiger Beetles (T) hunt small insects, hide 'neath vegetation. **Ant Lions** (A.L.) excavate conical pits to trap ants.

T

A.L.

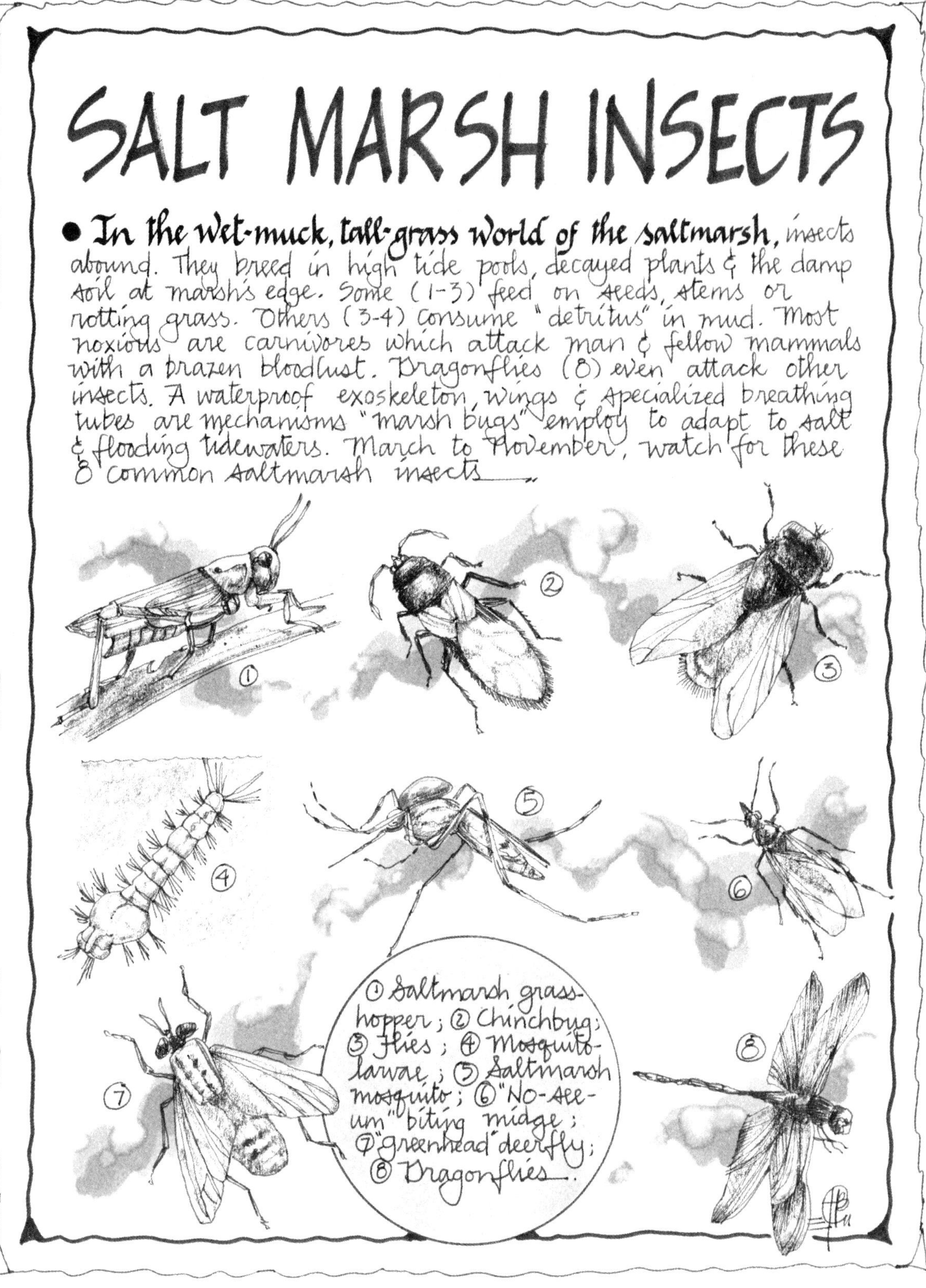
SALT MARSH INSECTS
• In the wet-muck, tall-grass world of the saltmarsh, insects abound. They breed in high tide pools, decayed plants & the damp soil at marsh's edge. Some (1-3) feed on seeds, stems or rotting grass. Others (3-4) consume "detritus" in mud. Most noxious are carnivores which attack man & fellow mammals with a brazen bloodlust. Dragonflies (8) even attack other insects. A waterproof exoskeleton, wings & specialized breathing tubes are mechanisms "marsh bugs" employ to adapt to salt & flooding tidewaters. March to November, watch for these 8 common saltmarsh insects...
①
②
③
④
⑤
⑥
⑦
⑧
① Saltmarsh grass-hopper; ② Chinchbug; ③ Flies; ④ Mosquito-larvae; ⑤ Saltmarsh mosquito; ⑥ "No-see-um" biting midge; ⑦ "Greenhead" deerfly; ⑧ Dragonflies.

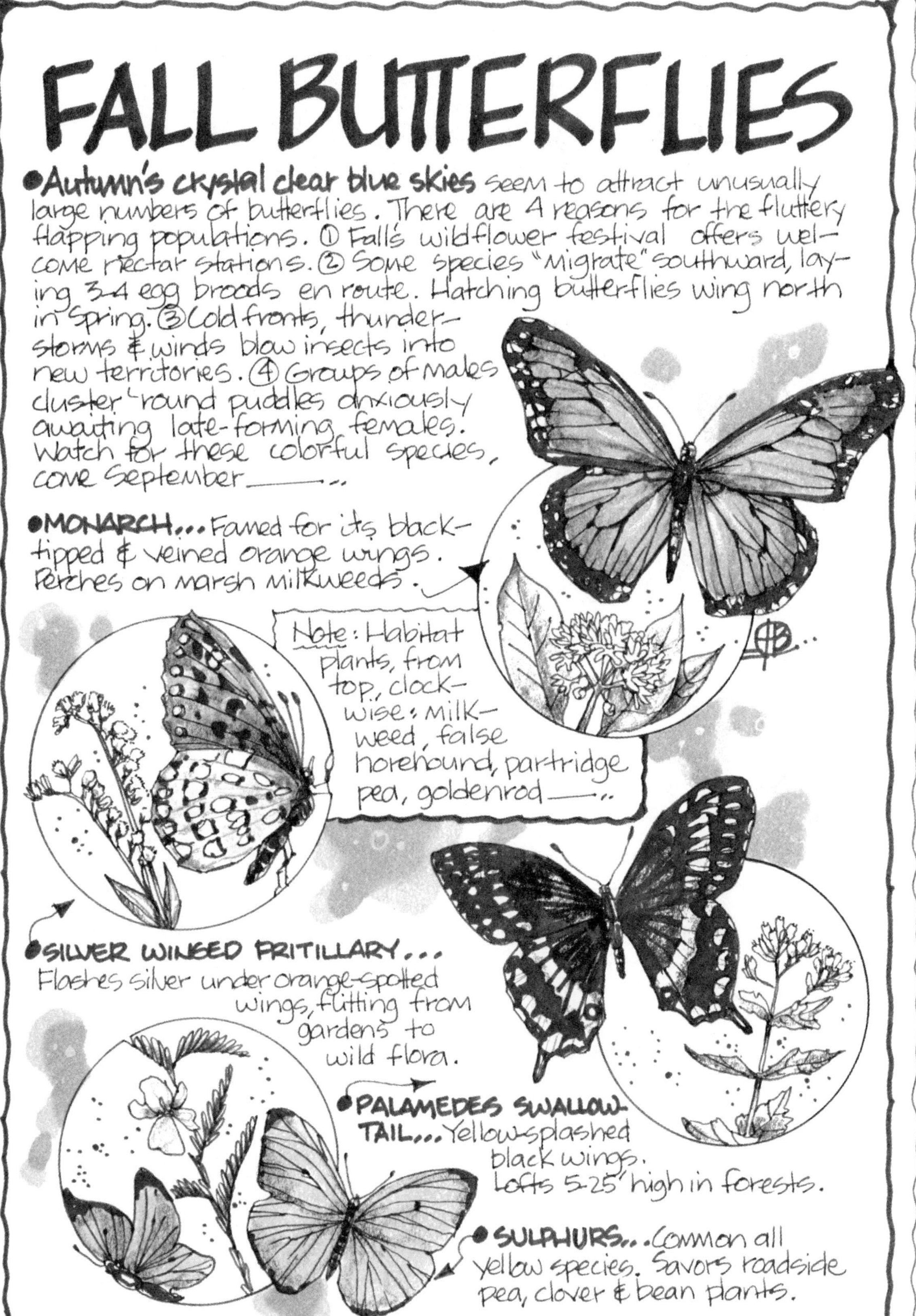
FALL BUTTERFLIES
●Autumn's crystal clear blue skies seem to attract unusually large numbers of butterflies. There are 4 reasons for the fluttery flapping populations. ① Fall's wildflower festival offers welcome nectar stations. ② Some species "migrate" southward, laying 3-4 egg broods en route. Hatching butterflies wing north in Spring. ③ Cold fronts, thunderstorms & winds blow insects into new territories. ④ Groups of males cluster 'round puddles anxiously awaiting late-forming females. Watch for these colorful species, come September ——..
●MONARCH... Famed for its black-tipped & veined orange wings. Perches on marsh milkweeds.
Note: Habitat plants, from top, clockwise: milkweed, false horehound, partridge pea, goldenrod ——..
●SILVER WINGED FRITILLARY... Flashes silver under orange-spotted wings, flitting from gardens to wild flora.
●PALAMEDES SWALLOWTAIL... Yellow-splashed black wings. Lofts 5-25' high in forests.
●SULPHURS... Common all yellow species. Savors roadside pea, clover & bean plants.

INSECT SONGS

"If moonlight could be heard... it would sound like that."
~Nathaniel Hawthorne

● **Insects "sing"** by rubbing certain body parts together. Their musical messages stake out territories, attract mates & drive off rivals. Of these species, only adult males do the crooning. So, as the sexist saying goes: "Happy are cicadas' lives, for they have voiceless wives..."

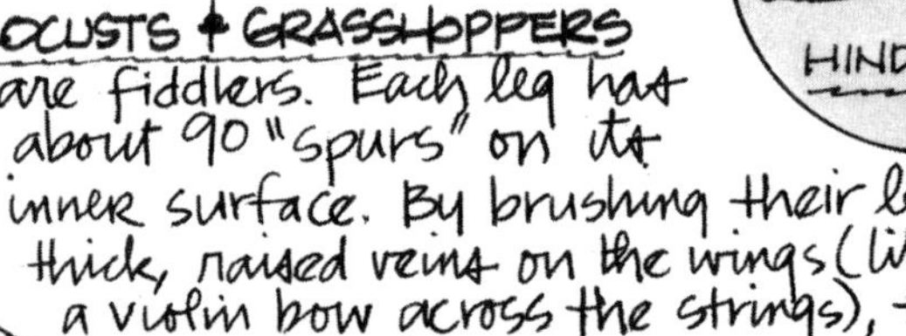

① **LOCUSTS & GRASSHOPPERS** are fiddlers. Each leg has about 90 "spurs" on its inner surface. By brushing their legs across thick, raised veins on the wings (like drawing a violin bow across the strings), they make a steady whistle.

SPURS
HIND LEG:

SCRAPER
FILE VEIN
WING:

② **FIELD CRICKETS** also fiddle, but rub wings together. Each wing is equipped with a heavy file-like vein & a sharp, ridged "scraper". When the wings brush together, the scraper of one wing rubs the file of the next, creating a strident "creet... creet... creet."

③ **CICADAS** are nature's snare drummers. Internal muscles vibrate a pair of big "drumheads", producing a sound like the creaking of a rusty door hinge. The hollow stomach resonates the late summer's song.

AIR CHAMBER
DRUM-HEAD
MUSCLES
ABDOMEN:

④a **KATYDIDS**, green as leaves, scrape wings 50 million times each summer, crying "Katy-did, katy-did, katy-did" over & over.

④b **SNOWY TREE CRICKETS** do the same, but shriek the familiar, rythmic chorus: "Tree... tree ... treeeee!...."

T. Bottontini

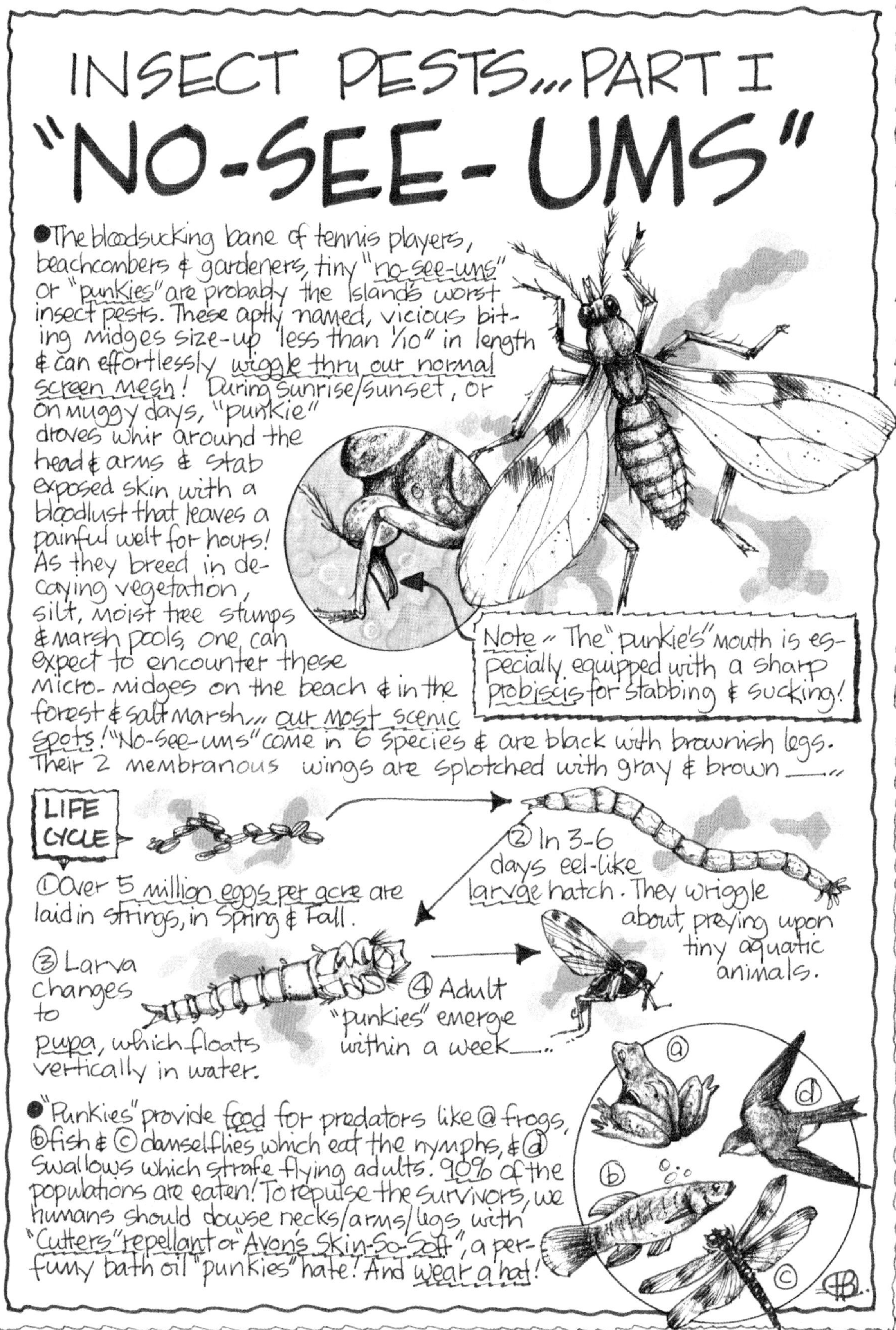
INSECT PESTS... PART I
"NO-SEE-UMS"
●The bloodsucking bane of tennis players, beachcombers & gardeners, tiny "no-see-ums" or "punkies" are probably the Island's worst insect pests. These aptly named, vicious biting midges size-up less than 1/10" in length & can effortlessly wiggle thru our normal screen mesh! During sunrise/sunset, or on muggy days, "punkie" droves whir around the head & arms & stab exposed skin with a bloodlust that leaves a painful welt for hours! As they breed in decaying vegetation, silt, moist tree stumps & marsh pools, one can expect to encounter these micro-midges on the beach & in the forest & salt marsh... our most scenic spots! "No-see-ums" come in 6 species & are black with brownish legs. Their 2 membranous wings are splotched with gray & brown —..
Note – The "punkie's" mouth is especially equipped with a sharp probiscis for stabbing & sucking!
LIFE CYCLE
① Over 5 million eggs per acre are laid in strings, in Spring & Fall.
② In 3-6 days eel-like larvae hatch. They wriggle about, preying upon tiny aquatic animals.
③ Larva changes to pupa, which floats vertically in water.
④ Adult "punkies" emerge within a week —..
●"Punkies" provide food for predators like ⓐ frogs, ⓑ fish & ⓒ damselflies which eat the nymphs, & ⓓ swallows which strafe flying adults. 90% of the populations are eaten! To repulse the survivors, we humans should douse necks/arms/legs with "Cutters" repellant or "Avon's Skin-So-Soft", a perfumy bath oil "punkies" hate! And wear a hat!
ⓐ
ⓑ
ⓒ
ⓓ

INSECT PESTS... PART II

DEER FLIES

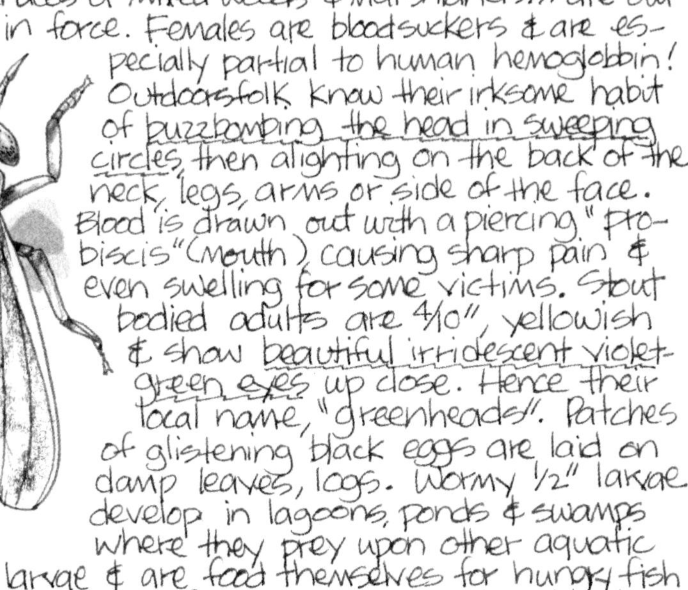

• **Joggers, dogwalkers & hikers beware!** May-Sept. deerflies... Mean menaces of mixed woods & marshlands... are out in force. Females are bloodsuckers & are especially partial to human hemoglobbin! Outdoorsfolk know their irksome habit of buzzbombing the head in sweeping circles, then alighting on the back of the neck, legs, arms or side of the face. Blood is drawn out with a piercing "proboscis" (mouth), causing sharp pain & even swelling for some victims. Stout bodied adults are 4/10", yellowish & show beautiful irridescent violet-green eyes up close. Hence their local name, "greenheads". Patches of glistening black eggs are laid on damp leaves, logs. Wormy 1/2" larvae develop in lagoons, ponds & swamps where they prey upon other aquatic larvae & are food themselves for hungry fish fry. Males feed on flower nectar, thus beneficially collecting pollen & cross-fertilizing numerous plant species!

HORSE FLIES

• **The worst way to meet "gadflies"** is in some swimming pool. These big (1") black cousins to deerflies land on protruding heads & are often mistaken for bees. Horseflies suck blood with an even more painful bite, but are slower & easier to swat! Locales near wetlands, where their egg clusters hatch on overhanging vegetation are horsefly haunts. Their life cycle is similar to deerflies ——..

Note.. Rather than 'bug spray,' wearing a hat, long sleeves & pants is your best precaution against bites by these big flies!

INSECT PESTS...PART III

MOSQUITOS

● **The high whine hum** of mosquitos a-buzz is music most annoying to outdoor folk here. Dozens of species... ranging from the "yellow fever" anopheles to the "house" culex to the huge 5/8" gallinipper inhabit Hilton Head. Each favors specific but separate breeding grounds: deep wet woods, swamp edges, marshes, ponds, lagoons, floodwater bogs, mud flats & even bird baths! Kin to flies (2 wings), 'skeeters are black, brown or gray, show 2 big eyes on the head, hairs on the long legs & hump-backed thorax & a tube-like abdomen. Both sexes feed on plant juices, but it's the female's lust for blood, needed to nurture her eggs, which makes 'em all so despised. Dawn & dusk are most active times for 'skeeter swarms hunting human, dog, livestock, snake or frog targets.

Stylet

Blood Vessel

Above... A belly full of blood!

● **About mosquito bites.** Oddly, these critters are attracted to dark clothing & high body heat/carbon dioxide respired when we swat nervously! The bite is really a stab & a sip. The long "proboscis" tube extending from the mouth is tipped with 6 needle-like "stylets" that poke skin & pierce right into blood vessels. 'Skeeter saliva inhibits blood clotting. To this saliva most humans are allergic, resulting in an itchy swelling around the bite area. Reddened females fly off engorged 1½ times their normal size! Commercial repellants keep mosquitos away, but dissolve with sweat, hence need be reapplied each hour.

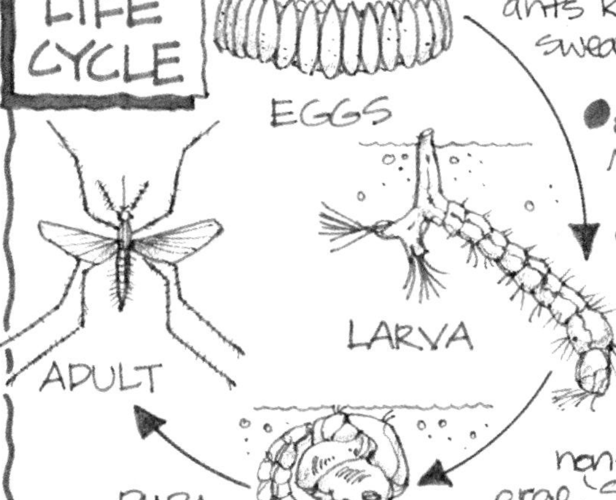

● **A month in the life.** Females attract mates by their wingbeats... their hum is higher, 1000 flaps per second! 100-300 eggs are laid in muddy/stagnant water nurseries, then nudged together with the legs into rafts. In days, wormy "wriggler" larvae hatch. Breathing thru siphon tubes, they eat tiny aquatic plants & animals. Wrigglers soon molt into pupa, a non-feeding stage from which adults immerge. 'Skeeters seldom live over 30 days, so many generations are to blame in our long summer's sting!

TICKS

Bloodthirsty vampires of the bush, ticks are parasites to man, dogs & cats here, Feb.-November. The 1/10" terrors are relatives to spiders. 8 legs stick out from their flat, oval bodies, resembling crabs. Tick's heads are movable. They draw blood... your blood... thru a big 2 pronged beak, bent backwards to anchor these sucking savages on moving, scratching hosts. Ticks inhabit high grass/shrublands. Plopping on passerby warm-blooded animals, they crawl up chosen bodies to a suitable soft spot, then bite. Engorged ticks swell up double-size, look like shiny gray berries. Eventually they'll fall off the victim. Females lay nearly 50,000 eggs in leaf litter. 6 legged, 1/16" larvae blood-suck rodents (but not man), must molt twice to become the adults we pluck off our jeans. Only adults attack man....

ENGORGED

EGGS

Lone Star Tick. Our commonest tick. Is reddish-brown, shows a white spot on its back.

Wood Tick. Duller brown/tan, is the "Spotted Fever" carrier.

About tick bites. Wood ticks are known to carry "Rocky Mountain Spotted Fever". Characterized by chills, severe muscle pains & paralysis sometimes leading to death, the virus is injected when ticks feed on the skull or base of the neck. Odds are 100 to 1 against catching the disease from any one bite, but all bites are bothersome. So after woodswalking, make a body check for ticks. An itchy calf, waist or arm pit may reveal the tiny brown pest with its head imbedded in your skin. Don't panic & yank it out! Calmly drop rubbing alcohol on its rear end (left). Wait a minute, the tick will loosen its grip. Pull & twist the critter out with tweezers. Make sure not to leave the head behind! Wash the bite with soap & water, administer antiseptic ointment & a band-aid. Spraying pant legs with insect repellant is a hiker's best precaution against attracting ticks...

Red bugs are a ton of trouble hiding in a tiny pest package. Nearly microscopic (1/100") chiggers are chrome-orange mites, or relatives to spiders, abiding in pine straw, leaves & tree bark (especially pines). The 6 legged larva is parasitic to man. Out on the prowl April to November, chiggers crawl up human hosts & bite where clothes are tight & body heat is high ... the lower legs, waist & arms. They'll dig right in skin pores to suck blood, causing non-stop itching bad enough to keep you awake at night & a battery of red spots on bite sites. After 1-7 days, red bugs usually drop off victims & toddle away to mature into 8 legged adults (who do not attack people). Females lay 3-8 eggs in leaf litter or under roots, then die by Autumn ... the cool end to a chiggar's sucking season ——— !!

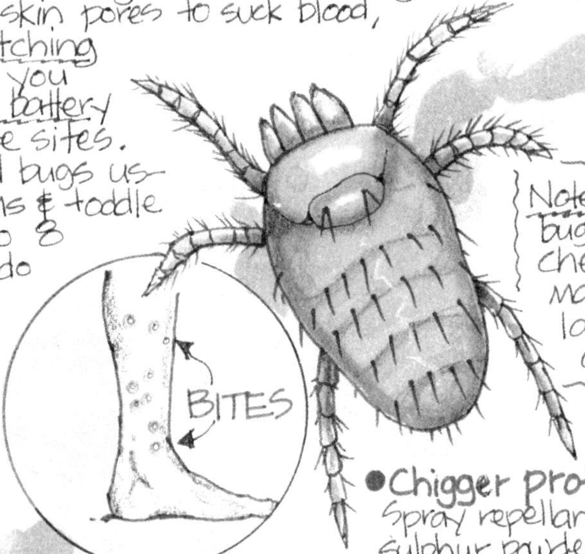

BITES

Note: Red bugs that chew humans are larvae, not adults.

Chigger protection. Spray repellant or dust sulphur powder (sold in pharmacies) on ankles, wrists & waist before hiking. Shower using strong soap upon returning. Treat bites with "Chigger Rid", an effective liquid medication containing collodion, camphor, phenol & oil of eucalyptus ———...

Below: Other animals chiggers attack ...

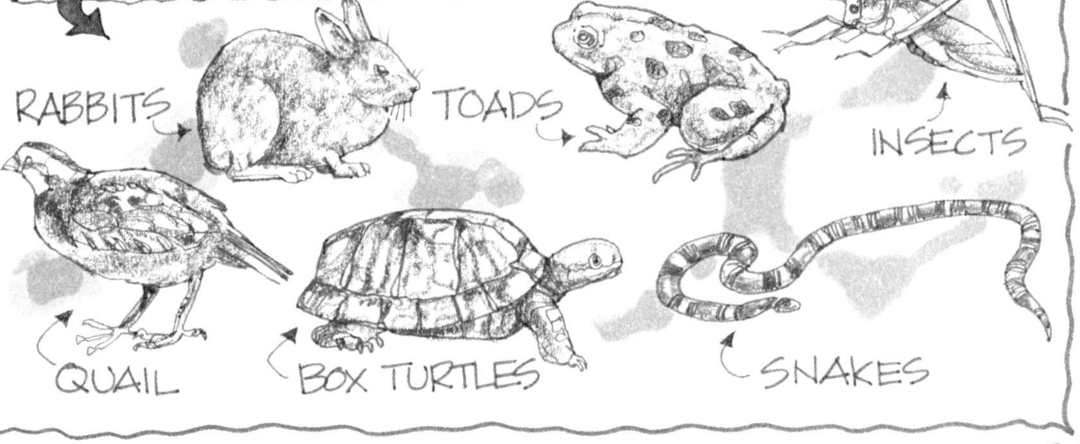

RABBITS

TOADS

INSECTS

QUAIL

BOX TURTLES

SNAKES

● **Devilfish** is a misnomer coined by frightened fishermen for the ferocious appearing, but harmless Manta Ray. This awesome sized fish weighs nearly 2 tons. Brown to slate black above, blotched whitish below, its great dark "wings" (pectoral fins) spread 22 ft. tip to tip; nose to tail, it spans 17 ft.! Two hornlike fins project in front of the head. Located around the mouth, these "arms" sweep in food while the ray swims. Large eyes are placed on the far sides of the broad black head. Mantas range from the Carolinas to Brazil. Here they frequent the rich estuarine creeks/sounds & the open Atlantic to the Gulf Stream.

"FLYING"

● **Like bats on the surf,** Mantas are known for their surprising "flying" routine. They leap 15 ft. out of the water, seeming to sail above the surface before belly-flopping into the drink with a roaring "clap!"... startling nearby boaters, for sure! These acrobatics may be used to rid the ray of parasites, or to precipitate giving birth. Normally Mantas bask near the surface, their wings splayed out in the waves, or rest calmly on the seafloor. They are not dangerous to humans, in fact are considered a tasty game fish. During the cotton era, a planter named William Elliot was known to harpoon the devilfish for sport. The powerful ray would tow his dory miles across Port Royal Sound. Hopefully today islanders do not waste sea life so capriciously___.

SHRIMP

MULLET

PLANKTON

● **Manta young** hatch from eggs in their mother's bodies, then develop there to maturity. Fully formed juvenile "bats" feed on shrimp, copepods & small fish___...

Note.. "Arms" wave food (inset) to the wide mouth.

STING RAY

• **Docile but dangerous** sting rays inhabit beach shoals, muddy salt creeks & rivers here. Close relatives to sharks & skates, rays have skeletons of cartilage (the mushy stuff in the end of your nose) rather than bone & 5 pairs of gill clefts on their underside. Pectoral (chest) fins fan out like wings joining the head. The long tail extending back makes the creature look more like some bizarre, overgrown water weed than a fish. It's this whip-like appendage that gives the ray its bad reputation____.

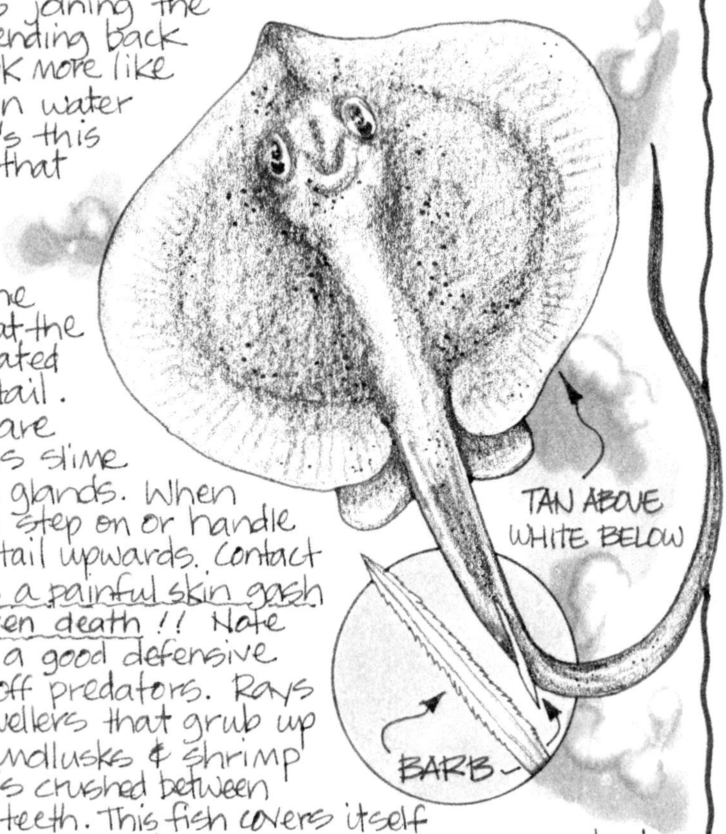

• **A tale of a tail.** The name 'sting ray' hints at the 1-3 flattened barbs located near the base of the tail. These toothed spikes are coated with a poisonous slime made by nearby venom glands. When bathers/surf fishermen step on or handle the ray, it flails the tail upwards. Contact with the barb causes a painful skin gash leading to paralysis, even death!! Note this stinger is merely a good defensive weapon used to fight off predators. Rays are secretive bottom dwellers that grub up urchins, sand dollars, mollusks & shrimp with their snout. Food is crushed between strong, flat teeth. This fish covers itself with sand to hide, or hustles away when approached.

TAN ABOVE
WHITE BELOW

BARB

• **Our resident ray** is the Atlantic Sting Ray. Average size is 2ft. long, 5 lbs; yet it is known to weigh up to 600 lbs! Young develop as embryos within eggs carried by mothers. They are nourished from the egg yolk, not the female's bloodstream. 4-6 baby "stingarees" are born totally able to feed & fend for themselves____..

CAMOUFLAGED

SKATES

● **Poor cousins** to sharks & rays, skates are seldom seen by bathers or boaters, but are commonly snared by inshore fishermen. They are characterized by their broad pectoral fins that fan out to join the head, giving them the flattened look of a ray. Used as a rudder, their long tail is marked with 2 dorsal (back) fins & 1 caudal (tail) fin, & lacks any poisonous barb. Tho' this fish is generally smaller than sharks or rays, it can grow 1-4 ft., weighing 100 lbs____.

● **The Clearnose Skate** is common from Fla.-Cape Cod. Reddish-brown dorsal parts speckled with dark spots & bars contrast a white underbelly. Average size: 6 lbs., 3 ft. long. The clearnose abides in shallow water to 60 ft. depths, scrounging crabs, clams, snails, urchins & fish off the mud bottom. The mouth underneath makes sea floor hunting easy. Flat teeth that fit together into tight plates grind up shells & bones like a garbage disposer! To avoid swallowing water while feeding, the skate employs its "spiracles"... water intake valves behind the eyes that aid gill breathing while the mouth is agape____.

CLEARNOSE SKATE

● **Warm water months** find skates migrating inshore (Sounds, creeks) to spawn. Each egg a female lays is protected in a horny, flattened capsule called a "Mermaid's purse". This black egg case is formed when passing through the mothers oviduct & hardens in sea water. The 1-3" purse is sticky on the underside & adheres to seaweed, sponges & debris. Embryos take from 3-15 months to hatch. Castoff purses (noted by a small rip) found awash in tidal flotsam puzzle beachcombers, but are evidence of skates in our vicinity____.

"MERMAID'S PURSE" WITH EMBRYO INSIDE

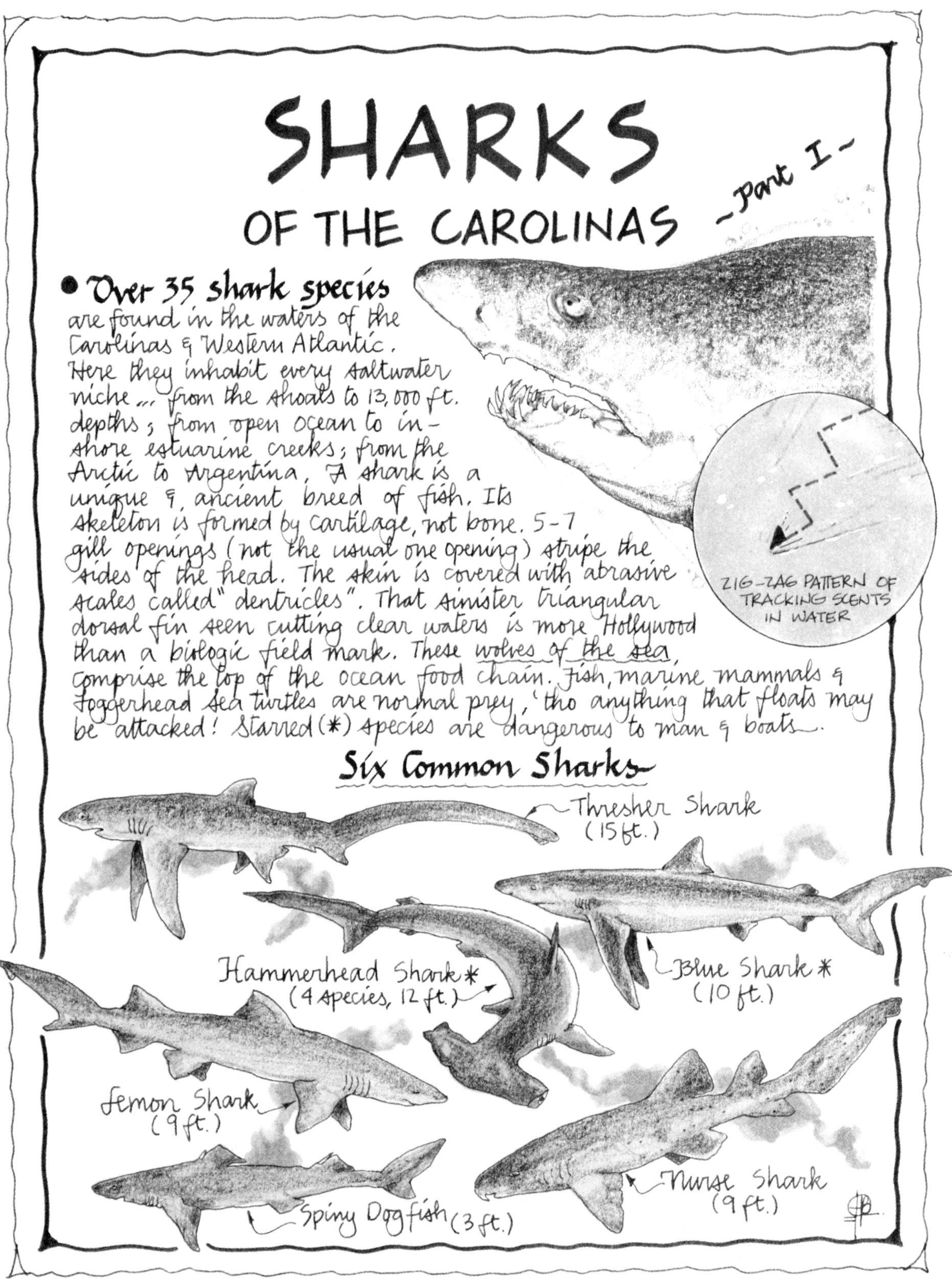
SHARKS
OF THE CAROLINAS
-Part I-
• Over 35 shark species
are found in the waters of the
Carolinas & Western Atlantic.
Here they inhabit every saltwater
niche ... from the shoals to 13,000 ft.
depths; from open ocean to inshore estuarine creeks; from the
Arctic to Argentina. A shark is a
unique & ancient breed of fish. Its
skeleton is formed by cartilage, not bone. 5-7
gill openings (not the usual one opening) stripe the
sides of the head. The skin is covered with abrasive
scales called "dentricles". That sinister triangular
dorsal fin seen cutting clear waters is more Hollywood
than a biologic field mark. These wolves of the sea
comprise the top of the ocean food chain. Fish, marine mammals &
Loggerhead sea turtles are normal prey, 'tho anything that floats may
be attacked! Starred (*) species are dangerous to man & boats.
ZIG-ZAG PATTERN OF TRACKING SCENTS IN WATER
Six Common Sharks
Thresher Shark (15 ft.)
Blue Shark * (10 ft.)
Hammerhead Shark * (4 species, 12 ft.)
Lemon Shark (9 ft.)
Nurse Shark (9 ft.)
Spiny Dogfish (3 ft.)

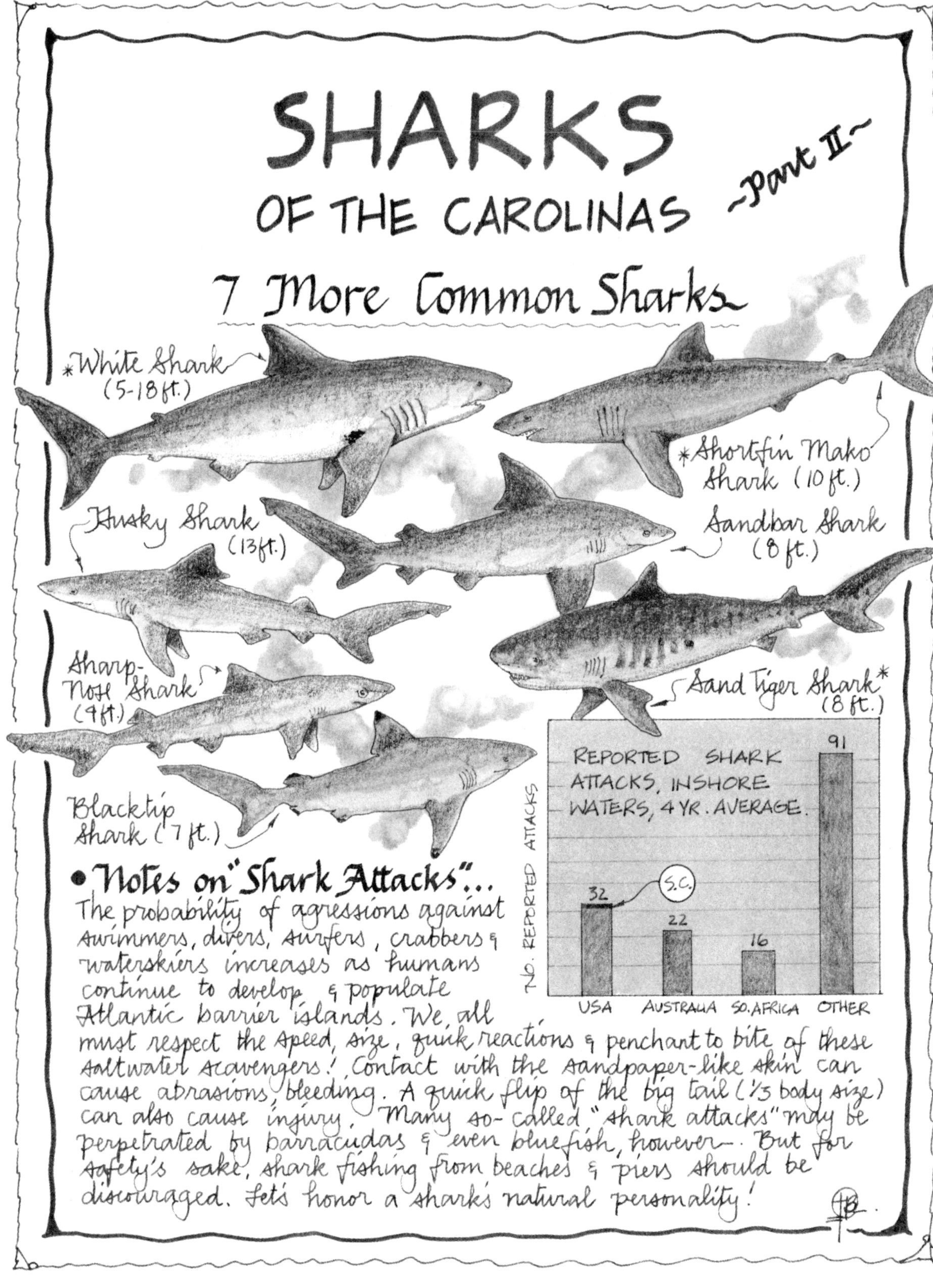
SHARKS
OF THE CAROLINAS ~Part II~
7 More Common Sharks
*White Shark (5-18 ft.)
*Shortfin Mako Shark (10 ft.)
Dusky Shark (13 ft.)
Sandbar Shark (8 ft.)
Sharp-Nose Shark (4 ft.)
Sand Tiger Shark* (8 ft.)
Blacktip Shark (7 ft.)
REPORTED SHARK ATTACKS, INSHORE WATERS, 4 YR. AVERAGE.
NO. REPORTED ATTACKS
32
S.C.
22
16
91
USA
AUSTRALIA
SO. AFRICA
OTHER
• Notes on "Shark Attacks"...
The probability of agressions against swimmers, divers, surfers, crabbers & waterskiers increases as humans continue to develop & populate Atlantic barrier islands. We, all must respect the speed, size, quick reactions & penchant to bite of these saltwater scavengers! Contact with the sandpaper-like skin can cause abrasions, bleeding. A quick flip of the big tail (1/3 body size) can also cause injury. Many so-called "shark attacks" may be perpetrated by barracudas & even bluefish, however. But for safety's sake, shark fishing from beaches & piers should be discouraged. Let's honor a shark's natural personality!

SHARK LORE

~Sharks, Part III

• **The name, shark** probably evolved from the German root, "schurk", meaning greedy parasite. Today the word is applied to either elasmobranch fish (cartilage skeletons, uncovered gill slits) or human villians, rogues & lowlifes.

• **Largest shark, smallest shark:** 250 species haunt the seas worldwide. Whale sharks (60 ft., 15 tons) are largest, yet only feed on microscopic plankton. Smallest is the Japanese "Dwarf Shark with a Long Nose", or Tsuranagakobitozame (4 in., 1 oz.).

Whale Shark

Six foot man

• **About shark teeth:** Sharks sport several rows of teeth on the jaw. When a tooth is lost, a new one grows in to replace it. Fossil shark teeth (appear black) may be unearthed in quarries, borrow pits & eroding shore banks. They are found in upland regions because sealevels were higher in prehistoric times.

• **Shark Products**

Meat: Steaks & fillets are sought by anglers. Dried shark flesh is the meat portion of British "fish & chips". Orientals cook a tasty soup from the dried fins.

Shark oil was a major source of vitamin A before 1950. The oil was extracted from the liver.

Fertilizer is made from ground carcasses.

Skin called "shagreen" has been used as a sandpaper or as leather after the toothlike "placoid" scales are removed.

FISHES
OF THE SEASHORE

●**The beachfront** we humans casually visit as a playground is in fact a waterworld teeming with fish. When tidal currents & surf stir up bottom debris & marine creatures, schools gather in the shoals to feed. Below are 6 common seashore fishes snarred by casters & sein netters, or found awash upon the strand, dashed dead on sandbars during storms here—...

HB...

●**MULLET...** 30", 15 lbs. The snub-nosed, silvery fish which leaps out of water, surprising swimmers! Mullets feed on seaweeds & bottom particles.

●**SEA CATFISH...** 12", 2 lbs. Bite on cut shrimp. Note dangerous sharp spine on dorsal & pectoral fins can cut skin, trigger a release of poison into the wound. Beware!

●**DOGFISH SHARK...** 2-3 ft., 15 lbs. Note the long tail on a slate gray body. Tiny teeth in the corners of its mouth render this "Jaws" harmless to man!

●**STING RAY...** 2 ft. Cruises inches deep water. Beware the serrated barb on the long thrashing tail used to slash enemies!

BARB

●**FLOUNDER...** 20", 3 lb. Flat-bodied fish of shoals/mud bottoms. Both eyes located on top side. Commonly dragged up in shrimp nets.

●**SPINY BOXFISH...** 8", ½ lb. Its flat-bottomed body is covered with a shell of porcupiney spines for defense.

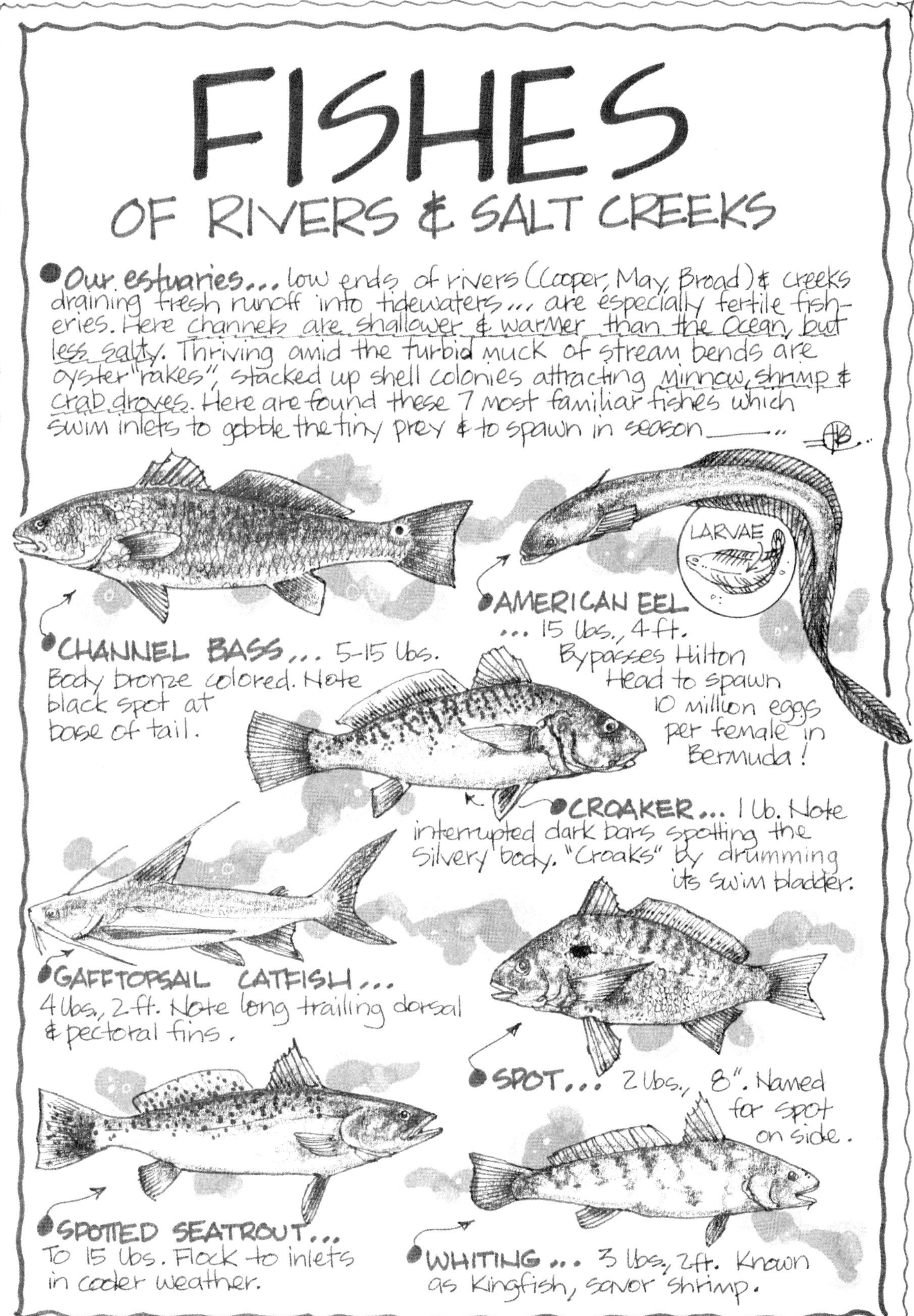
FISHES
OF RIVERS & SALT CREEKS
Our estuaries... low ends of rivers (Cooper, May, Broad) & creeks draining fresh runoff into tidewaters... are especially fertile fisheries. Here channels are shallower & warmer than the Ocean, but less salty. Thriving amid the turbid muck of stream bends are oyster "rakes", stacked up shell colonies attracting minnow, shrimp & crab droves. Here are found these 7 most familiar fishes which swim inlets to gobble the tiny prey & to spawn in season ——..
LARVAE
AMERICAN EEL ... 15 lbs., 4 ft. Bypasses Hilton Head to spawn 10 million eggs per female in Bermuda!
CHANNEL BASS... 5-15 lbs. Body bronze colored. Note black spot at base of tail.
CROAKER... 1 lb. Note interrupted dark bars spotting the silvery body. "Croaks" by drumming its swim bladder.
GAFFTOPSAIL CATFISH... 4 lbs., 2 ft. Note long trailing dorsal & pectoral fins.
SPOT... 2 lbs., 8". Named for spot on side.
SPOTTED SEATROUT... To 15 lbs. Flock to inlets in cooler weather.
WHITING... 3 lbs., 2 ft. Known as Kingfish, savor shrimp.

FISHES

'ROUND DOCKS & PIERS

• **Algae slickered pilings** of weathered docks & piers are rich inshore habitats to observe/catch saltmarsh fishes. Warm, placid, brackish waters of protected harbors swirl on running tides, swashing scads of stick-on-the-post filter feeders... barnacles, mussels, oysters..., with plankton soup. Fiddler crabs scuttle the mud basins. Slow bottom-loving fish graze with ease on these "benthic" creatures, darting in & out of shadows docks make, & debris boaters discard. From So. Beach to Skull Creek Marina watch for these 5 fishes —..

• **TOADFISH...** 1/2 lb., 1 foot. Slimy brown. Big toad-like mouth delivers a nasty bite! Males hide in rusted cans, guarding eggs. It's the brunt of Hilton Head's infamous "Toadfish tournament"!

HOLED UP

• **SHEEPSHEAD...** 2-20 lb., 16". Called "convict fish" for its black & white stripe camouflage. Crunches up shellfish with large buck teeth.

• **SEAHORSE...** 2-4". Hides in grasses/shoal-water plants, attaching self with tail. Males carry eggs in tummy pouch, Kangaroo style!

• **PINFISH...** 3/4 lb., 8". Black verticle/yellow horizontal stripes decorate a blue tinted body. Matching underwater shadow patterns, these stripes help the fish hide. Note black spot by gills —..

• **MUMMICHOG...** 5". A quick, darkish fish with dull vertical stripes. Gobbles up rafts of insect larvae from marsh plants.

"UNFISH"

• What's in a name? Not much... biologically speaking. Many varieties of sealife carry the word "fish" as a suffix to their common name. Yet, each creature is in no way a fish, defined as a finned, backboned animal which lives in water & breathes using gills. To clear up the confusion, below are shown 5 "unfish"... well-known swimmers, bottom-dwellers & look-alikes for the *true* scaly denizens of the deep.

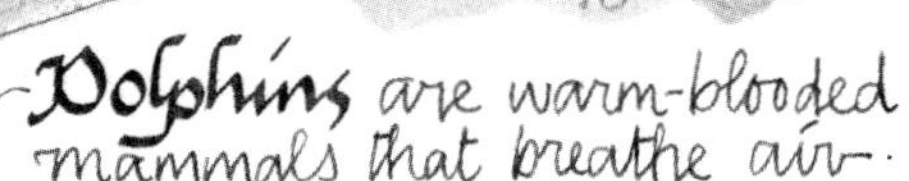

Dolphins are warm-blooded mammals that breathe air.

Jellyfish are coelenterates with a simple bag-like body lacking a backbone.

Starfish have spiny, radial arms & do not have a backbone.

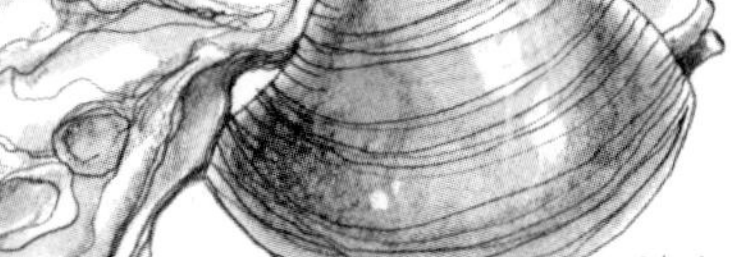

Ribbon Worms are fish-like swimmers without a backbone.

Shellfish... oysters & clams... are bivalves or 2-shelled mollusks that breathe & feed through siphons.

LOGGERHEAD SEA TURTLE

* A FEDERALLY THREATENED SPECIES

● **A wandering giant comes to nest.** It's a glad midsummer's eve when still another loggerhead sea turtle crawls ashore to lay eggs. Named for bark-like shields that plate its long head, this is a turtle of deep sea waters; but it also wanders our estuary mud bottoms... feeding, sleeping & hibernating in the insulating muck. The yellowish creature 'neath the 3½ ft. rusty-brown carapace peppered with barnacles weighs as much as 350 pounds. Yet, bouyed by its featherweight bones with air pockets, a loggerhead can flipper its way through the sea at 25 m.p.h. On land, this reptile moves one step faster than a snail!

● **Loggerheads have the strongest beaks** of the 6 kinds of Atlantic sea turtles. They use beaks to crunch thick calcium shells of: ① whelks; ② horseshoe crabs; & ③ blue crabs. Even fishermen's crab traps (#4) are yanked apart... the turtle getting good leverage from 2 strong claws on each flipper.

● **For 175 million years** loggerheads have mated at sea & come ashore to nest. May-Aug., often during Spring Tides, females trudge above the high tide line to nest. They lay 82-150 white, ping-pong ball sized eggs in 4 ft. long x 1 ft. deep crescent-shaped trenches, excavated with flippers. Next, they camouflage the clutch with sand & lumber back to sea. In 2 months, 5" hatchlings pop out of the den at night & scamper down the beach to the sea. 3 batches of eggs are laid each summer. Ghost crabs, coons, fish & weather kill 99.99% of the young.* Survivors may live 100 years.

DIAMOND-BACK TERRAPIN
• Plop! Every fisherman & salt marsh explorer knows the sound a Diamond-back Terrapin makes slinking off a cordgrass cliff into some soupy creek below. Named for its kaleidoscopic shell designs, the 4-8", 1 lb. Terrapin is our only small salt water turtle. Its tideland/brackish lagoon home, plus its spotted white head, legs & tail makes for easy identification. Look especially for that gray-brown carapace studded with 5 and 6 sided concentric rings. Actually these are a series of thin scales which add on one per year as the Diamond-back grows. From time to time, Terrapin shells will wash up in the surf... bleached out, but still in tact. The plastron or bottom shell is the color of burnt bone...
• Typically turtle, Diamond-backs are big eaters. Strong webbed feet help 'em dive deep or walk soggy flats hunting ① crabs, ② snails (Terrapins crack up periwinkles so hard you can hear a "popping" sound!), ③ insects & ④ fish. Even ⑤ burrowed worms are quarried by the flippers. Terrapins will dig themselves into marsh mud to hide or hibernate (Oct.-April).
• A Terrapin two-step! To get the larger female's attention prior to mating, the dwarfish male Diamond-back swims around her, waving his claws in her face! May-June, Mothers scoop out a 6" hole on sandy/bushy berms above the high-tide line. Here 5-12 pinkish eggs will incubate under a cover of packed earth for 6 weeks. 1" hatchlings grow about 1" a year. 'Coons & Fish Crows are the reptile's raiders today. But in the early 1900's humans harvested tons of Terrapins for their meat. A 7" Diamond-back once brought $10.00 ... before over-hunting exhausted the market!
T. Ballantine...
Floating head-high. Note the face's "mustache".
①
②
③
④
⑤

ALLIGATOR
RECORD LENGTH: 19 FT., 2 IN.
•That floating log you notice in our freshwater lagoons/golf course hazard ponds just may have teeth, eyes, 4 legs & a tail. Chances are, it's one of our common American Alligators... direct descendants of 45 ft. crocodiles that scuttled about with dinosaurs. This leather-plated, black "swamp dragon" with the wide, flat snout grows 14 ft. long, weighing 500 LBS. But this is no mean crocodile, which is larger, greener, has a pointed nose & ranges far south (FLORIDA TROPICS). 'Gator watchers know this reptile sunbathes on grassy banks to maintain a steady 89° body temp. In summer, 'gators submerge, so only the eyes & nubby nostrils show.
CRABS
FISH
IN-SECTS
BIRDS
SNAKES
NOTE: 70-80 cone-shaped teeth bite (do not chew) prey. Chunks are torn off, gulped down whole. Even your golf balls are swallowed for ballast when swimming...
•Slow digestion means 'gators need just 1 LB. of food per week. They can fast 2 yrs. Stealthy hunters, they'll upend prey with their thrashing, muscular tails... then hold it underwater 'til it drowns (includes dogs!).
7" STRIPED BABY & NEST
•'Gators hibernate Dec.-Mar., in underground dens, scooped out with jaws & claws. Rounded-up by the bulls' roaring bellow, females mate by Easter. They lay 30-70 oblong, white eggs in mounds of mud, stems, stalks & fronds "mama scrapes up in secluded marshes. She'll guard the nest against hogs, 'coons & male 'gators, 'til composting debris incubate the young to hatch. Be warned that 'gators will charge if bothered. They can outrun humans for 50 yards... so always stay clear!

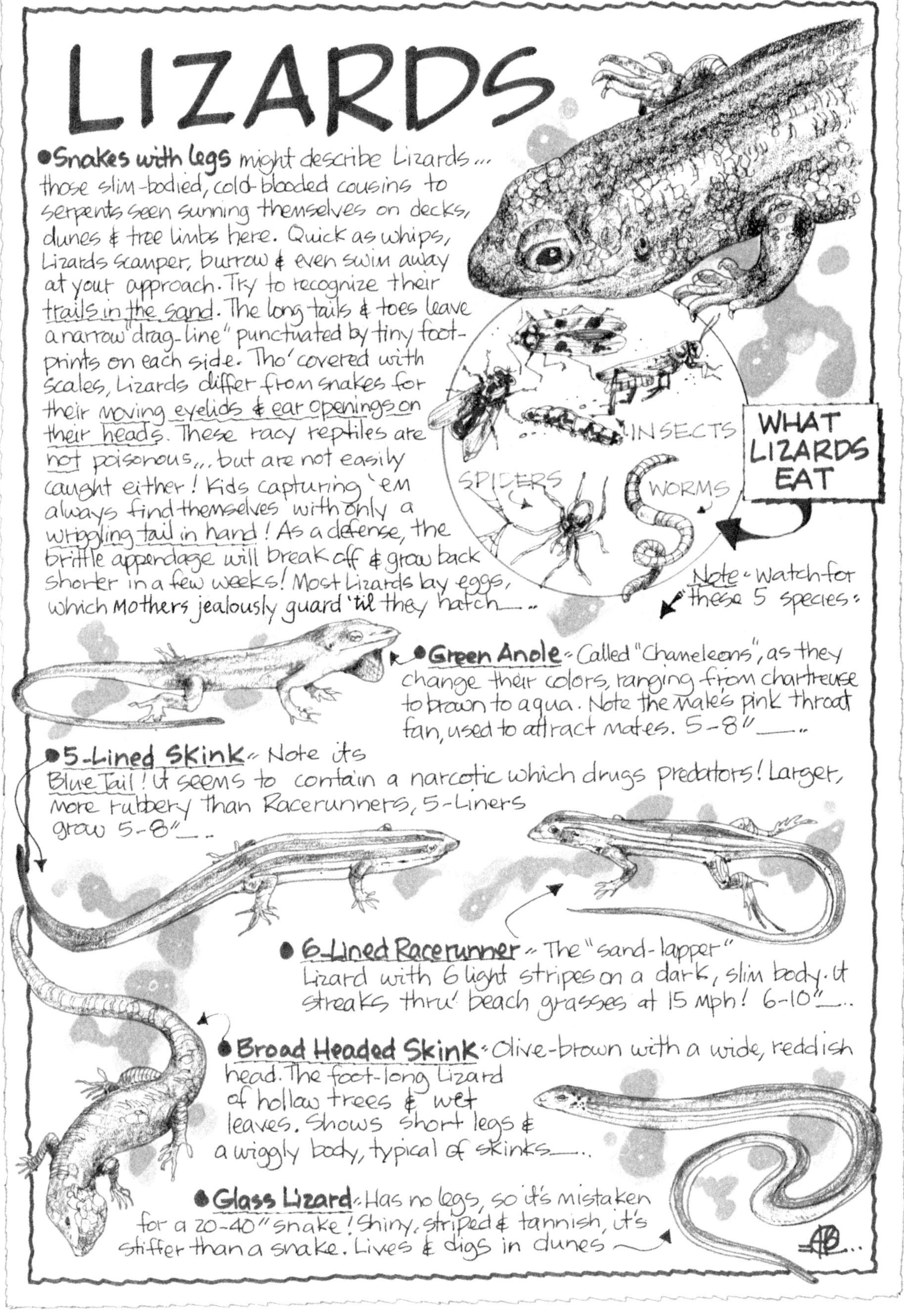
LIZARDS
Snakes with legs might describe Lizards... those slim-bodied, cold-blooded cousins to serpents seen sunning themselves on decks, dunes & tree limbs here. Quick as whips, Lizards scamper, burrow & even swim away at your approach. Try to recognize their trails in the sand. The long tails & toes leave a narrow "drag-line" punctuated by tiny footprints on each side. Tho' covered with scales, Lizards differ from snakes for their moving eyelids & ear openings on their heads. These racy reptiles are not poisonous... but are not easily caught either! Kids capturing 'em always find themselves with only a wriggling tail in hand! As a defense, the brittle appendage will break off & grow back shorter in a few weeks! Most Lizards lay eggs, which Mothers jealously guard 'til they hatch...
INSECTS
SPIDERS
WORMS
WHAT LIZARDS EAT
Note - Watch for these 5 species:
Green Anole - Called "Chameleons", as they change their colors, ranging from chartreuse to brown to aqua. Note the male's pink throat fan, used to attract mates. 5-8"...
5-Lined Skink - Note its Blue Tail! It seems to contain a narcotic which drugs predators! Larger, more rubbery than Racerunners, 5-Liners grow 5-8"...
6-Lined Racerunner - The "sand-lapper" Lizard with 6 light stripes on a dark, slim body. It streaks thru' beach grasses at 15 mph! 6-10"...
Broad Headed Skink - Olive-brown with a wide, reddish head. The foot-long Lizard of hollow trees & wet leaves. Shows short legs & a wiggly body, typical of skinks...
Glass Lizard - Has no legs, so it's mistaken for a 20-40" snake! Shiny, striped & tannish, it's stiffer than a snake. Lives & digs in dunes...

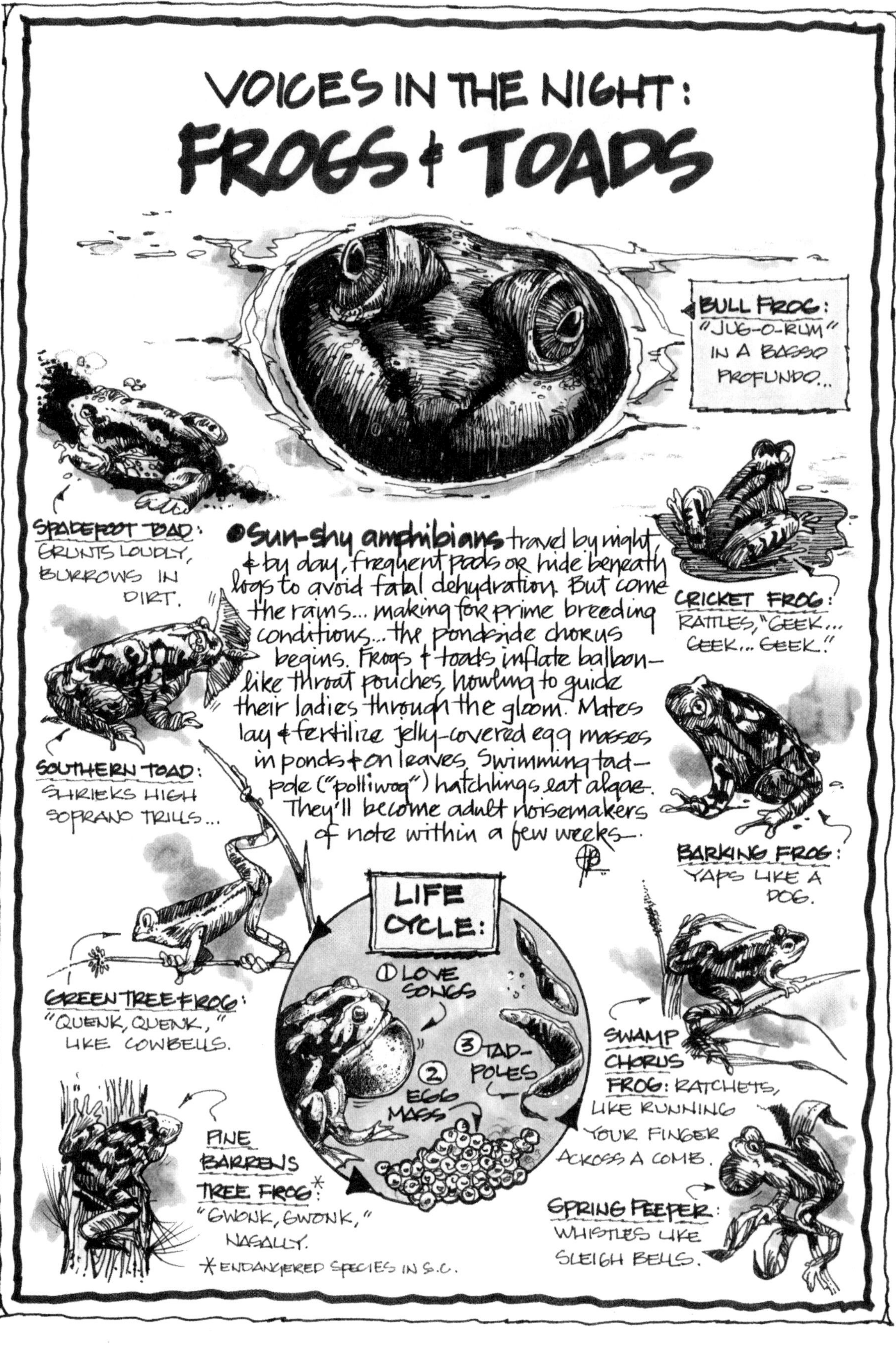

VOICES IN THE NIGHT:
FROGS & TOADS
BULL FROG: "JUG-O-RUM" IN A BASSO PROFUNDO...
SPADEFOOT TOAD: GRUNTS LOUDLY, BURROWS IN DIRT.
Sun-shy amphibians travel by night & by day, frequent pools or hide beneath logs to avoid fatal dehydration. But come the rains... making for prime breeding conditions... the pondside chorus begins. Frogs & toads inflate balloon-like throat pouches, howling to guide their ladies through the gloom. Mates lay & fertilize jelly-covered egg masses in ponds & on leaves. Swimming tadpole ("polliwog") hatchlings eat algae. They'll become adult noisemakers of note within a few weeks.
CRICKET FROG: RATTLES, "GEEK... GEEK... GEEK."
SOUTHERN TOAD: SHRIEKS HIGH SOPRANO TRILLS...
BARKING FROG: YAPS LIKE A DOG.
LIFE CYCLE:
① LOVE SONGS
② EGG MASS
③ TAD-POLES
GREEN TREE FROG: "QUENK, QUENK," LIKE COWBELLS.
SWAMP CHORUS FROG: RATCHETS, LIKE RUNNING YOUR FINGER ACROSS A COMB.
PINE BARRENS TREE FROG*: "GWONK, GWONK," NASALLY.
SPRING PEEPER: WHISTLES LIKE SLEIGH BELLS.
* ENDANGERED SPECIES IN S.C.

BROWN PELICAN

● **Still-winged, ungainly, dramatic, big-mouthed...** the colorful demeanor of the Brown Pelican makes it one of the island's most memorable wildlings. Our largest shorebird measures 50" with a wingspan over 6½ ft.! Adults are silvery-brown & show white on the head & neck. Immature birds have a dark head & palish underparts. You'll find Pelicans wherever salt water runs... the ocean, salt marsh flats or upon channel markers/wharf piling perches. A graceful wedge formation of 4-10 birds is commonly seen silently strafing the wave tops, alternately flapping & gliding with wingtips poised just inches above the swells.

Note: Pelicans can skim the wave tops at 30 m.p.h.!

● **"A wonderful bird is the pelican... his bill will hold more than his belican."** Donald Merritt's limerick best expresses 'big brown's' dive-bombing dining style. The bird drops from 30 ft. up, splashing beak-first into the drink. 'Neath the surface it nets small fish in its elastic "gular pouch" below the long (14") bill. This 6-7" deep sack will hold quarts of fish & water. Buoyed up by small air sacks behind the feathers, the pelican allows water to drain out narrow side gaps in the bill, then jiggles the quarry headfirst down its throat. Schooling fish such as Menhaden (left, inset), mullet, minnows & herring are prime pelican 'pickins.

● **Pelicans nest** on offshore sand bars. 2-5 chalky-white eggs are laid in bulky stick roosts. White fledglings feed on regurgitated fish from parents' beaks for 8-10 weeks. Here the big danger is flooding storms.

DOUBLE-CRESTED CORMORANT

Cormorants come to coastal S.C. in Autumn, giving chase to southward migrating fish schools. When their ragged "V" formations flap by, skimming low over the Atlantic/nearby sounds, the birds resemble long-necked, black geese! At rest on channel markers or bunched 50-to-a-wire on utility lines, Cormorants reveal their true colors. These glossy-black, 2½ ft. tall kin to pelicans flash an orange face/throat patch surrounding a lengthy, hooked bill. A long, stiff tail which sticks out when Cormorants fly is used as a brace, supporting the birds at perch. Strong swimming Cormorants paddle about for hours, buoyed-up on stout feathers made waterproof when the birds preen special oil glands near the rump. But... to really know a Cormorant is to see it dive ——...

Note: Cormorants have no nostrils & only breath thru' the mouth... an adaptation to avoid drowning during deep dives!

"Shag"... Cormorants' nickname referring to their fishing fame... streak 100 ft. down to capture fish... their sole food. Pulling water with their wings, propelling themselves with huge webbed feet (all 4 toes webbed) & steering with their rudder-tails, Cormorants actually out-run small fish (at left, inset)! Surfacing "shag" flip the catch skyward & swallow it headfirst, avoiding cutting spines. Sportsmen have complained "shag" compete for game fish, but studies show that: ① mostly undersize "trash fish" are taken; ② the birds' abundant guano nourishes the growth of plankton eaten by fry! Chinese fishermen, in fact, train Cormorants to snare fish. Tethered by a line to avoid escape & a loose noose preventing swallowing the quarry, the birds dive on command... & may bring up 100 fish-an-hour ——!!

MEN-HADEN

MINNOWS

Note: The long beak is ribbed with sharp edges to grab & cut thru' slimy fish skin.

Rocky ledges along the NE coast are sites where Cormorants nest after April. 2-4 little black babies hatch in May in a bundle of twigs/sticks bound with seaweed. Regurgitated seafood from the parents is the hatchling's first food, but whole fish chunks are chomped within 7 days ——...

TIDEWATER DUCKS... PART I
BUFFLE•HEAD

• "Little wool-head" is seen off our seashores & in nearby sounds & ponds, beginning December. This stout, 14" duck is named Bufflehead for the stand-out white patch adorning its iridescent purple/green head like ear-muffs. Tho' females are duskier than the black & white men-folk, bird watchers can distinguish 'em by the smaller white cheek spot on their gray heads. Gregarious Buffleheads spirit about in flocks of 10-40, & will hurtle away on silent, blurred wings if you advance within 50 ft. Down-range, the entire bunch slides back into the brink, slicing across the ripples as smoothly as would some pontoon-plane! To avoid real danger, Buffleheads will simply dip underwater, posting one sentry up-top to quack out an "OK.!!" when the coast is clear—!

♂ ♀

• Animals & the seeds/roots of a few aquatic plants make up the Bufflehead's banquet here. Its muscular gizzard helps digest even the crunchiest of estuarine edibles, at left. As these ducks take minnows which eat the eggs of game fish, they should be considered a friend-of man, & be protected as such!

"WATER WEEDS"
SHRIMP
SNAILS
FISH

Note.. When these "bumblebee ducks" whiz by, a flurry of black & white back stripes shows on males. Watch also for fleshy-orange feet.

• Around Febuary the males here strike-up their wild mating "disco"... a macho display of colors made by stretching necks & fluffing glossy head feathers. Rival males quarrel over wives, then will migrate with mates to breed, by April. From Maine to Ontario, Buffleheads nest in hollow trees or rotted stumps near marshes/fresh water lakes. The hen broods approx. 12 creamy/buff eggs atop a grassy thatch lined with feathers & down. A month later, she'll lead hrs. old hatchlings to water, teaching 'em swimming graces & how to dabble for insects.

F. Bottontine...

TIDEWATER DUCKS... PART II
LESSER • SCAUP
♀
♂
●So many Lesser Scaup over-Winter 'round Hilton Head, they've come to be known as "troop fowl". Beds numbering 40-50 of the hardy 14" Black Heads congregate in both the open sea/sounds & fresh water lagoons. Males reveal glossy black heads, necks & breasts tinted in purple. The rufous female is easily spotted by the white band between its bill & eyes. When freezing temps. drive 'em closer to land, Scaup can turn tame, paddling within 10 ft. of your dock or deck! They may even peck up breadcrumb handouts. But during hunting season they naturally remain skittish, barnstorming off in high, erratic lines if alarmed. Listen for a throaty, "huh, huh, hah!" they utter when they fly... & look for long white wing stripes on both sexes ___..
AB...
♀
♂
●The byname Scaup translates as "broken shellfish"... & that tells all about the diet of these "Mussel Ducks". Mollusks, crustaceans & other sluggish mud-bottom creatures feed our Scaup. Hunting in flocks, the webbed wonders can deep-dive 150 feet to clam beds/mussel flats to pull up chunky chow! The addition of a web on the hind (4th) toe gives 'em the extra subsurface skill ___..
MUSSELS
SNAILS
CRABS
Note.. A prominent "nail" on the bluish bill is used to break apart shells, & tear apart water plants.
●Lesser Scaup breed far North into Canada & even Central Alaska. Roosting back from the water's edge in marshy prairies or in damp bogs, parents cushion tussocks of grass with down/feathers to cradle 8-12 pale-olive eggs. By mid-July, the fluffy brown chicks jump out of the nest to nibble widgeon grass & insect larva. 11 wks. hence, fledglings & adult Scaup'll stream South.

TIDEWATER DUCKS... PART III
RED-HEAD

● Like bouncy barometers of bleak weather, Redhead Ducks frequent Hilton Head during the really hard Winters. Throughout the big freezes of '77-'78, scads loitered our brackish feeder creeks & inland waterways, like Sprunt pond (near South Beach). But in 1979, Redheads rafted well out to Sea, & most migrants moored-in far North, from Cape Hatteras to the Chesapeake Bay. These "pochards" love to chum around with Scaup Ducks, so distinguish the males from kindred quackers by their round chestnut head, blackish breast & silver-gray backs. Dull cinammon females show a white cheek patch 'neath the bill, that fades into a "chocolate" breast. Note... the best in-flight field marks - black neck & rump highlighted against a grayish back....

● Typical of offshore ranging "Bay Ducks", Redheads dive to dine. Tho' animals are a small % of the Winter diet, it's the roots/shoots/seeds of widgeon-grass, pondweed, water lillies & rushes that really "fill the bill"! Foggy-day & nocturnal feeders, Redheads dive deep, propelled by strong webbed feet equipped with a fleshy lobe on the back toe.

AQUATIC PLANTS (SEEDS)

MOLLUSKS

LOBE

● Unique to Redheads is their April "latitudinal migration". Following the receding frost-line, successive "V" waves of ducks string due-west along the 41-44° parallels to breed. From Utah to Manitoba, 8-20 light-buff eggs are roosted in clumped reeds/cattails in deep sloughs. "Chamois" colored ducklings sip away the Summers on grasshoppers, midges & caddisflies... & the big Autumn flights East begin in October. At left, the youngsters at about 2½ weeks of age...

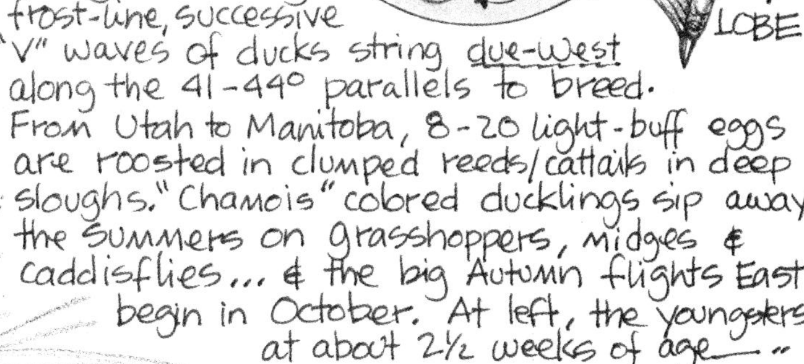

T. Ballantine...

TIDEWATER DUCKS... PART IV
RING-NECKED DUCK

● November's Duck migrations find "Blackjacks" hobnobbing S.C.'s old rice fields & flooded sloughs. At a glance, Ring Necked Ducks resemble Scaup, & often raft with 'em. But the black headed/breasted Males have black backs & a showy splash of white before the closed wings. A white eye-ring best identifies tannish females from their near-twins ... female Redheads. Up close, both sexes show a white ring on the bill. Tufting head feathers & arching swan-like, Ring-Necks are heard "booing" a hollow, hooting call as they swim. Flushed flyers wing off in 3's & 4's (not in long lines, like Scaup), & will splash down again without circling——..

Note.. Call these Ducks "Ring-Bills" for the notable white beak band. Field glasses alone will spot the Male's namesake chestnut neck ring——..

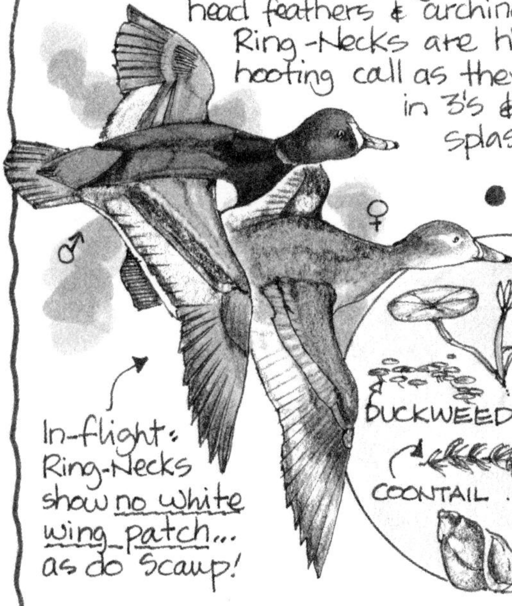

♀

♂

● Look for Ring-Necks where the lily pads & "Water weeds" grow. 'Round sunrise, Winter feeders dabble & dive for seeds (favorite fare), roots & bulbs of inshore plants. Here too they muck-up mollusks... 25% of their Menu, at left. At night/mid-day they'll paddle out to the refuge of open water——..

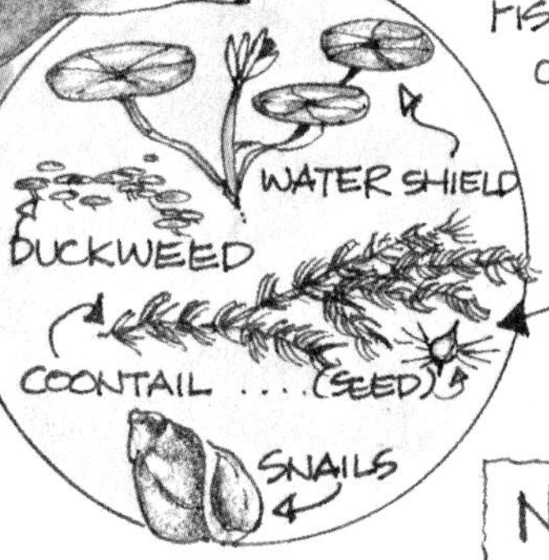

♀

♂

In-flight: Ring-Necks show no white wing patch... as do Scaup!

WATER SHIELD

DUCKWEED

COONTAIL ....(SEED)

SNAILS

NEST and EGGS

● From April on, breeding Blackjacks range from Central No. America into Saskatchewan/W. Ontario to nest on wetground amid thick Marsh grasses. Females alone roost 6-12 off-white eggs in matted masses of fine grass, moss & down. 8" beige-buff youngsters put away hordes of insect larvae &, as they grow, tadpoles, frogs & minnows. Juvenile "Ringers" attain adult plumage by their second Autumn——..

+. Ballentine

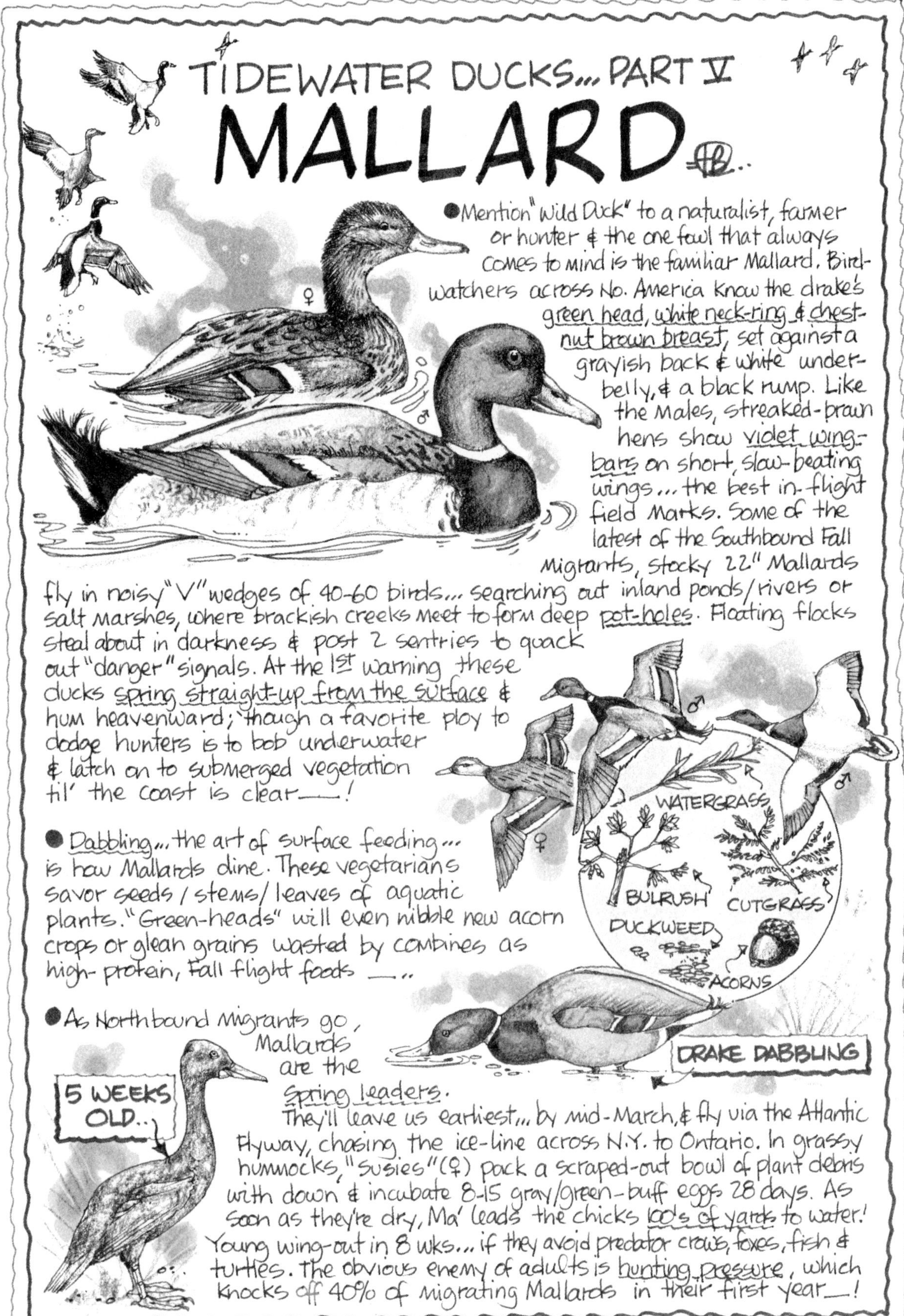
TIDEWATER DUCKS... PART V
MALLARD
●Mention "Wild Duck" to a naturalist, farmer or hunter & the one fowl that always comes to mind is the familiar Mallard. Bird-watchers across No. America know the drake's green head, white neck-ring & chestnut brown breast, set against a grayish back & white underbelly, & a black rump. Like the males, streaked-brown hens show violet wing-bars on short, slow-beating wings ... the best in-flight field marks. Some of the latest of the Southbound Fall Migrants, stocky 22" Mallards fly in noisy "V" wedges of 40-60 birds... searching out inland ponds/rivers or salt marshes, where brackish creeks meet to form deep pot-holes. Floating flocks steal about in darkness & post 2 sentries to quack out "danger" signals. At the 1st warning these ducks spring straight-up from the surface & hum heavenward; though a favorite ploy to dodge hunters is to bob underwater & latch on to submerged vegetation til' the coast is clear—!
●Dabbling... the art of surface feeding... is how Mallards dine. These vegetarians savor seeds / stems / leaves of aquatic plants. "Green-heads" will even nibble new acorn crops or glean grains wasted by combines as high-protein, Fall flight foods —..
●As Northbound Migrants go, Mallards are the Spring leaders. They'll leave us earliest... by mid-March, & fly via the Atlantic Flyway, chasing the ice-line across N.Y. to Ontario. In grassy hummocks, "Susies" (♀) pack a scraped-out bowl of plant debris with down & incubate 8-15 gray/green-buff eggs 28 days. As soon as they're dry, Ma' leads the chicks 100's of yards to water! Young wing-out in 8 wks... if they avoid predator crows, foxes, fish & turtles. The obvious enemy of adults is hunting pressure, which knocks off 40% of migrating Mallards in their first year—!
♀
♂
♂
♂
♀
WATERGRASS
BULRUSH
CUTGRASS
DUCKWEED
ACORNS
DRAKE DABBLING
5 WEEKS OLD..

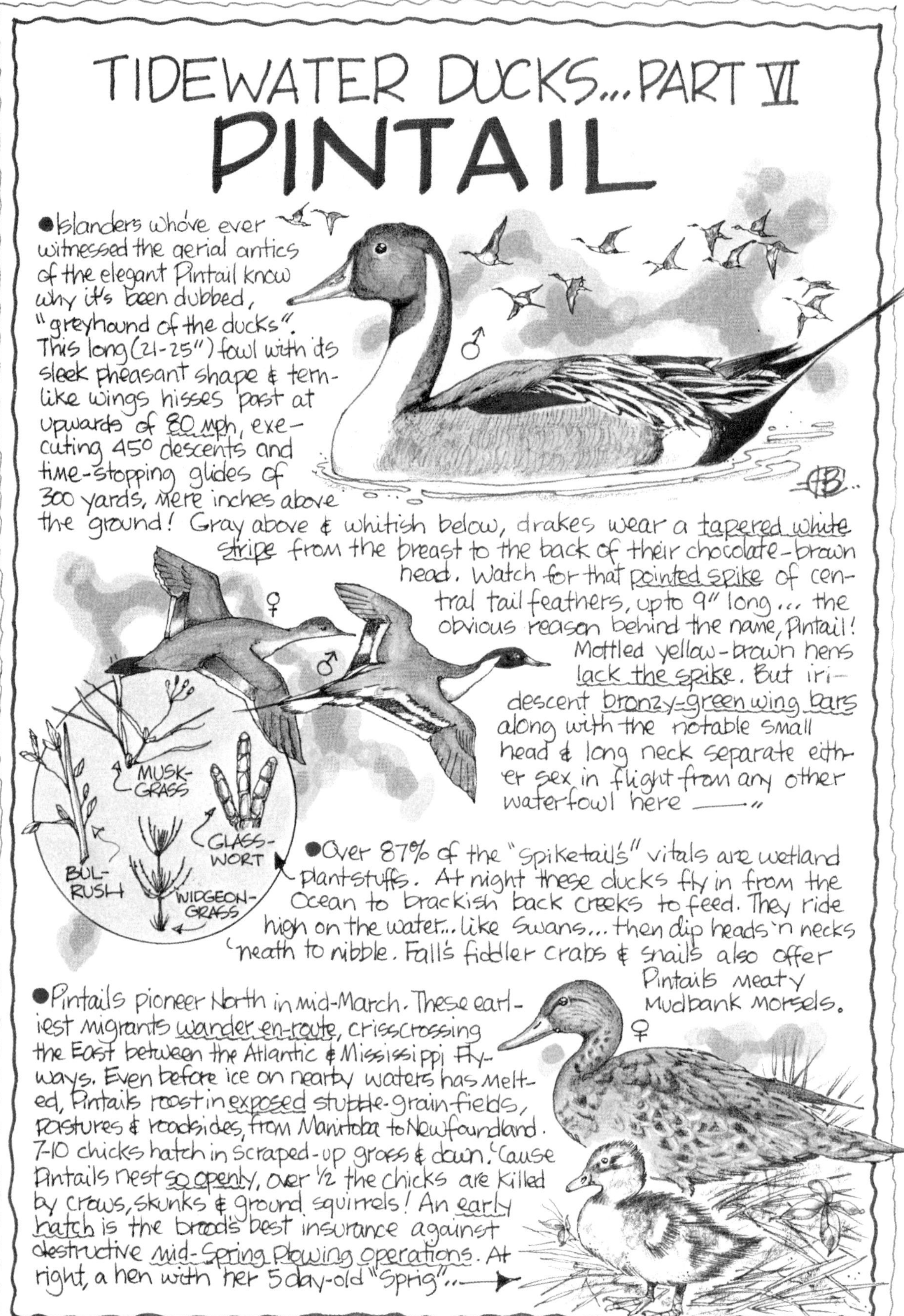
TIDEWATER DUCKS... PART VI
PINTAIL
●Islanders who've ever witnessed the aerial antics of the elegant Pintail know why it's been dubbed, "greyhound of the ducks". This long (21-25") fowl with its sleek pheasant shape & tern-like wings hisses past at upwards of 80 mph, executing 45° descents and time-stopping glides of 300 yards, mere inches above the ground! Gray above & whitish below, drakes wear a tapered white stripe from the breast to the back of their chocolate-brown head. Watch for that pointed spike of central tail feathers, up to 9" long ... the obvious reason behind the name, Pintail! Mottled yellow-brown hens lack the spike. But iridescent bronzy-green wing bars along with the notable small head & long neck separate either sex in flight from any other waterfowl here ——"
♂
♀
♂
MUSK-GRASS
GLASS-WORT
BUL-RUSH
WIDGEON-GRASS
●Over 87% of the "spiketail's" vitals are wetland plantstuffs. At night these ducks fly in from the Ocean to brackish back creeks to feed. They ride high on the water... like Swans... then dip heads 'n necks 'neath to nibble. Fall's fiddler crabs & snails also offer Pintails meaty mudbank morsels.
●Pintails pioneer North in mid-March. These earliest migrants wander en-route, crisscrossing the East between the Atlantic & Mississippi Flyways. Even before ice on nearby waters has melted, Pintails roost in exposed stubble-grain-fields, pastures & roadsides, from Manitoba to Newfoundland. 7-10 chicks hatch in scraped-up grass & down. 'Cause Pintails nest so openly, over ½ the chicks are killed by crows, skunks & ground squirrels! An early hatch is the brood's best insurance against destructive mid-Spring plowing operations. At right, a hen with her 5 day-old "Sprig"...
♀

TIDEWATER DUCKS... PART VII

BLUE-WINGED TEAL

♂ ♀

● For Nature-lovers or hunters, this bantam-weight duck makes a tiny target. A shade above 15", Blue-Winged Teal whistle by Hilton Head in Fall & Spring flocks, & are credited with speeds near 130 mph! They keep out to sea, but do migrate during day-light, when birdwatchers can spot the cobalt-blue shoulder patches, glistening in the sun like stainless steel, that give the bird its name. By March drakes in nuptial colors sport a white facial crescent on their slate-black face. Tawny-tan hens are quite streak-ed & like the brownish males show dark spott-ing on the breast. Folks 'round Calibogue Sound are familiar with this white-faced fowl, as it's enamored of the wood decoys residents love to place in local lagoons there. Bouyant on the surface, the duck bobs about with gulls & shows "mallard-green" wing bars when afloat.

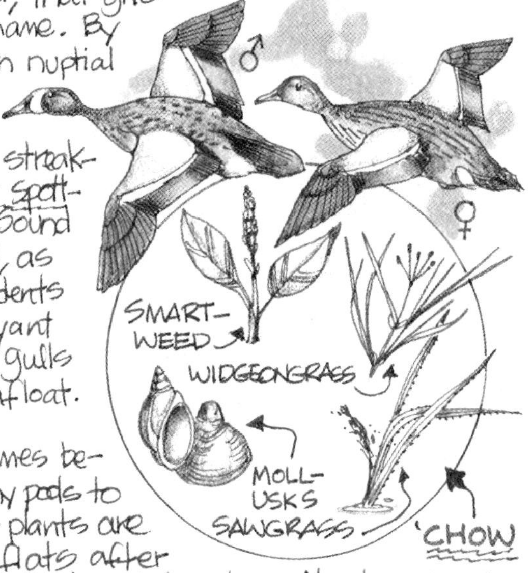

♂ ♀

SMART-WEED

WIDGEONGRASS

MOLL-USKS

SAWGRASS

'CHOW

● Blue-Wings strafe the wetlands 2 or 3 times be-fore settling in favored fresh/brackish marshy pools to dabble. Tender stems/shoots of shoalwater plants are especially savored. They'll also waddle mudflats after flood tides, pecking up stranded seeds, snails, clams & crabs.

CHICKS AT 4 WKS.

● This warm-weather waterfowl is the 1st to migrate South for the Winter & the last to head North for Summ-er breeding. From OCT. 1st on, they flee to Florida/Cuba/So. America; then thru' April they fly back to the Da-kotas/Canada. Devoted drakes guard hens roost-ing 8-12 tannish eggs in prarie-grass bowls, hood-ed with stems, feathers & down. But "summer teal" pay the price for their late-nesting (June) habit... just 35% of the chicks survive attacks by skunks, crows & Magpies hunting to feed their hungry broods!!

T. Ballantine

TIDEWATER DUCKS... PART VIII

GREEN-WINGED TEAL

● What these pigeon-size ducks lack in size, they certainly make up in speed & color. After mid November, 100's of 13-14" Green-Wing Teals veer & twist overhead in tight flocks with the same percision flight maneuvers as Sandpiper squadrons. The word teal which means, "a greenish-blue tint," describes the glossy green "speculars" (wing-bars) bordered by black, that both sexes show. Cinnamon-headed males wear a green eye-patch & sport splashes of spots on a pinkish-tan breast. Their backs & sides are gray. Mottled brown hens are identified by a darkish eye-stripe. After Winter's 1st freezes drive 'em South, 70% of the E. Coast's Green-Wings settle in S.C. Marshlands & flooded rice fields. Here they'll be seen dabbling away their days, rumps pointed heavenward; or high-stepping bank to bank, walking well away from water! In a pinch, the frightened fowl will dive underwater & scoot 20 yards to safety... like "hell diver" Grebes—!

● These shoalwater ducks are called "mud teal" for their marsh-flat eating habits. Here they gobble washed-up seeds/stems of emergent grasses & rushes... 90% of their diet. Insects & snails are also a small % of their "meals-in-the-muck"—...

● Once April breezes in, Green-Wings begin their zany courtship ritual... where the drake that spits water out of his bill farthest gets the girl! Flocks migrate via the Atlantic Flyway to Newfoundland/Labrador, or across Tenn./Ohio to No. Ontario to breed. For 3½ wks. hens roost 8-12 pale-buff eggs in secluded nursuries of woven grass/twigs/leaves, padded with down. The nests are so well camouflaged in willow clumps/bushes at the forest edge, that few humans ever happen upon a hatch. But the cover-up doesn't fool predator skunks/crows that devour ⅔ of the nestlings. No wonder mama teal skeedaddles chicks to safer sloughs within 24 hours of the hatching!

J. Bottontine...

TIDEWATER DUCKS... PART IX
BLACK DUCK

• I had to work hard to spot my 1st Black Ducks on Hilton Head. While exploring a winding Tupelo swamp flowing south from Pope Ave., I flushed a pair which bolted up 10 ft. in the air & made a beeline for some secret sapling hummock 100 yds. downstream! My next introduction was a twilight meeting with a flock of 20 circling into the December salt marsh for the evening. So, Black Ducks range Island-wide... from brackish estuaries to fresh ponds to bottomland woods... yet are so secretive that to see 'em is a naturalists reward! This 22-24" fowl really isn't black, rather it's dusky brown, resembling female Mallards. Except for the bills (see note), both sexes are look-alikes & show purplish-blue wing bars in flight. "Blacks" aloft will flash white underwings that stand-out against the chocolate body—.

• Like phantoms of the night, our "dusky ducks" flock out to open waters to feed as soon as the sun goes down. Their diet is a multiple menu of Fall's seeds, roots & shoots, and Springtime's mollusks, frogs, fish & worms. At right... the favored Island delicacies—

• Right around Heritage time, Black Ducks fly up the coast to breed, from Cape Hatteras to E. Canada. A loud, quacking game of aerial "tag" is how mates woo each other! In April 7-12 pale buff-green eggs are laid in upland, camouflaged cups hens scrape out with their feet & line with plant debris & down. Monthling chicks string after Ma' miles to sloughs & beaver ponds where they all feed & hide from predator 'coons 'til Autumn—..

TIDEWATER DUCKS,,, PART X
WOOD DUCK
The gaudiest of all No. American ducks, this swamp beauty calls our Island "home" year-round. Just to see the 20" Wood Duck drake's royal robes of bronze, green, blue & purple, bordered with splashes of black & white, once is enough Nature to make the heart skip 2 beats! Drabber gray-brown hens show a white ring & streak about the eyes. Both sexes wear a noticeable slick crest on their big heads.
♀
♂
Note.. Males molt in Autumn. They look like hens, but have more white on necks.
'Woodies' long, square tails are good fly-by field marks,,, tho' you'll have to crook to see 'em, as these ducks can whir thru' the trees, magically threading the maze of moss & limbs without dropping a feather, whistling "peeet.. peeet!" a-wing!
♂
Extra-long claws help Wood Ducks hop-scotch across floating deadwood in flooded Cypress/tupelo swamps to feed. They also dive, or tromp deep into the forest to gulp down relished acorns, 4-5 at a time! A heavy-duty gizzard will crunch up even the roughest of plant/animal foods, at left —..
ACORNS
DUCKWEED
INSECTS
These "tree ducks" nest in hollow cavities like Pileated Woodpecker borings in oak/Maple trunks, 20-40 ft. above ground. In early March, hens lay 8-14 whitish eggs in down/leaves there. In a month, day-old 'Woodies will high-dive to the duff & migrate with Ma' to protected timbered ponds. Note.. you can build a 10x10x24" nest box with roof & elliptical entry-hole. Fill with sawdust & attach to a pole or tree, 10-20 ft. up, near a pond —..

● December's chill & Ocean temps. sinking below 60° herald the arrival of migrant Scoters. The more common SC/GA. visitor is the Black Scoter, a dark-as-coal duck, face to tail (males). Thru' field glasses you'll spot its buttery yellow bulb at the bill base. These "Sea Coots" are divers... squat, tough fowl which power down flapping both legs & wings for propulsion. Reported to reach 100 ft. depths, Scoters wear stout feathers that shield their bodies against deep water pressures. Both Scoters here dive to catch protein-rich mollusks/crustaceans (inset) as well as starfish/grass/seaweed. Our estuaries offer abundant hunting grounds, so here Scoters feed... ...at night & sleep days, banded in long, bobbing black rafts visible on the horizon.

♂

MUSSELS

RAZOR CLAMS

PERIWINKLE SNAILS

BARNACLES

♂

SURF SCOTER

● Bigger (21") but just as black as its "Sea Coot" cousin, the Surf Scoter stands out for its "Skunk-head". White patches on the forehead & neck are seen with the naked eye. Binoculars bring close its harlequin bill, swashed with red at the base & yellow on the tip. Tho' they skitter along the surface, dragging their heavy bodies on a labored lift-off, Scoters are fast in flight. Jagged "V" lines led by a large drake zip along at 60 mph. Note.. the duck's odd name, Scoter is derived from the old Norse, "Skoti"... meaning, "to shoot along at great speeds"! On overcast days, these dark divers paddle closer inshore, seeking shelter from the Atlantic's angry surf. Listen for whistling wings when airborne flocks short-cut over tips of the Island. In late March both Scoters will migrate back to northern nurseries located anywhere from the Hudson/James Bay region on West into Alaska —!! JB..

RED-BREASTED MERGANSER

• A few short weeks after Thanksgiving, Red-Breasted Mergansers will migrate to our brackish sounds/back creeks. These 17" slim-shaped "Sheldrakes" (means 'Many light & dark colors') ride low in the water, dragging their tails. Most obvious is both sex's head crest... no other duck here bears such a fuzzy tuft. The male's glossy blackish-green head stands out strikingly against its white neck, robin-red speckled breast, & black & white back feathers. Ashy brown hens show chestnut heads. Watch these noiseless navigators fly by in straight lines, skimming near wave tops with their streamlined bodies! A good flight field mark: the drake's white wing patches.

♀

♂

Note: These Mergansers raise & dip their crests while swimming.

♂

• Red-Breasts are named "serrator" in latin. The title denotes the long, cylindrical bill with saw teeth. Diving sheldrakes lay into schools of small fish (minnows, sunfish) & crustaceans (see inset, right), mouthing squirming prey with their jagged beaks. The ducks submerge for nearly a minute & may teamwork to herd quarry into dead-end shoals!

FISH

CRABS

SHRIMP

• Spring's warmth sends Red-Breasts flapping to Maine/E. Canadian nurseries. By July hens hatch 6-12 olive-buff eggs in leaf/moss/down nests, near pond water. Here "saw bill" ducklings can swim away from predator ravens 'til flight feathers form in August ___ ..

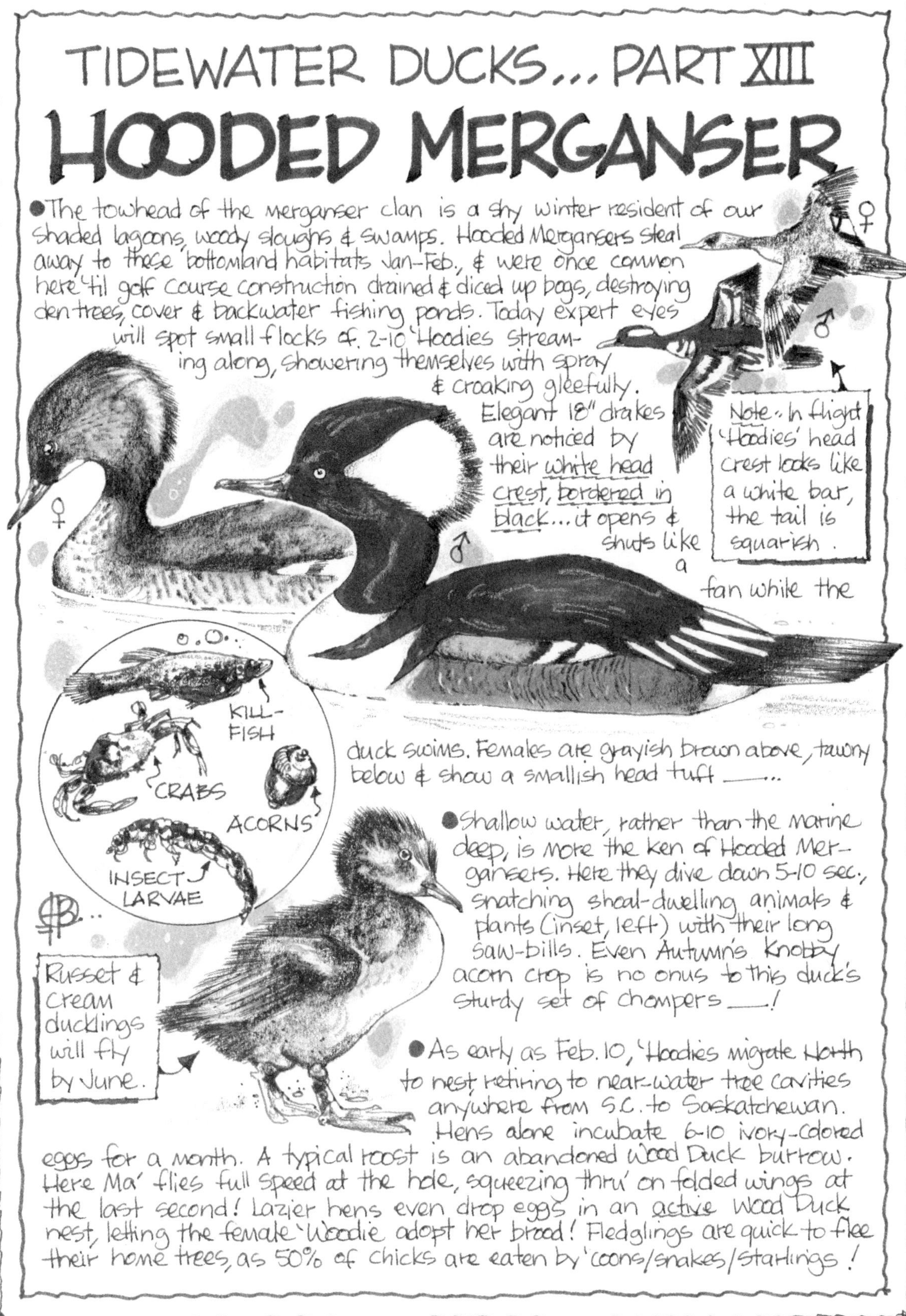
TIDEWATER DUCKS... PART XIII
HOODED MERGANSER
●The towhead of the merganser clan is a shy winter resident of our shaded lagoons, woody sloughs & swamps. Hooded Mergansers steal away to these bottomland habitats Jan-Feb., & were once common here 'til golf course construction drained & diced up bogs, destroying den trees, cover & backwater fishing ponds. Today expert eyes will spot small flocks of 2-10 'Hoodies streaming along, showering themselves with spray & croaking gleefully. Elegant 18" drakes are noticed by their white head crest, bordered in black... it opens & shuts like a fan while the duck swims. Females are grayish brown above, tawny below & show a smallish head tuft ___..
♀
♂
Note: In flight 'Hoodies' head crest looks like a white bar, the tail is squarish.
♀
♂
KILL-FISH
CRABS
ACORNS
INSECT LARVAE
●Shallow water, rather than the marine deep, is more the ken of Hooded Mergansers. Here they dive down 5-10 sec., snatching shoal-dwelling animals & plants (inset, left) with their long saw-bills. Even Autumn's knobby acorn crop is no onus to this duck's sturdy set of chompers ___!
Russet & cream ducklings will fly by June.
●As early as Feb. 10, 'Hoodies migrate North to nest, retiring to near-water tree cavities anywhere from S.C. to Saskatchewan. Hens alone incubate 6-10 ivory-colored eggs for a month. A typical roost is an abandoned Wood Duck burrow. Here Ma' flies full speed at the hole, squeezing thru' on folded wings at the last second! Lazier hens even drop eggs in an active Wood Duck nest, letting the female 'Woodie adopt her brood! Fledglings are quick to flee their home trees, as 50% of chicks are eaten by 'coons/snakes/starlings!

Wading Birds... Part I

GREAT BLUE HERON

• **Our largest heron** haunts the lagoons, sloughs & salt creeks of the islands. "Great Blue" stands 4 ft. tall on dry ground. Its namesake plummage is unmistakable. Above, it is slate-blue; below, black & white with brown/white streakings. Long black plumes crest the white head. The dusty gray neck is dashed with rusty black & white marks. Its big, long beak is cadmium yellow.

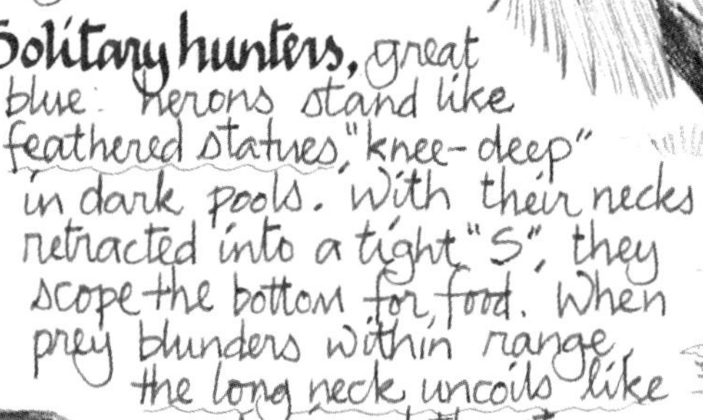

• **Solitary hunters,** great blue herons stand like feathered statues, "knee-deep" in dark pools. With their necks retracted into a tight "S", they scope the bottom for food. When prey blunders within range the long neck uncoils like a spring, & the strong beak spears a morsel in a micro-second. "Blue Cranes" are also seen stalking prey in still waters, step by step placing long toes, quietly 'neath the surface without exciting a ripple. Here they hunt fish, crabs, frogs, insects (inset, left), snakes & even baby 'gators 'til well after sundown. Small mammals are commonly caught in fields & grasslands nearby.

• **Social only during breeding season,** great blues nest in swamp-side rookeries, where nests are clustered near dozens of like roosts used by kindred wading birds. 3-6 greenish-blue eggs are laid in April-May, in large platforms of twigs, leaves, grass, Spanish moss... all cemented with guano. Brown, crestless young are fed a fishy gruel regurgitated by parents. By mid-summer, they'll wing away from the nest.

Wading Birds... Part II

GREAT EGRET

- **"Long white"** is the South's most famous wader. Prized for its 50 dainty plumes ("aigrettes") which trail straight down, shoulders to tail, the bird was hunted to near extinction before 1900. These plumes brought $10-a-bunch on the millinery market! Because the Audubon Society saved the great egret, today islanders commonly observe the 35-42", dazzling white bird with black legs & feet, & a long yellow bill here. Those beautiful plumes flare out as a mating display & are seen only between April-June.

Plumes

- **With quiet alabaster poise** the great egret wades shoalwaters of marsh creeks, ponds, sloughs & lagoons. They'll extend the lengthy crooked neck out near the surface, then spear crabs, snails, small fish or frogs. Grassy edges nearby yield mice, moles, lizards, young snakes (even cottonmouths!) & insects to the "long white's" diet.

- **A slip-shod platform** of sticks is nest enough for great egrets, which "rook" or nest colonially with anhingas & other waders in blackwater swamps. 2-5 mop-topped young hatch by June. They noisly croak, "me first!" to harried parents returning with a meal. Food is disgorged into babes' beaks, then off parents flap for another dozens-a-day food-finding sortie. Young gain flight feathers by midsummer.

Wading Birds... Part III

SNOWY EGRET

• **The little white egret with the golden slippers** is a one-liner description of the snowy egret that all birdlovers can remember. 24" long, this heron is noticeably shorter than its lanky cousin, the great egret. A snowy's plummage is also ivory-white... but far softer & fluffier looking. Note the bill is black, as are the legs. In flight the snowy's yellow feet are obvious.

• **50 long plume feathers** adorn the lower back between the wings during nesting season (March-June). Mates proudly fan-out these silken feathers in the roost as (1) a claim to territory; (2) a nuptial display. At the turn of the 20th Century, many U.S. women demanded these "cross aigrettes" for bonnets or hair ornaments (the market price was $32/ounce!). Hunters martyred tens of thousands of breeder adults for their fluff, leaving their helpless young to starve to death. Now protected by S.C./Federal laws, snowy's thrive in our sloughs, marshes & mudflats. They hunt fiddler crabs, shrimp, snails, fry fish, frogs, reptiles & insects in shallow water (their legs are the shorter of our 2 egrets), & pluck grasshoppers from banks closeby.

In full display: Feathers fluff up from the head, breast & shoulders.

• **Several snowy families** nest in a shared cypress, tupelo or shrub in the Spring. 2-5 pale blue-green eggs are laid upon haphazard tree-beds of swamp sticks & twigs. Pure white young are fed regurgitated prey from parents' bills. The namesake aigrettes grow in the plummage a full year following the hatch.

Wading Birds... Part IV

CATTLE EGRET

• **A wader of pastures, highway shoulders & marsh banks,** the cattle egret occupies a feeding niche all its own. The stocky, white 17-20" bird with the short yellow bill & pink legs is most often seen strutting summers' grasslands in the company of cattle & horses. Here it gleans flies, crickets & grasshoppers stirred up by stomping livestock, or ticks pecked directly from the animals' backs. This pest-preening service must be welcome relief to creatures of the field, for they are typically seen grazing oblivious to 1 or more "cowbirds" perched securely on their heads & haunches.

Note: Spring breeding plummage reveals an orange wash on the crown, back & breast...

• **World travelling cattle egrets** made ornithological history when they migrated 3,000 miles across the Atlantic from Africa to British Guiana, in 1937. It is a mystery why the birds left their So. European & African homeland... perhaps for lack of sufficient insect foods in a drought. They winged to Hilton Head in 1953. Now the cattle egret ranges north to Massachusetts, South thru' Florida & the gulf states, & even thrives as far West as Hawaii!

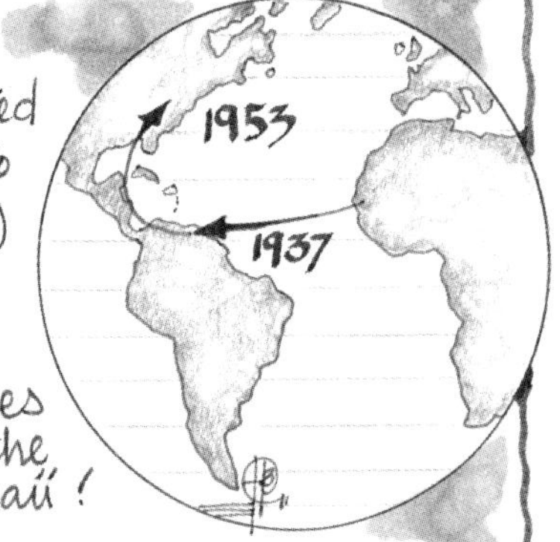

1953

1937

• **Migrant cattle egrets** nest in April here. 3-4 hatchlings are raised in swampland rookeries. By June the whole family takes to the pastures. Abandoned nests are adopted by breeding white ibis..

Wading Birds... Part V

NIGHT HERONS

• **Black Crowned Night Herons** are 26" chunky-gray, short-necked waders always identified by their black cap & shoulders. The bill is black, the shortish legs yellow to pink. To spot this heron in sunshine is a birdwatcher's surprise. By day it is most inactive & roosts perched on over-water limbs. But the last liquidamber rays find black-crowns silhouetted against the twilight sky, 100 feet up, winging off to savored swampland hunting holes. Listen for their loud, "quawk!" call, yelled in flight. Feeding black-crowns <u>wander-wade</u>... pacing the shoals with heads held by the surface. Frogs, fish or snakes are easy targets for the quick-stabbing bill guided by the big red eyes with refined night vision.

white

gray

• **Yellow-Crowned Night Herons** (24") look like black crowns only at a distance. These herons wear a cream-white patch on the crown (tinted with a faint yellow by the bill) & white on the cheeks. The bill is black. Their long yellow legs trail out behind the tail in flight. Yellow-crowns are known to feed in fresh/salt water marshes, sloughs or swamps, by both night & day. Favored prey: mussels, crayfish & small crabs. Like their black-capped kin above, they fetch food using strong eyesight & split-second beak thrusts. But their longer legs will carry them into deeper waters.

Note: Both night herons nest colonially in swamp forests. 3-6 blue-green eggs are laid in May, in loose masses of twigs, leaves & spanish moss.

Wading Birds... Part VI

LOUISIANA·HERON

● **Lady of the waters,** as Audubon lyrically labeled it, the graceful Louisiana heron is a common, permanent resident to these barrier isles. This 26" wader is tri-colored. Purplish-blue on the neck & back contrasts the obvious white underparts. Dusky chestnut aigrettes plume out from the back to the tail. The head & neck may show shorter plumes—.

● **No Louisiana local,** this heron ranges the E. Coast from the Chesapeake Bay to Texas. On Hilton Head, the bird feeds in streams/sloughs/marshy meadows & along the borders of swamps/ponds. Here it wades on long strides with its slender, slate neck craned out far over the water. The sharp, black bill swiftly strikes: ① killifish, ② worms, ③ frogs & tadpoles, ④ snails, ⑤ insects & ⑥ lizards (inset, left). Note ... the Louisiana heron is tamer in disposition than most other waders; so birdwatchers may approach them more closely in their hunting habitats—.

● **Bushy islands** or gum/willow swamps are the Louisiana herons' favorite nesting nooks. In close commune with egrets, other herons, ibis & anhingas, mates raise 2-5 young in a fragile platform of twigs, 2-20 ft. above the black waters. Russet hues wash the head/neck/wings of the young, which clamber about the jungle-gym of nursery limbs using bills & feet. Once old enough to fend for themselves, immature Louisianas abandon the rookery & feed away the Summer in our fertile wetlands—»

Wading Birds... Part VII

LITTLE BLUE HERON

● **The slate-blue heron with the purplish red head & neck** is commonly viewed in the company of great blue herons & egrets. "Little blues" are permanent residents in coastal S.C. They inhabit grassy ponds, slough creeks & river flats (especially the Savannah R.). Here they stalk on measured strides, hunting small fish, crabs, frogs & water insects. Mature birds (24" tall) are easily recognized in a feathered crowd by their dark-all-over plumage and bluish bills & feet.

● **Young adults resemble snowy egrets** in early Spring. Feathering may appear pure white, but at closer inspection, it shows hints of blue molting. Note, too, the bill is bluish & the legs are light green, compared to the Snowy's black bill, black legs & "golden slippers". It has been observed that little blues do rear their young while still arrayed in that youthful white flue. May-June, 2-4 bluish eggs are nested in trees or bushes, in bottomland swamps. Once downy young fledge flight feathers, they wing far northward from the parents' range. 'Old timers' frequent local hunting sites & will be seen flying to favorite swampy, rookery roosts in the early evening duskglow of Summer.

Above, the mature adult. Right, the little blue in juvenile white.

Wading Birds... Part VIII

GREEN HERON

• **Our smallest heron,** the green heron is 16-22" with a wing-span of about 2 ft. This crow-sized wader is a common, permanent resident here, but is inconspicuous due to natural camouflage. The neck is deep chestnut (streaked on immature birds). Back & wings are bluish-green, the underbelly whitish. Legs are short, but the greenish-yellow-to-orange hue is a familiar in-flight fieldmark—.

• **With true heron stealth,** the 'green' silently stalks thru' the reeds & grasses along pond/lagoon waters' edges, keeping its head pinched down upon its shoulders. A lightning-quick thrust of the 2" beak, spikes fish, frogs, salamanders, crabs & insects. One naturalist even observed the bird swiping prey out of the shoals with its feet & then stabbing the landlocked quarry! When startled, a green heron stretches its neck, pumps up its bushy crest & jerks its tail. Eventually it will flap off to a nearby perch where it "freezes" into motionless merging with the greenery—.

• **March to June** is the green herons' nesting cycle. They'll roost off by themselves in low willow/tupelo branches over or near water. 3-6 pale green eggs are laid in a frail interlace of loose sticks. Hatchlings (left) are covered with a fine streaked down which is brownish-gray in color—

Wading Birds... Part IX

AMERICAN BITTERN

• **The genius of the bog** was Thoreau's characterization of the ooze & reed loving American Bittern. Chunky for a heron, the 24" Bittern is brownish above; dark streaks freckle its tawny underparts. A brown "mustache" on the side of the throat is obvious, if one is fortunate enough to capture a close-range view. For the furtive, earth-toned Bittern is a master at camouflaging itself amongst high grasses, rushes & cattails. By cocking-up its bill, it matches the pitch & bend of cover plants. When flushed, the airborne bird reveals blackish outer wings.

To discover this Bittern, a bird-watcher must traipse the soft mire in our freshwater marshes, sloughs or ponds. Here the "bog bull" picks off snails, small fish & insects at water's edge while rarely exposing itself. Its 4 long toes lend traction & support in the muck.

Outer wings blackish in flight.

• **A hiccough more than a song,** the Bittern's courting call is a repeated "plunk-a-lunk." The percussive, thunderpump, nuptial noise is sounded during Spring's dawn & dusk interludes. The birds nest in the protection of dense aquatic vegetation... laying 3-5 mottled brown eggs in piles of dead plants. Born at pondside, helpless young are preyed upon by 'gators, snakes, coons, hawks & owls. Parents defend young by feathering out to twice-size & stabbing enemies with their dagger-like beaks.

Wading Birds...Part X

WOOD IBIS

• **Stork of the South,** the Wood Ibis is the only member of its family inhabiting North America. All storks (Ciconiidae) are characterized by a bill very thick at the base & slightly curved at the blunt tip. The Wood Ibis is a 4 ft. snow white giant with a buzzard-like, featherless black head & neck. Graceful aloft, its long neck & "ironhead" stretch straight ahead. Black-rimmed wings span 5½ ft. as it loops high on Summer's thermals.

• **Shallow potholes & sloughs** attract hungry "Wood Stork" congregations which stir the silt with their big feet. When fish, crayfish & snakes surface for oxygen, the waiting Woodies snap them up in 1/40 sec. (less time than the blink of an eye!) with the submerged 9½ inch beak. Gorged to the hilt, the birds retire bankside to digest dinner, resting their bills so low on their breasts that they appear to be praying!

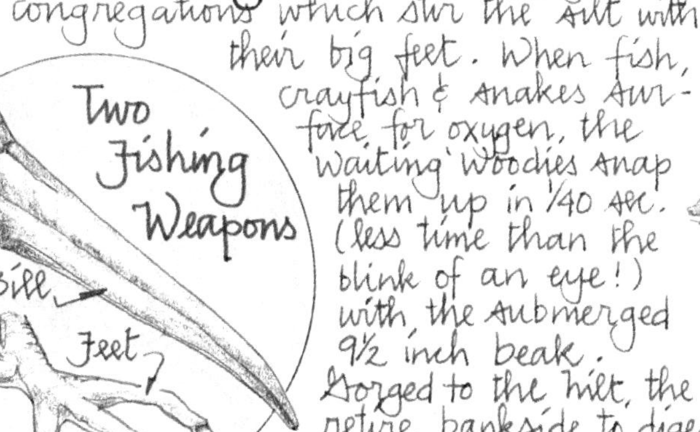

• **Wood Ibis hordes** colonize cypress tree tops, building spindly homes of live willow sprigs cemented with Spanish moss & guano. Spring's 3-4 nestlings, woolly head to knee, bellow out hunger pangs. Parents respond, flying 40 miles a day to feed their habit. By Autumn, the fledgling clan will have consumed over 400 pounds of fish!

Wading Birds... Part XI

WHITE IBIS

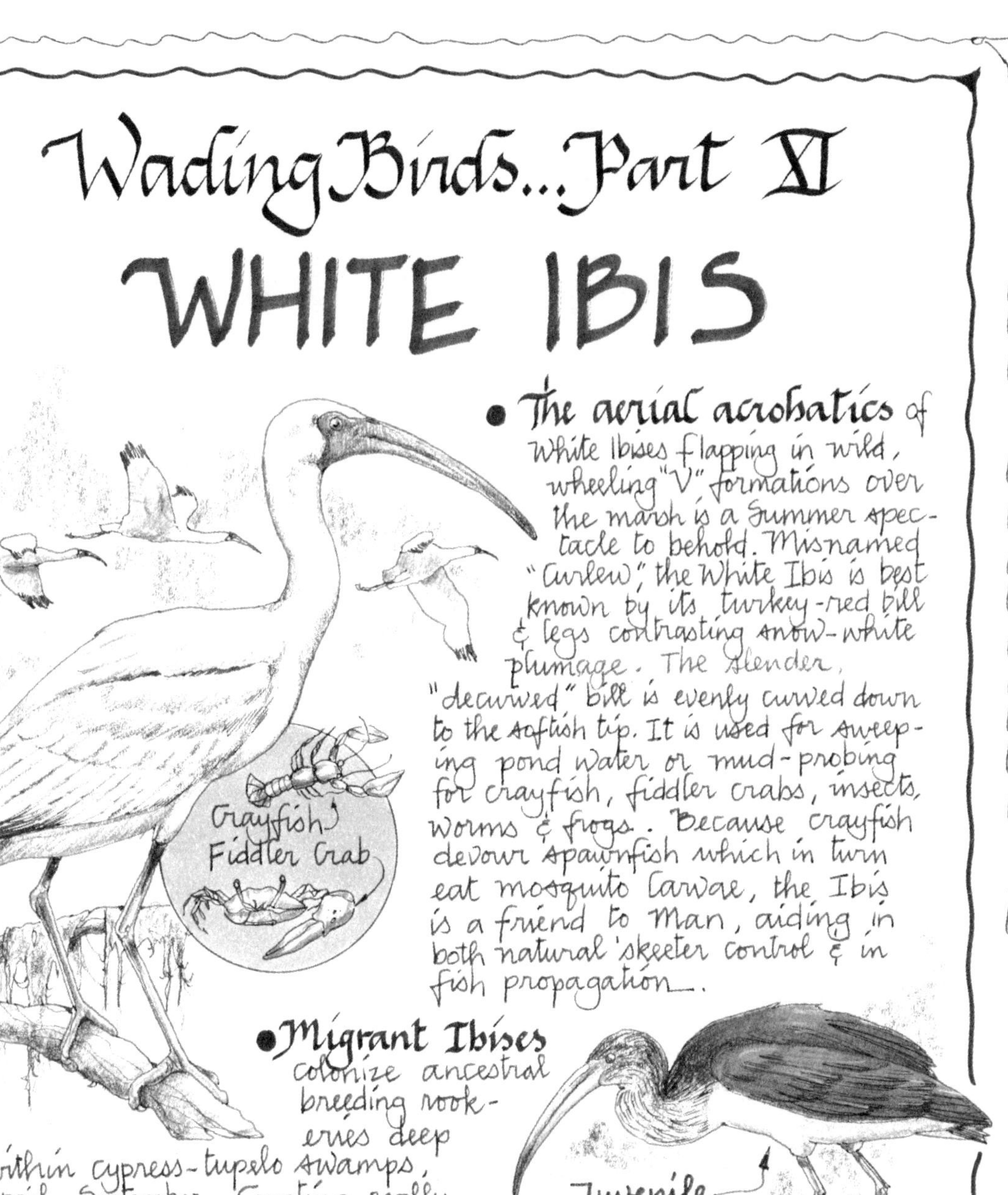

• **The aerial acrobatics** of White Ibises flapping in wild, wheeling "V" formations over the marsh is a Summer spectacle to behold. Misnamed "Curlew," the White Ibis is best known by its turkey-red bill & legs contrasting snow-white plumage. The slender, "decurved" bill is evenly curved down to the softish tip. It is used for sweeping pond water or mud-probing for crayfish, fiddler crabs, insects, worms & frogs. Because crayfish devour spawnfish which in turn eat mosquito larvae, the Ibis is a friend to Man, aiding in both natural 'skeeter control & in fish propagation.

• **Migrant Ibises** colonize ancestral breeding rookeries deep within cypress-tupelo swamps, April-September. Courting really swings when show-off males barnstorm the boughs, showering twigs with flailing wings. Somehow, their flimsy stick nests, often jammed 30 per tree, hold 4 bluish-speckled eggs (right). Fattened & energized by regurgitated fish parents ram down their gullets, fledglings oftimes topple from the roost & must bill & claw their way back home. Note juveniles show a mottled head, an olive-brown back & white underparts.

Juvenile

CLAPPER RAIL
"OUR SALT MARSH HEN"
•All talk & no show… such is the secretive style of Clapper Rails. Anyone who listens to the salt marsh knows the bird's monotone "tick, ticks" (4/sec.), or those wild cackling calls… but to see 'em is another story! Pure patience & luck reveals a "compressed" 14 in bird colored olive-gray above, with a pale cinammon breast & a whitish abdomen patterned by dull gray stripes. Rather than flying, Clappers run on long legs amid the shady coverts of marsh greenery, easily slipping their slender bodies between the blades. The hours between sundown & dawn are times this Rail ventures forth to hunt in mud banks & brackish tidal creeks___.
Note: Only as a last resort will Clappers fly when flushed. Flapping short wings & dangling long legs behind, the birds skim the grass tops & then plop down suddenly in reeds a few ft. away!
SHRIMP
SNAILS
FIDDLER CRABS
CLAM WORMS
Note: Strutting & bobbing like hens, Clappers ably tread the wet sod on wide-spreading toes. Their long, barely curved bills are used to probe the soft mud at low tide for burrowing animals (to the left..). Seeds of spartina grass & needle rush are savored cereals in the diet.
NEST & EGGS
•Mating April–June, Clapper Rails roost in loose colonies. Dead stalks are piled into an exposed platform nest. Propped on rushes 8" above the mud, the home is anchored to sturdy stems as protection against wash-away (Rails' worst enemy). 6–10 glossy black chicks hatch from grayish spotty eggs by July. The footloose brood will learn to run along reedy runways around the nest mere minutes after birth___!
J. Ballantine

AMERICAN
OYSTERCATCHER
• Cragged oyster rakes, tideflats & ebb-water beaches are S.C. habitats the American Oystercatcher trods year-round. Recognize this large (17-21") wader by its elegant colors... a black head, brown back, snow white underparts & a bright red, straight bill. Swift, short flights display a white rump & wing stripes. If you are close enough to behold the beak's striking vermillion, you should hear the Oystercatcher call... a noisy, shrill, "Kleep!"____.
• A bird that brings its own oyster knife to feast, the Oystercatcher is named for its big, wedge-shaped bill. Upon locating oysters, mussels & clams by striding shell colonies or probing nose-deep in mudflats, it thrusts the beak in the narrow gap bivalves display when tides run. Here it deftly snips the adductor muscle fastening the 2 shells together & devours the helpless creature inside! Oystercatchers also wade to the breast to capture shrimp, small crabs &
Note probe holes
marine worms. Stomping stout feet is their way to scare up a Summer's meal of swarming insects!
• S.C. breeders, Oystercatchers nest on high, dry bars/beaches. In May, 2-3 speckled, creamy eggs are laid in a slight, sandy depression. Females seldom roost, rather, they cover the clutch at night/on cloudy days, & during fair weather expose it to the gentle Spring sun, achieving passive solar incubation! In 3 wks., precocial buffy chicks spirit the shoals....
Note: The 5" bill is flattened at the tip, like a blade, to force apart bivalve shells!

PLOVERS...PART I
KILLDEER

• Noisemaker of the plovers, the Killdeer is named for its shrill "Kill-dee! Kill-dee!" cry broadcast in flight when alarmed. Outdoor folk commonly see these 9-11" birds with 2 black bands on their white breast scampering around Autumn's grassy lagoon/creek/lake banks, fields & yards. Tho' classified as wading birds, plovers with their plump body, short neck & dove-like bill are best suited to high ground feeding rather than wet mud/sand probing... as are sandpipers.

WATCH FOR THE RED RUMP AND LONG TAIL

• Stalking exterminators, Killdeer hunt grass-scapes & plowed earth, gorging on insects & invertebrates. Many of their prey are pests to man... grasshoppers & crickets (eat foliage), wireworms (eat roots, seeds), billbugs, weevils & curculio beetles (damage fruit), ticks, horseflies & marsh mosquitoes (may harbor diseases), & marine worms (attack oysters).

• A simple scrape in the dirt concealed by grassy stalks is nest enough for a Killdeer female. Here she incubates 4 black-spotted, buffy white eggs, April-June. If predators or birdwatchers should approach, she'll feign injury... gasping, limping, fluttering, dragging one wing behind her as if it were broken... to decoy danger from the clutch. Well-camouflaged chicks actively devour bugs soon after hatching. Note nesting range: Central Florida to New Brunswick.

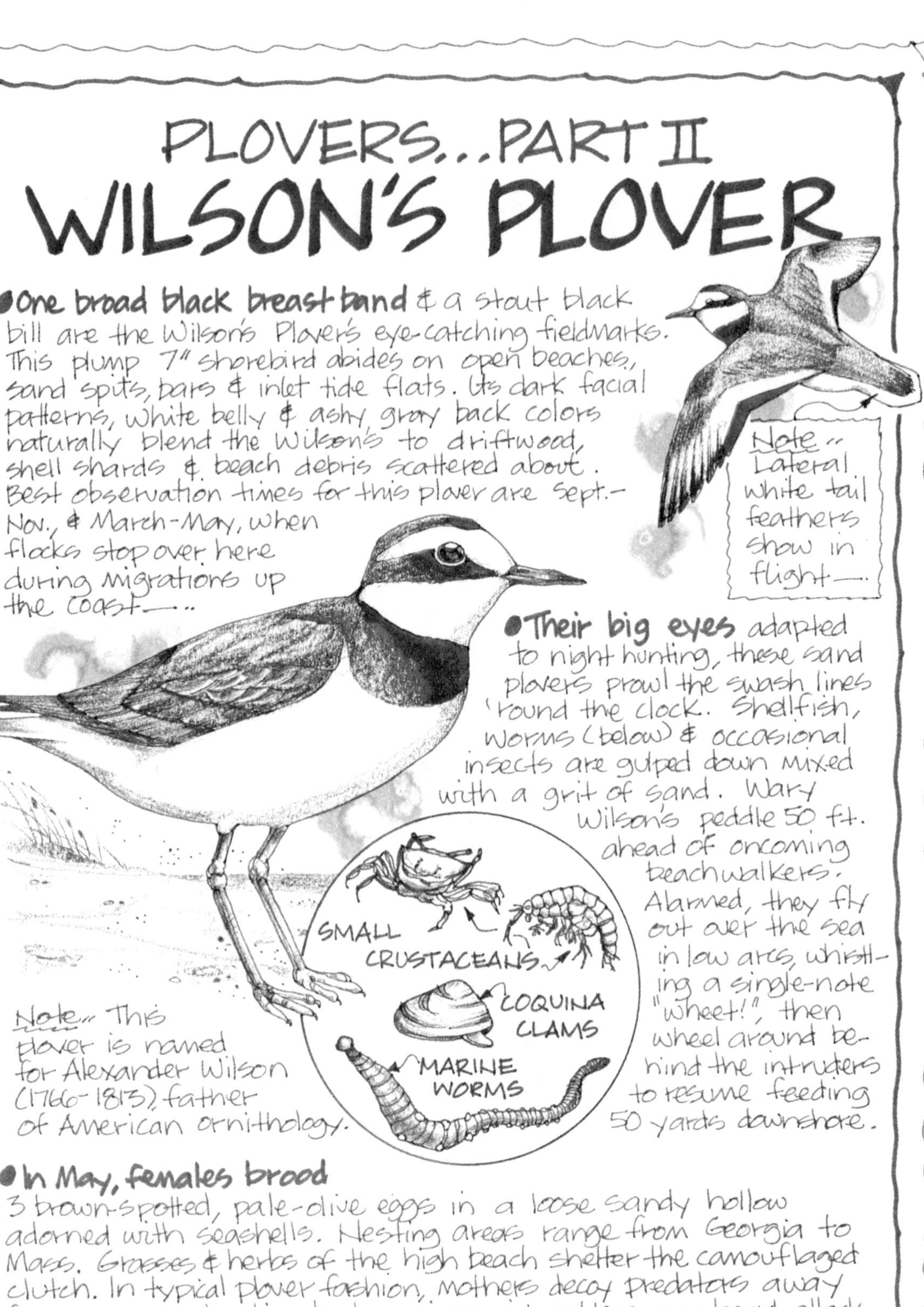
PLOVERS...PART II
WILSON'S PLOVER
One broad black breast band & a stout black bill are the Wilson's Plover's eye-catching fieldmarks. This plump 7" shorebird abides on open beaches, sand spits, bars & inlet tide flats. Its dark facial patterns, white belly & ashy gray back colors naturally blend the Wilson's to driftwood, shell shards & beach debris scattered about. Best observation times for this plover are Sept.-Nov., & March-May, when flocks stop over here during migrations up the coast....
Note... Lateral white tail feathers show in flight—
Their big eyes adapted to night hunting, these sand plovers prowl the swash lines 'round the clock. Shellfish, worms (below) & occasional insects are gulped down mixed with a grit of sand. Wary Wilson's peddle 50 ft. ahead of oncoming beachwalkers. Alarmed, they fly out over the sea in low arcs, whistling a single-note "wheet!", then wheel around behind the intruders to resume feeding 50 yards downshore.
SMALL CRUSTACEANS
COQUINA CLAMS
MARINE WORMS
Note... This plover is named for Alexander Wilson (1766-1813), father of American ornithology.
In May, females brood 3 brown-spotted, pale-olive eggs in a loose sandy hollow adorned with seashells. Nesting areas range from Georgia to Mass. Grasses & herbs of the high beach shelter the camouflaged clutch. In typical plover fashion, mothers decoy predators away from eggs, pretending broken wings, injured legs or a heart attack, but springing aloft with a cheery peep when her audience is suckered out of range! Mottled chicks hatch within 25 days & soon skitter among Summer's dense dune overgrowth....

PLOVERS...PART III
SEMIPALMATED PLOVER

● **"Ringnecks"** are the most common beach plovers seen here during transcoastal migrations, Oct.-May. Squat 7" Semipalmated Plovers huddle in flocks with sandpipers, hunting ebb tide sands, mudflats & salt marsh creeks. Their brownish-gray back matches the dun of wet sand, so identify the single dark neck ring, short dark bill (in winter) & yellowish-orange legs. Call: a plaintive, "chee-wee", whistled in twisting flight.

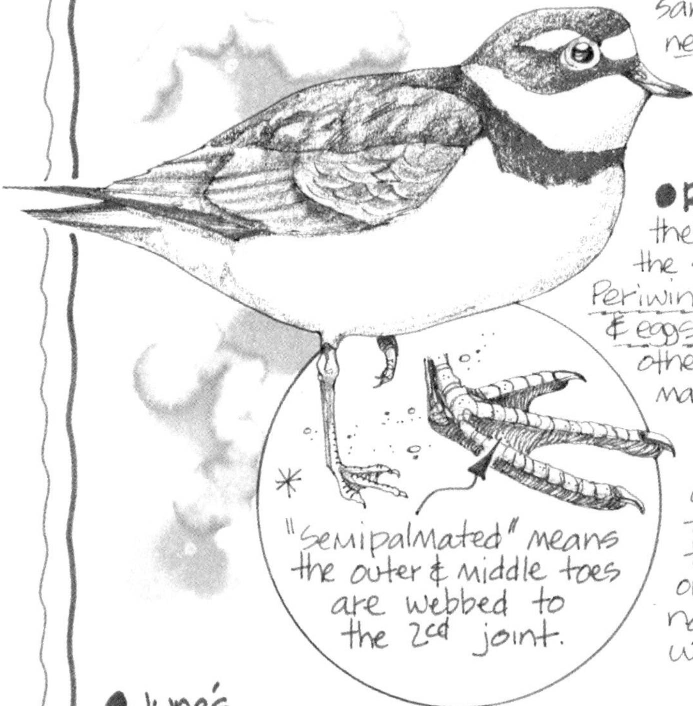

● **Running erectly,** then dabbing the flats from time to time is the semipalm's feeding personality. Periwinkle snails, gribbles, beach fleas & eggs of saltmarsh mosquitos & other marine animals comprise its maritime menu. Partially webbed feet* give stability to traverse slimy mud zones without slipping. When high tides blanket feeding grounds, this plover sleeps, resting on one foot with its head nodding down into its plump white breast —.

* "Semipalmated" means the outer & middle toes are webbed to the 2cd joint.

● June's **breeding semipalms** migrate as far north as the Yukon Territory/Beaufort Sea area to nest... a 2,640 mi. round-trip from Hilton Head! 3-4 blotched, olive-buff eggs are roosted in a 1" cavity lined with leaves, grass, seaweed & moss, nearshore. In 23 days ground-colored hatchlings hop out of the nest on their "knees". Parents act in tandem to lead away trespassing predators. While one skulks off feigning mortal injury, its mate leads the chicks out the "back door" to the shelter of seaside vegetation!

CHICK

PLOVERS... PART IV
PIPING PLOVER

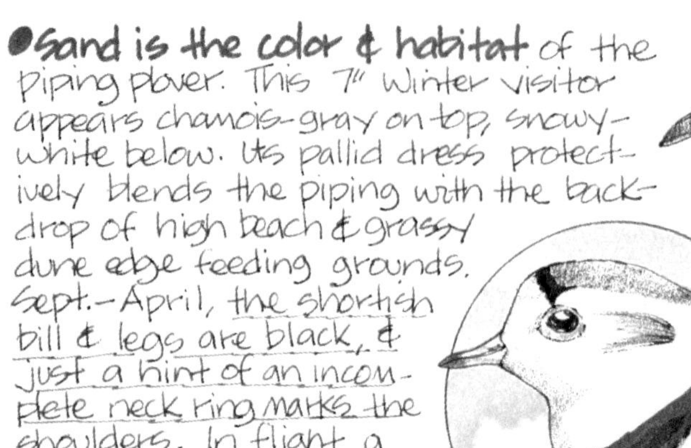

● **Sand is the color & habitat** of the piping plover. This 7" winter visitor appears chamois-gray on top, snowy-white below. Its pallid dress protectively blends the piping with the backdrop of high beach & grassy dune edge feeding grounds. Sept.–April, the shortish bill & legs are black, & just a hint of an incomplete neck ring marks the shoulders. In flight a noticeable white rump patch is seen —.

SUMMER PLUMAGE

WINTER COLORS

● **Run & pause, run & pause...** so goes the pipings nervous beachcombing for burrowed prey. These plovers feed individually, first staring at the sand with head ajar, then stabbing at the slightest wiggle from mollusks, crustaceans, maggots or marine worms (which are slurped down whole!). Awaiting receding tides, pipings tend to bob back & forth... a curious plover resting behaviour —.

Note: With no 4th toe for balance, pipings must feed in harder, dry sand.

● **By May,** pipings in their nuptial colors migrate to Chesapeake Bay–Newfoundland breeding zones. 4 finely specked, clay-colored eggs are laid in sand hollows lined with pebbles, shells & driftwood crumbs. Day-old youngsters, camouflaged to the stones & grains of their shoreside home, scamper strongly about & will even swim away from danger when predators like crows approach!

SWIMMING CHICK

PLOVERS...PART V

BLACK-BELLIED PLOVER

● **Few shorebirds compare colors** with the regally dressed Black-Bellied Plover. Its rich sable throat, cheeks & breast contrast vividly against the white forehead, nape, sides & underbelly. Black & white speckling on the back completes the Summer "nuptial" plummage which may be seen here worn by non-breeding adults that do not migrate North. Overwintering Black-Bellies turn whitish flecked with dark brown above. 12" long, this is our largest local plover. Call: a wailful, whistled, "whee-u-ree".

● **Wary Black-Bellies** tread far out on sand-bars, mudflats & to tide pools to feed. Heads held high, they patter along the waterline, stopping at intervals to strike prey... (A) Crabs, (B) Marine worms, (C) beach fleas, (D) Mollusks, (E) salt marsh Mosquitos. Frequently these plovers flop right into the tidewater to bathe, splashing cool brine over themselves with wild, fluttery wings!

Note: In-flight winter-color field marks (above)... White rump & black wing pits (axillars).

● **Massed flocks** migrate (commonly with Ruddy Turnstones) to the Arctic Circle to breed, in May. Nest-builder females scoop out a 6" wide hollow & cushion it with moss & grass. Their mottled back & the 4 heavily spotted eggs blend perfectly with the ambient close-cropped tundra. If this protective coloration isn't defense enough against predator gulls & jaegars, parent plovers will boldly divebomb & head-peck aggressors away from the clutch! Pale-bellied young splotched with yellow, black & white hatch in 23 days. Fledglings fly South up to 2 months (September) after adults (July)—..

AB..

RUDDY TURNSTONE

• **Adorned in its harlequin hues,** the Ruddy Turnstone is our most colorful shorebird, & hence the easiest to identify. 9" Spring Males display chestnut back feathers, & black bands streak their white underparts from face to breast. The short legs are red, the stout bill is black. By Autumn, the "ruddy" chestnut will fade to mottled gray & the black neck markings will break into patches. Beaches, sand-flats & muddy inlets are hunting haunts Turnstones prefer when they migrate thru' Hilton Head. Note.. in flight, Ruddys show a short tail, long wings & a white rump patch on their calico backs. Call... a line of slurred, "kek-kek-kek" whistles—..

Above.. The male in Winter dress. Right.. Spring colors.

• **The name, "Turnstone",** refering to its feeding habits, fits this little sand trotter to a "T". Traipsing back & forth across the shore, it pokes into every nook 'n cranny for marine morsels with its specialized beak. The bill is slightly upturned & is used as a wedge to upend shells, pebbles, seaweed & sticks. By tossing its head, the Ruddy flips over the obstacle & gobbles the goods hiding underneath! If objects prove too heavy, Turnstones will "turn" as a team! Ruddys eat food ranging from fresh mollusks to parasites of carcasses (left), tho' it has been discovered they lack the internal antiseptic Crows/Vultures have, & will suffer serious food poisoning from digesting bacterias found in beach carrion—..

Note.. The bill is turned up at the tip

• **World traveling Turnstones** breed in the Artic tundra, north of the Hudson Bay. 4 spotted, greenish-gray eggs hatch in mossy hollows lined with grass blades/seaweed. Young are perky at birth & will forage shellfish & shrimp their first day of life—!!

T. Ballantine...

SANDPIPERS... PART I
WILLET
"Shorebirds"... those sandside pips & peeps... are notoriously shy & hard to identify. But not Willets! These "white-wing curlews" stand taller (15") & have longer bills & legs than any of our other Sandpipers. While smallish beach fowl teeter across the dry strand, Willets tend to strut on stiff legs, bobbing their heads as they stride right into the surf to feed! Gray-backed adults may show brown streaks/spots on their white underparts. Beachwalkers will flush hunting Willets at 50 yards & will hear the lanky loudmouths lament, "bill-willie!" "bill-willie!" as they flap away, flashing eye-catching white-wing patches. The birds will usually land 200 feet downshore & resume dining —..
FEET
Note Webs
In many ways, Willets resemble herons in their hunting habits. They stand alone, or in pairs, away from other shorebirds. Wading the waves on long blue legs, Willets are supported against currents & wet sand by their big webbed feet (above). With that bigger-than-the-head sized bill, the birds can either stab 8" underwater for fish, or peck up prey burrowed 'neath the hard-packed sands —!
IN-FLIGHT Note white wing patches.
RIGHT... What Willets eat
FIDDLER CRABS
COQUINA CLAMS
WORMS
KILL-FISH
In May, Willets balance platform nests of woven grass & caked mud on stiff-stemmed salt marsh plants (like Sea Oxe-eye daisies). 4 gray-brown eggs, speckled with lilac/brown spots, are staunchly defended by the parents. Willets wheel around the trespassers to the lair, whaling loudly, & even ganging up on predators like Fish Crows (which eat chicks or move into the nest!) Soon after the hatch, Ma leads... or carries... downy youngsters to protected marshy sloughs. Here 'neath the cover of the high grasses, the Willet family gobbles insects & crabs 'til late August... when they return to the shore, & are first spotted by birdwatchers —..

SANDPIPERS... PART II

SANDERLING

● Scatterings of shorebirds that swarm about our Autumn beaches are guaranteed to include dozens of familiar Sanderlings. These 7-8" sandpipers are plumper & a tad taller than their kindred "peeps". When you spot a batch of beach birds, observe their underparts. Sanderlings are so pure white, neck to belly, that folks here call 'em "whities". No other sandpiper is so unmarked below. Ashy gray above, the bird wears a dusky line from bill to eye. When approached, "whities" swing out to sea in tight circling formations & show a line of white spots on their fast-flapping wings—..

● **Wave dodgers extraordinaire,** Sanderlings are famous for the way they play tag with the surf while feeding. Unlike their big cousins, Willets, "whities" have only 3 toes & thus are unstable in soft sand. So they skip along the foam line, fleeing incoming breakers that threaten to soggy up their feathers,.. & then chasing the backwash seaward, probing for food in the bubbly flats. Note: Sanderling's 1" beak is the perfect length for digging up burrowed sandhoppers, worms, isopods, shrimp & shellfish, such as cockles (right). Slightly flattened at the tip, the bill is a useful wedge for prying open shells—..

● 'Though they hunt here thru' the Winter, Sanderlings migrate as far North as Greenland/Iceland to breed! "Whitey" nests are grass-padded hollows hidden 'neath tufts of vegetation. In June, 4 chicks hatch from speckled, light olive-brown eggs. When the entire family wings back to Hilton Head in September, the over-fed youngsters look especially pudgy. Well enough... for they'll need all that downy insulation to weather out bitter Nor'Easters which scrape across the strand, November–March—!!

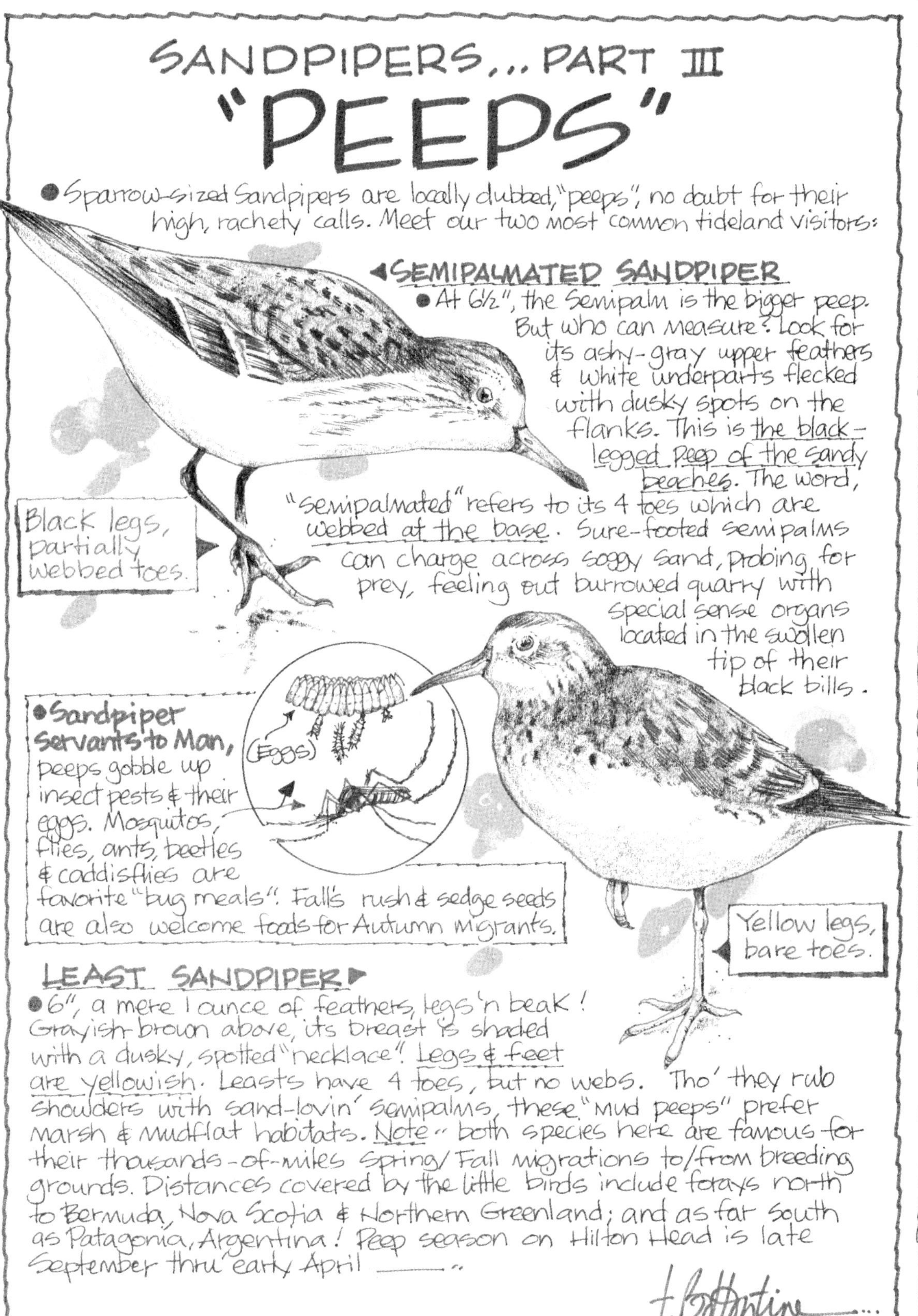
SANDPIPERS... PART III
"PEEPS"
●Sparrow-sized Sandpipers are locally dubbed, "peeps", no doubt for their high, rachety calls. Meet our two most common tideland visitors:
◄SEMIPALMATED SANDPIPER
●At 6½", the Semipalm is the bigger peep. But who can measure? Look for its ashy-gray upper feathers & white underparts flecked with dusky spots on the flanks. This is the black-legged peep of the sandy beaches. The word, "semipalmated" refers to its 4 toes which are webbed at the base. Sure-footed semipalms can charge across soggy sand, probing for prey, feeling out burrowed quarry with special sense organs located in the swollen tip of their black bills.
Black legs, partially webbed toes.
●Sandpiper Servants to Man, peeps gobble up insect pests & their eggs. Mosquitos, flies, ants, beetles & caddisflies are favorite "bug meals". Fall's rush & sedge seeds are also welcome foods for Autumn migrants.
(Eggs)
Yellow legs, bare toes.
LEAST SANDPIPER►
●6", a mere 1 ounce of feathers, legs 'n beak! Grayish-brown above, its breast is shaded with a dusky, spotted "necklace". Legs & feet are yellowish. Leasts have 4 toes, but no webs. Tho' they rub shoulders with sand-lovin' semipalms, these "mud peeps" prefer marsh & mudflat habitats. Note: both species here are famous for their thousands-of-miles Spring/Fall migrations to/from breeding grounds. Distances covered by the little birds include forays north to Bermuda, Nova Scotia & Northern Greenland; and as far south as Patagonia, Argentina! Peep season on Hilton Head is late September thru early April ——..
T. Ballantine

SANDPIPERS...PART IV

SPOTTED SANDPIPER

• **Round black spots** pepper the white breast & belly of this common shorebird, a permanent resident here. The 7½" Spotted Sandpiper's namesake tummy marks, an ashy-olive back & a white line above the eye are summer colors. By late fall, the spots fade to whitish....

• **A solitary hunter,** the Spotted Sandpiper stalks the margins of salt marsh creeks, mud pools & ponds. Dull back hues camouflage the bird to its marsh muck background as it gingerly steps along lumpy knolls, advancing on insects, crabs, clams & marine worms. Its nervous habit of see-sawing its body up & down has earned this sandpiper the nickname, "teeter tail". This body pumping routine along with a well-extended head & strong grasping toes ensures balance on slimy terrains. If alarmed, the Spotted soars out over the water on stiffly held quivering wings (watch for a white wing bar)*... whistling, "peet-weet-weet" via a semicircular return route to, or near, its original perch.

TAIL TEETERING

*Note how wings are bowed in flight.

• **Breeding Spotted Sandpipers** range up the Atlantic Seaboard to the Hudson Bay. The male shares incubating chores, roosting 4 blotched, cream-buff eggs in a clawed-out hollow lined with stems, leaves & grass. Nearshore nests are disguised in grassy clumps. Soon after breaking from their shells, fluff-ball hatchlings show their family colors, wagging downy plumes like true teeter tails! To escape enemy hawks, young lie down in the sand to hide, or dive right into ponds, submerging 3-4 sec. 'til the perplexed predator wings away—!

AB...

SANDPIPERS... PART V
DUNLIN

Our bent-beak sandpiper, the Dunlin is commonly seen here Sept.-May. This 8-9" shorebird is notable for its longish black bill, curving downward at the tip. Dunlin winter dress is ashy-gray above with an obvious gray wash across the breast. Shortly before Spring migrations, the back turns chestnut & a broad black patch splashes the belly area ___.

Dunlins gather with gulls, plovers, turnstones & "peeps" to hunt quiet beaches, tidepools & mudflats. Here they probe the soft mud with slightly open beaks which they jockey around 'til locating wiggly, burrowing prey (inset, below) down to 1" deep. These surefooted sandpipers will wade belly deep into small pools & plop their heads completely underwater to snatch crabs, snails & marine worms. Unlike their kindred sandpipers, Dunlins do stoop to scavenge, supping on scads of maggots found in dead fish & carrion___.

SUMMER...
WINTER

MOLLUSKS
SAND FLEAS
FIDDLER CRABS
PROBING FOR...

June brings Dunlin migrations to the upper Hudson Bay area to breed. Dry grass stems & leaves are clawed into simple hollows or ruts in the tundra permafrost for nest padding. 4 spotted, pale green eggs are incubated about 3 weeks by both parents. By July, tawny fledglings will freely fly to nearby marshes & ponds where they'll gobble abundant aquatic insects & seeds___...

HB...

GULLS ... PART I
HERRING GULL
• No beach walk would be complete without enjoying a "close encounter" with a Herring Gull or two. The largest, most abundant local Gull, this 24" snow-white bird with the grey-blue mantle & white wing tips shows a chrome-yellow bill with a tiny red spot, in summer & fall. Its beak color is the key to distinguishing it from the smaller, near-twin, Ring-Billed Gull. In the winter, the head & neck plumage turns dusky & streaked, & the bill pales. Though Islanders spot Herring Gulls pecking nearby mudflats or begging breadcrumbs from humans, these "Sea Gulls" range far from land too... sailing on broad, wide wings & fan-tails, with their bills pointed ahead, ever-scanning the horizon for shrimp trawlers & other seaside scavenge —!
• These "beach vultures" scrounge up storm wash-ups & tideland animals (shown at left) with relish. Dead or alive, food is torn up with the strong, hooked bill. A famous dinner-time coup is "clam-cracking", their trick of dropping shellfish from 50 ft. in the air to the hard beach (or your auto hood!) below 'til they pop apart, gaping, raw & ready to eat —!
FISH
SHELLFISH
CRABS
INSECTS
Note.. Herring Gulls are our swimming shore birds. Rafts of 10-20 Gulls will bob & paddle using large webbed feet for propellers. The sharp claws aid in picking up food on-the-fly, scratching out nests & even climbing trees.
• Gregarious Herring Gulls nest in crowded communes from S.C. sandbars to the rocky isles off Maine. Various Gull species stay segregated. For 26 days both parents incubate 3 blotched, grey-green eggs in a simple sandy hollow, or tightly packed nests of moss/grass in available trees. Downy, splotched, hours-old hatchlings wander about freely thru' the rookery, but are often pecked to death by not-so-sociable adult neighbors! Watch the shore for sooty-brown yearlings gaining white on wing-tips as they grow. In 3 years adults will complete the familiar "Sea Gull white & grey" colors —...
YEARLING...
HATCHLING
F. Ballantine

GULLS... PART II

RING-BILLED GULL

●There is one sure way to pick out Ring-billed Gulls from the gang of Gulls that throng to our beaches August–May... **BEHOLD THE BEAK!** No other Gull has that broad black band encircling the yellow-green bill. Winging aloft, these white headed/bodied birds with the blue-grey mantles do appear like their close cousins, the Herring Gulls. But note 18 in. "Ringers" are 6 in. shorter and show black-tipped primaries in flight. Their Winter plumage is similar... a dirty spotting about the head 'n neck. Like any self-respecting shoreline scavenger, this Gull tags along after shrimp boats, bobs the brine, or works the mudflats/rock groins for supper. Yet remember this "Lake Gull" also flocks to lagoons, sloughs & even open fields, hunting well within the "upland" arenas of this Carolina isle—.

●Although fish provide 50% of their diet, our Ring-billed Gulls are not above supping on some juicy insect protein. Their habit of following the plow, snapping up grasshoppers, crickets & weevils out of the fresh furrows makes these birds a welcome winged exterminator of farmers' pests. Those arch-grain-gobblers, Mice & Voles are hunted around woody margins of cleared fields. Always hungry, never timid, the birds are as much at home in a garbage bin as crowding with crows, nibbling January's store of fermented palm fruits!

●In May, mates migrate to No. N.Y – Ontario to breed. Parents weave reeds, weeds & feathers into nests hidden in high marsh grasses. Mottled & downy, 2-3 June hatchlings per nest merge naturally with their stemmed surroundings, but in emergencies, they'll paddle away from predators, bouyed up by their oily fluff & tiny webbed feet. Yearlings returning here by Fall are streaked with brown/grey & most noticeably, their flesh-colored bills have a black cap, not a ring! —AB...

GULLS... PART III

LAUGHING GULL

● Life is one big chuckle for the Laughing Gull, which is christened for its "hah-ha-ha-hah-hah!" cackling call. Learn to listen for this raucous serenade as the birds fly 100 ft. overhead. The smallest of our local Gulls, the 16 in. "Laugher" stands out in a shorebird crowd, for its slate-black hood covering the head. Its white body has a slight rosy tint & the dark-grey wings show black tips. The tail is white. Adults will lose the hood in Winter & will grow white head feathers with a dusky band on the nape. 'Though Laughing Gulls range far 'n wide with their kindred species, they delight in estuarine habitats like creeks, spits, harbors & docks. Here wheeling, swooping flocks fill the salty air with their noisy namesake banter as they hunt ——..

● Laughing Gulls devote every waking hour to finding food. Rotting trash & the eggs of sandpipers are big helpings in their diet (at left). Adept piscators, they'll skim the wave tops or follow feeding dolphins to scavenge mullet & minnows. But their most daring fishing trick is picking on Pelicans... robbing their catch by alighting on their heads & reaching right inside the big throat pouch to lift out fresh, finny morsels —— !!

● These "Black Headed Gulls" nest up & down the Atlantic coast, crowding their May nests on isolated sand bars, dunes & keys. 3-4 off-white, heavily streaked eggs are laid in a bulky thatch of woven grass, sedge & seaweed. The spotted, buff-brown brood hatches in 3 weeks & zips about the colony within 48 hrs., hiding under vegetation to avoid predators. Young'ns fly by July & show up shoreside cloaked in brownish-black immature feathering for their first year of life. 2 annual molts are needed before they will wear adult breeding colors (Spring-Summer) shown at the top, right ——..

NEST & EGGS

T. Bottontine

GULLS ... PART IV
GULL ECOLOGY
●"Gulls, Gulls everywhere & always a bite to eat" is the lyric answer to why so many Gulls sail our seacoast. Wherever feed is found, these hungry aeronauts will fly on broad wings, glide with fan-tails or swim using webbed feet to grab it! Tho' our 3 common species party together, ea. has its favored feeding niche: Herring Gulls, the open sea; Ring-billed Gulls, farther inland; Laughing Gulls, estuaries/marshes.
●BIRDS OF FORTUNE.. Gull's ability to glean shrimp-boater's sweep-over "trash" is far-famed. Flocks over open seas may indicate feeding Dolphin. Pilfering fish from Pelicans & begging breadcrumbs/popcorn from tourists are stock-in-trade. Some Gulls do kill baby Terns/Sandpipers, thus balancing overpopulation in shorebirds.
●A BOON TO MANKIND.. Gull's hooked upper bill is a perfect tear-up tool for scavenging. These "Health Officers of the Coast" clean up rotting debris & bacteria. Their penchant for insects (& rodents) makes Gulls true Farmers' Helpers, as immortalized by the "Sea Gull Monument" located in Salt Lake City, Utah. From 1848-50 flocks of Gulls saved Mormon settlers' grain fields by gobbling-up swarms of ravaging black crickets.....
FLYWAY ROBBERY!
THE SEAGULL MONUMENT
● DANGER!.. Feathered from birth, Gull chicks are always on-the-run from these predators, below. But their big enemy is killing cold or storm washover. So many youngsters die in floods that a Gull's lifespan averages just 1¾ years!
HAWKS
OWLS
FOXES
'COONS
●SPRING & FALL MIGRANTS.. Most Gulls wing far Northward via the Atlantic Flyway to breed. May & August migrations to & from their teeming rookeries follow the oceanic "plankton bloom" & abundant fish schooling in turbulent Spring & Fall waters.....
ATLANTIC FLYWAY

TERNS... PART I
CASPIAN TERN

•**The spirited swallows of the sea,** Terns are the noisy, diving black-capped white birds that hustle along the shores here. The imperial member of the clan is the Caspian. At 20-23", this biggest Tern is about gull-sized. Its back/wings are gray-blue & it bears a "flat-top", jet-black crown atop pure white face/neck/underparts. The tail is barely forked. Watch for the vermillion bill... no other Tern sports such vivid red-orange chompers! Heads pointing down to scan the waters, Caspians fly to fish for live prey in our sounds, salt creeks & lagoons. Long, pointed wings & a forked tail help these "strikers" maneuver like Nature's P-38's... darting about on the winds, then folding wings in for the headlong plunge into the drink! Minnows are snared with the spear-like beak. Caspians hunt in groups, taking baby birds, squid, shrimp & mussels as well as fish, bantering "craak!" "craak!" back 'n forth as they jockey down-wind for diving position——..

Note.. In the dead of Winter, the crown is broken by white flecks——..

TERN
GULL

•**The difference between Terns & Gulls:** ① Terns generally smaller. ② Terns show long-pointed wings & forked tails for maneuvering, Gulls broad wings & fan-tails for gliding. ③ Tern bills sharp for fishing, pointed down. Gull bills hooked for tearing flesh. ④ Terns dive to fish. Gulls float/land on water to pick up prey—..

•**Caspians breed in bunches** in S.C., nesting with Gulls on sparse, offshore bars like Joiner's Bank, located just east of Ft. Walker, Port Royal Plantation. 3 buffy eggs, spotted in chocolate-brown, are laid in a mere scoop in the sand or reeds. Tho' hundreds nest wing-to-wing, anti-social Caspians will beat & peck to death any neighbor chicks that trespass their sand spot! Tern broods will return to our shores in September——..

JOINER'S BANK
ATLANTIC OCEAN
HILTON HEAD (PORT ROYAL PLANT'N.)

TERNS ... PART II

ROYAL TERN

Even Aububon himself confused Royals with Caspian Terns at 1st glance, labeling both white divers, "Cayenne Terns". But birdwatchers now know Royals are smaller, at 20"; wear a regal, swept-back black crest, for which they are named; and show a "cadmium-orange" bill (far less red than the Caspian's). Even its tail ... deeply forked for ½ its length ... sets the Royal apart from its big, red-billed cousin —...

Lofting in line formations, Royals fly at great heights on calm days. We ground-huggers will be attracted by their high-pitched, "Kak-kak-kak!", bantered 100's of feet above salt marshes, harbors & the beachfront. Flocks fish here, on overcast days, circling, circling ... then splash-down-diving for fingerling menhaden. In cloudy weather, surface schools stand out as dark silhouettes in the gray water. For variety, long-winged, agile Royals will rob fish from slow-moving Brown Pelicans, or hunt shrimp & crabs from oyster bars / mud flats —...

Thousands of thronging Royal Terns colonize nearby remote islands & shoal bars to nest in June. 2-3 yellowish eggs adorned with lilac/brown spots sit in an exposed, sandy hollow. Sociable Royals brood so closely together that a visitor to the rookery could touch 5-10 nests within an arms-length ... if adults would allow it! I learned how protective parents are in 1975, when I sailed to Joiner's Bank, via Hobie-Cat to investigate the local Royal nestery. But the strafing, screaming birds dive-bombed me into retreat, to the far end of the sand bar! Out there the big enemy is Gulls, who prey on the toddling teams of pinkish chicks —!

TERNS... PART III
COMMON TERN

● Only during Fall & Spring migrations is the agressive little Common Tern truly "Common" here. Winter flights may carry the birds as fas South as the Straits of Magellan, tho' flocks do loiter on our beaches/ mud flats for months at a time. Commons are the mid-sized Terns (15") with the black crest covering the head down to eye level (the cap fades up the forehead in Winter). The vermillion-red bill is tipped with black, ½ its length. The naturalist's name, "Red Shank", advertises this Tern's coral-red feet which highlight against snowy underparts, a deeply forked tail & a pearly-blue mantle. Wing tips are noticeably dark —..

WINTER CROWN

● **Fishermen's friends...** Commons hover in hordes above waters where predatory game fish feed, & thus act as winged range finders for boated anglers! The terns catch 3-4" minnows the big fish chase & plunge like missles into the boiling seas, screaming "tee-ar! tee-ar!" non-stop. Sometimes, for sheer sport, the quarry is tossed aloft & deftly struck again in mid-air before it falls a foot! "Red Shanks" also dart like swallows to nip crabs, shrimp & even butterflies off marshy grounds —..

Two adult Common Terns "hen-peck" an immature Gull over the rookery —...

● Common Terns nest in secluded colonies from Maine to Massachusetts. 3 speckled, light brown eggs are roosted in pebbly hollows lined with grass & spaced a yard apart. After the June hatch, parents play off-shore, paddling around with webbed feet & winging cool spray over their backs. But all adults keep an eagle-eye out for gulls, hawks & owls which prey on the chicks. Protective to-the-death of their broods, swooping Tern teams will strike at the heads of nest-robbers, piercing their brains with spear-sharp beaks! Getting the hang of hunting comes slowly to youngsters. Parents are still seen flipping finny morsels to their babes when they all settle in on Hilton Head in mid-Autumn —!!

T. Bottorline...

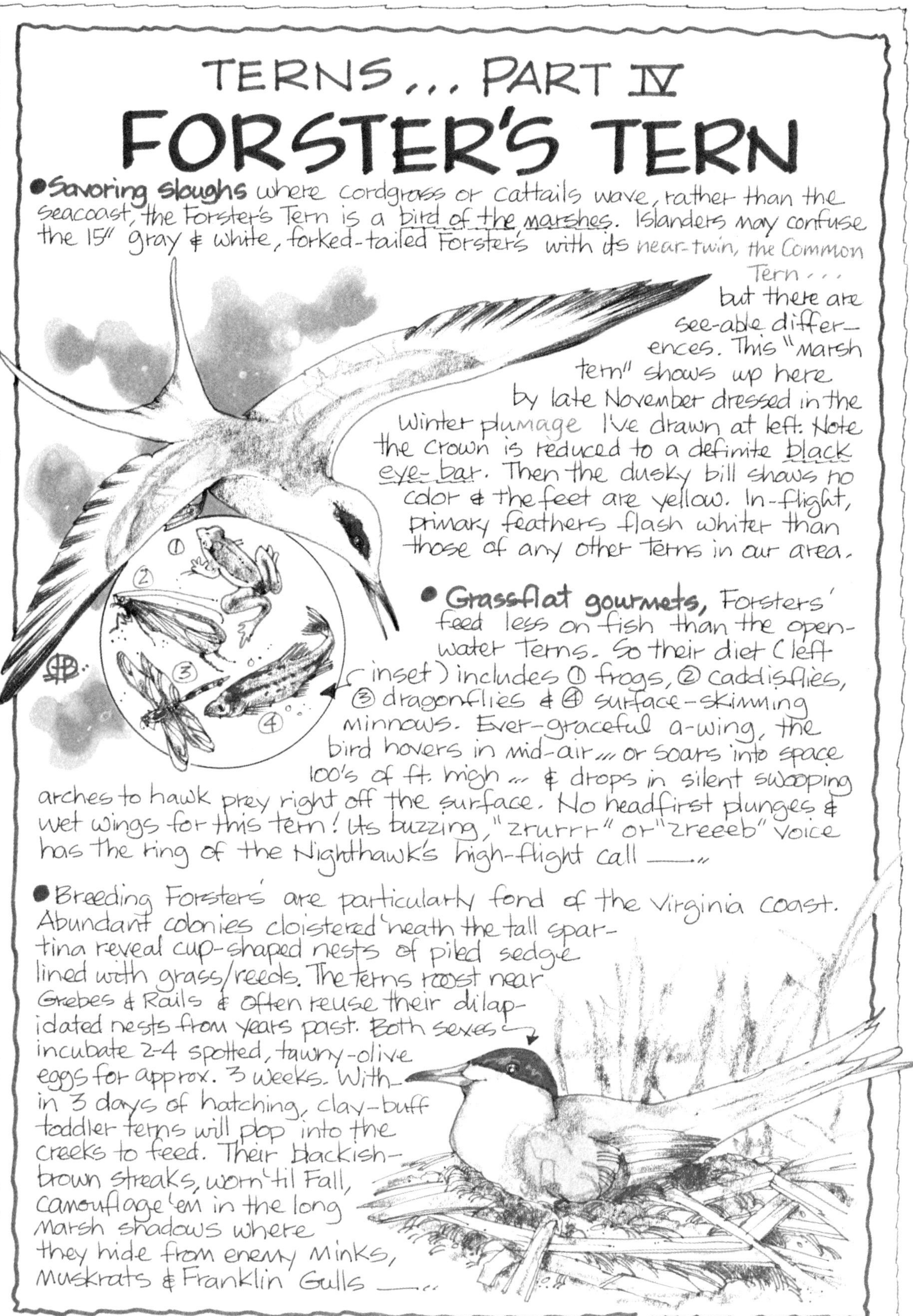

TERNS... PART IV

FORSTER'S TERN

● **Savoring sloughs** where cordgrass or cattails wave, rather than the seacoast, the Forster's Tern is a bird of the marshes. Islanders may confuse the 15" gray & white, forked-tailed Forster's with its near-twin, the Common Tern... but there are see-able differences. This "marsh tern" shows up here by late November dressed in the winter plumage I've drawn at left. Note the crown is reduced to a definite black eye-bar. Then the dusky bill shows no color & the feet are yellow. In-flight, primary feathers flash whiter than those of any other terns in our area.

● **Grassflat gourmets,** Forsters' feed less on fish than the open-water Terns. So their diet (left inset) includes ① frogs, ② caddisflies, ③ dragonflies & ④ surface-skimming minnows. Ever-graceful a-wing, the bird hovers in mid-air... or soars into space 100's of ft. high... & drops in silent swooping arches to hawk prey right off the surface. No headfirst plunges & wet wings for this tern! Its buzzing, "zrurrr" or "zreeeb" voice has the ring of the Nighthawk's high-flight call ——.

● Breeding Forsters' are particularly fond of the Virginia coast. Abundant colonies cloistered 'neath the tall spartina reveal cup-shaped nests of piled sedge lined with grass/reeds. The terns roost near Grebes & Rails & often reuse their dilapidated nests from years past. Both sexes incubate 2-4 spotted, tawny-olive eggs for approx. 3 weeks. Within 3 days of hatching, clay-buff toddler terns will plop into the creeks to feed. Their blackish-brown streaks, worn 'til Fall, camouflage 'em in the long marsh shadows where they hide from enemy Minks, Muskrats & Franklin Gulls ——..

TERNS ... PART V

LEAST TERN

• **Summer's the season** for our peppy "little striker", the Least Tern. Well named, it's the 'least' in its family, only 9" long. No other Tern is so small. Thru' field glasses adult Leasts show a unique blackish crown, broken by a white crescent on the forehead, located between the eyes & the area above the bill. The yellow beak itself is tipped with black. Feet are yellowish-orange. With the naked eye any stroller along shoal edges... e.g. creeks & sounds such as the waters 'round South Beach... can spot the bird's blue-gray mantle & satiny-white underparts; a long forked tail; & dark wing-tips splashed with a silvery tinting——..

• **"Yip! Zree-yip!"** squeals this pint-sized piscador, hovering motionless, parallel to shore over a minnow school. Up & down fidgets the head & bill, the tiny bird quavering high & low on breezy drafts. Then... swoop!... splash!... gulp!... the Least makes the most of its meal, swallowing, on-the-wing, shallow-water fish, floating shrimp & even swarming insects——..

• **Dark days fell upon Least Terns** in the early 1900's. Nationwide, their colonies were exterminated by millinery hunters. 1400 birds a-day died for their feathers! Sadly, Hilton Head Island bears guilt for the more recent demise of the local Leasts. Real estate "development" steam-rolled an abundant rookery on a high, broad sand-spoil at the mouth of Braddock's Cove, at South Beach. The quaint hamlet now called "Land's End" eradicated a once thriving nursery where Leasts nested May-July. There, on close approach, I learned the nests are simple scoops in the dry sand, ½ the size of 'yer fist. 2 broods of 1-4 drab, spotted eggs are incubated 2 weeks by both parents. Mouthfuls of morsels are brought like 'breakfast in bed' by one adult to its roosting mate & later to the downy chicks! Sand-colored to blend with their grainy world, baby Leasts actively jog around the colony, but hit-the-dirt to hide when danger... rats, cats, dogs or bulldozers... threatens. Families fly by August. Winter broods wander inland & migrate south from Louisiana to faraway Argentina——..

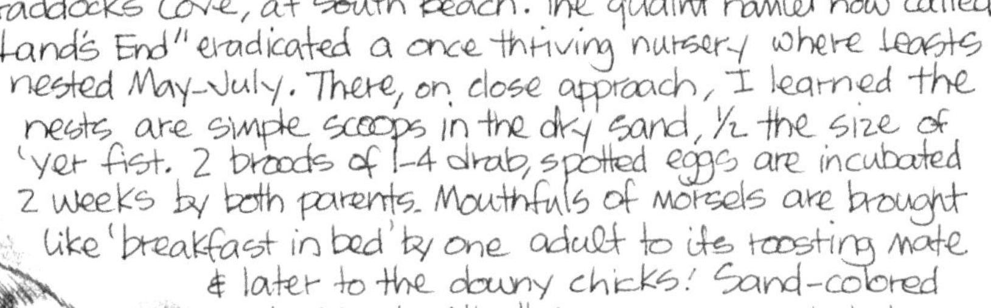

BLACK SKIMMERS
When it comes to scraping up a meal from the Sea, the Black Skimmer doesn't miss a trick. This 16-20", long-winged speedster with the jet-black cap, back & flight feathers; white underparts; & carmine-red bill feeds on-the-fly. It slurps in small marine life by cutting the surface with its long lower jaw while flapping mere inches above the brine! Outracing & outdistancing soaring Gulls or diving Terns, these "shearwaters" have thus captured their own niche as masters of the wave-tops. Skimmers are nocturnal, so watch tidal creeks/estuaries for straight-line feeding flocks, numbering 5-25 birds, barking out "auw! auw!" around dusk & dawn —.
In late June, Black Skimmers nest in colonies near, but not with, cousin Terns & Gulls, on close-by offshore sandbanks. Home is a simple shell-strewn hollow parents scoop out by gyrating 'round & round. The entire rookery rests in formation with bills & bodies facing windward. 4-5 spotted, sandy-colored chicks hatch from spotted-buffy eggs in July. Both parents raise the youngsters 'til they gain primary feathers in the Fall. Then the tag-along brown fledglings first fall in line with the sweeping, skimming ranks of the black & white "razor-bills."
MEN-HADEN
SHRIMP
Note: The lower mandible is over 1 inch longer than the movable upper! Thin as knife blades, the jaws come together like scissors on prey. Skimmers may also feed in tide pools, wading well on "notched" webbed feet.
F. Bottontine ...

OSPREY
● Lord of the sky, the osprey soars the skies over sounds, creeks & inland ponds. Over 2 feet long with a 5 ft. wing-span, the bird is easily identified by its bent wings, forming a "V." Don't confuse the osprey with an eagle. Remember: Only ospreys are brown on top & white underneath. Eagles (more common each year in the south) are brown below.
NOTE: Crooked wings help the osprey shake off water after high dives.
● Bone breaker, the Latin meaning for "osprey" aptly tells how this hawk catches fish... 98% of its diet. Madly flapping 30 stories over water, the bird crashlands, feet-first, to ambush Mullet, Menhaden, catfish & bass. It scores a direct hit 1 in 3 times. Ospreys have strong *barbed talons with reversible toes, so they can grip 1½ lbs. of struggling prey... half their own body weight. They carry fish with heads forward to cut down wind resistence, then gobble the catch on a nearby tree limb.
*TALONS: Note the barbs on these fish traps
● Each March, mates-for-life re-nest in bulky bundles of branches, seaweed & beach trash, wedged atop baldcypress trees, utility towers, bridges & channel markers. Buff-brown at birth, fledglings fly at 8 weeks.
J. Bottontini

MARSH HAWK
Dawn in the salt marsh: an ashy spectre strafes the wet meadows, hovers for a moment, & then plunges deep into the grass below. This dark hunter is the Marsh Hawk, a 19" harrier seen gliding over lowlands/fields on a 4 ft. wingspan. Called "Blue Hawks", males are actually light grey with whitish abdomens. Larger females are dark umber above, tawny & striped below. The semi-circles of ruff around their eyes reminds us of the "owl-look". But in a pinch, the best field mark is their white rump patch, shown in flight. Listen for their call, a series of stacatto, "chit... chit... chit... chit's"—.
Note: Slim, lithe Marsh Hawks typify "harriers", the low-gliding hawks with long wings & tails for maneuverability.
♂
Note: Wings held in a "V". M. Hawks hunt ① rabbits, ② rodents, ③ frogs, ④ snakes. Prey, including insects & wounded waterfowl, is gobbled on the spot!
①
②
③
④
♀
Swooping somersaults & daring dives are tricks males use to court spring mates. Both parents build a neat, foot-wide nest of grass/stems/twigs at ground level in some cloistered marshland hammock. 4-6 downy chicks hatch from bluish-white eggs. They'll free-load in the "crib" for over a month, even after growing flight feathers! The folks will scrounge-up 1,000 rodents alone for the brood in the interim! Marsh Hawk families migrate South for the winter, so watch skyward for harrier hunting parties, numbering a doz. or more!

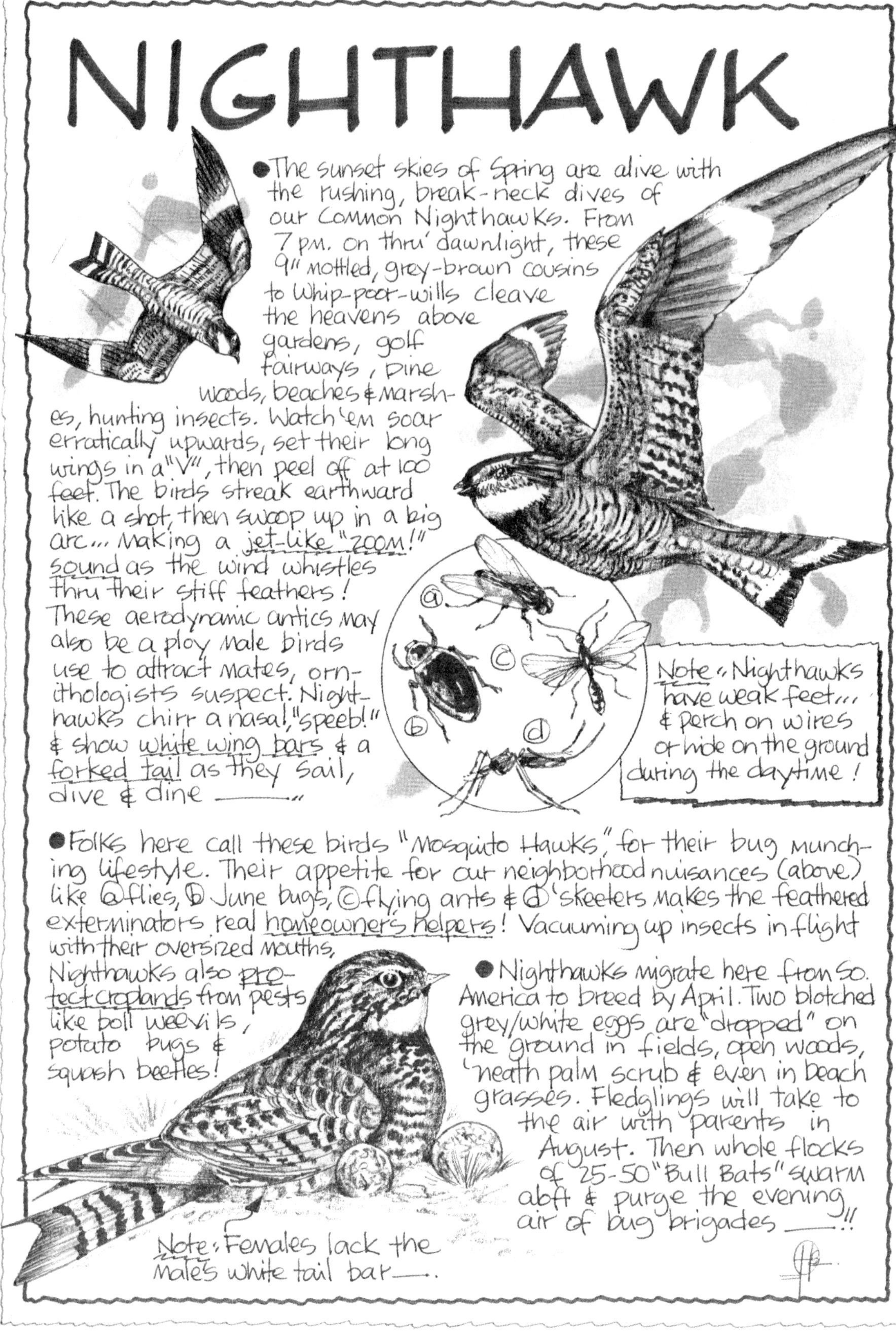
NIGHTHAWK
●The sunset skies of Spring are alive with the rushing, break-neck dives of our Common Nighthawks. From 7 p.m. on thru' dawnlight, these 9" mottled, grey-brown cousins to Whip-poor-wills cleave the heavens above gardens, golf fairways, pine woods, beaches & marshes, hunting insects. Watch 'em soar erratically upwards, set their long wings in a "V", then peel off at 100 feet. The birds streak earthward like a shot, then swoop up in a big arc... making a jet-like "zoom!" sound as the wind whistles thru their stiff feathers! These aerodynamic antics may also be a ploy male birds use to attract mates, ornithologists suspect. Nighthawks chirr a nasal, "speeb!" & show white wing bars & a forked tail as they sail, dive & dine ——."
ⓐ
ⓑ
ⓒ
ⓓ
Note: Nighthawks have weak feet... & perch on wires or hide on the ground during the daytime!
●Folks here call these birds "Mosquito Hawks," for their bug munching lifestyle. Their appetite for our neighborhood nuisances (above) like ⓐ flies, ⓑ June bugs, ⓒ flying ants & ⓓ 'skeeters makes the feathered exterminators real homeowner's helpers! Vacuuming up insects in flight with their oversized mouths, Nighthawks also protect croplands from pests like boll weevils, potato bugs & squash beetles!
●Nighthawks migrate here from So. America to breed by April. Two blotched grey/white eggs are "dropped" on the ground in fields, open woods, 'neath palm scrub & even in beach grasses. Fledglings will take to the air with parents in August. Then whole flocks of 25-50 "Bull Bats" swarm aloft & purge the evening air of bug brigades ——!!
Note: Females lack the male's white tail bar——.

TREE SWALLOW

● **Swirling swarms of swallows** fill the skies above our coastal isles October–May. The large flying flocks are composed of tree swallows migrating here to overwinter. The 5-6" bird is known by its steely blue-green back & wings, & snow white underparts. Its short tail is slightly forked. During warmish, still-air days, these "white bellies" will be seen winging above open salt marshes, beaches, shrublands, hedgerows, lagoons & lakes. In true swallow fashion, they'll glide in quick but graceful circles, rising at the end with a few short flutters. A chattering "cheet!" note is sounded when they stream overhead——.

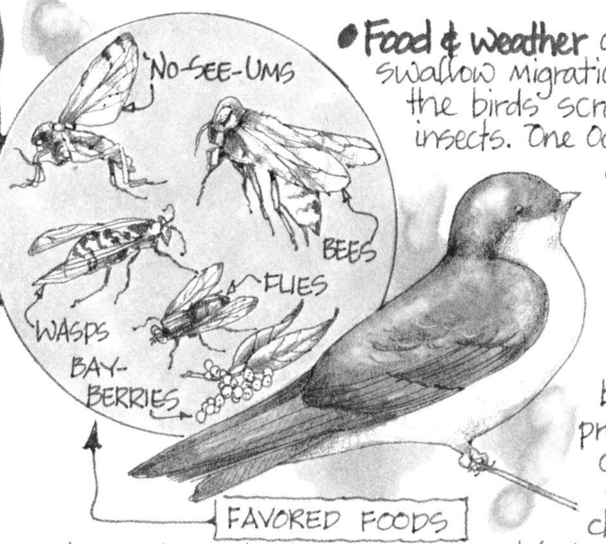

● **Food & weather** are the direct causes for tree swallow migrations here. During the cool season, the birds scrounge scads of fruits & winged insects. One October, I stood amidst a green cloud numbering over 500 birds razing bayberry shrubs in the Sea Pines Forest Preserve! No-see-ums, bees, wasps, flies, moths & leaf-cutting insects comprise 80% of tree swallows' diet year-round. Hence, the bird is a friend to Man, as it preys upon pests which destroy crops & carry disease. Tree swallows abhor the Northern chill & are normally comfortable riding out our benign winters on telephone wire perches. But when 'Nor-easters blow thru', they'll roost in the protection of high marsh grasses, or even under eaves & behind household shutters——.

● **White-bellies breed** from Virginia well into Canada. They prefer to nest in old woodpecker bore-holes or man-made nesting boxes. The Summer's clutch of 4-7 white eggs are brooded in a bed of feathers & grass. Tawny young are fed insects gleaned from the air & skimmed off nearby ponds——..

BELTED KINGFISHER
●Talk about fishing prowess: Few anglers rival our belted kingfisher. The big-headed, double-crested blue/white bird with a dark belt on its belly hunts from a perch... i.e., a powerline or exposed limb. There, scanning the surface with its big piercing eyes, "King of Fishers" is ever-alert to plunge in headfirst & snatch fish in its long, straight beak. The kill is hefted back to perch, beaten to death & devoured. Swift, swooping flight & hovering in place are possible, thanks to the bird's short, round wings. The kingfisher "rattles" on the fly to keep rival 'fishers from trespassing its fishin' hole.
Note: thick, oily feathers keep kingfishers dry despite repeated dunks for dinner.
♂
♀
●Humans needn't fret that kingfishers will pilfer game fishes. Shoalwater minnows, not prized bass or bream are fare. When choppy water makes for bad fishing, this bird picks on reptiles, amphibians, insects & even a wild berry or two (see inset drawing, left).
FISH
FROGS
BEETLES
LIZARDS
Note: The female, here stuffing at the roost, shows her characteristic 2nd russet band.
DOWN THE TUBE
●Kingfishers nest by their home ponds & creeks in May. Parents peck & claw underground tunnels with wide brooding chambers in mudbanks. Cushioned in feathers & disgorged fish parts, the 6-8 eggs hatch in 3 weeks. The adult's shadow in the tunnels cues babies to open their beaks for food. This goes on 4 weeks... 'til the cave stench drives the little stinkers into the open!
J. Boltentine

COASTAL WRENS

• **Four species of Wrens** frequent the Hilton Head area throughout the year. These smallish birds have long, slender bills curving downward at the tip ... a specialized tool for probing crevices and cracks for caterpillars, insects & spiders. Always adorned in a streaked-brown camouflage, Wrens are easiest to see in flight. Short wings propel them through reeds & boughs at 1-15 ft. At perch, the birds cock tails up or down. Wrens are loudmouthed for their stubby size. Many a morning will be welcomed with their tumbling, liquid songs. Their call of alarm, a harsh, rasping complaint, is often sounded when predator cats or squirrels are near!

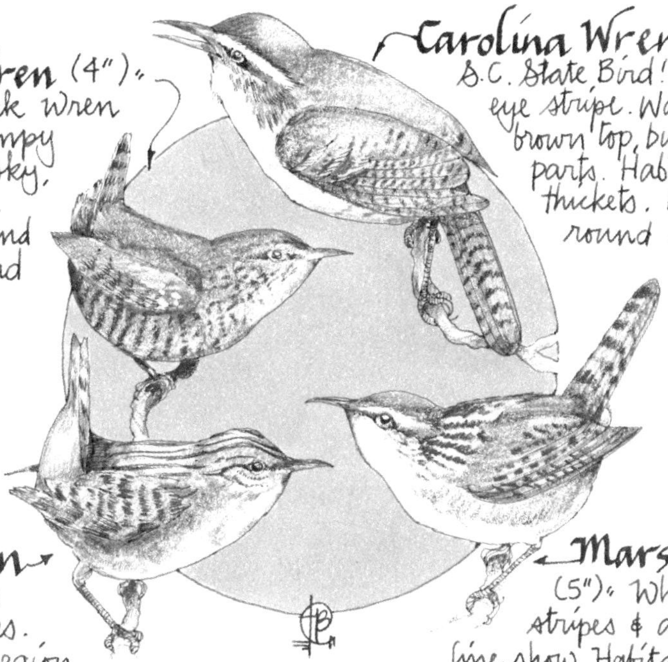

Winter Wren (4"). A small, dark Wren with a stumpy tail & a dusky, barred belly. Habitat: ground level woodland brush. A Winter visitor.

Carolina Wren (5 3/4"). S.C. State Bird! Note white eye stripe. Warm rusty-brown top, buffy lower parts. Habitat: woods, thickets. A year-round resident.

Sedge Wren (4½"). Crown shows streaks. Undertail region is warm buff. Back is streaked. Habitat: sloughs & sedge marshes. Also called Short-billed Marsh Wren. A Winter visitor.

Marsh Wren (5"). White back stripes & an eyebrow line show. Habitat: cattail marshes with water fresh or brackish. Also called Long-billed Marsh Wren. A permanent resident.

MOCKINGBIRD

• **Vocal artist of the feathered world,** the Mockingbird is one of the most conspicuous avians along the Southern coast. Islanders' ears hear its liquid, trilling songs day or night. The bird has a peculiar habit of warbling extra loudly on warm, moonlit evenings. Its Latin name, mimus polyglottos means, "mimic of many tongues." Well said! Mockers imitate the songs & calls of other birds, repeating each tune 4-6 times, then changing voice. Ornithologists have catalogued at least 58 different songs in its repertoire! These bootlegged bird melodies are so exact, they even deceive other birds into thinking their kind are nearby!

In flight: Note white wing patches & white outer tail feathers.

"Mockingbirds are 9-11". Plummage is dark gray above, buff below. At perch, the long tail flicks nervously.

• **An agressive sense of territory** may be the reason Mockers endlessly sing. Songsters warble from wire & shrubtop perches along gardens, roadsides, marsh borders & hammocks. If birdcalling alone doesn't claim space, they descend & threaten other winglings away from food sources. Mockingbirds eat insects (beetles, ants, bees, wasps, grasshoppers) during Spring-Summer. Fruits (holly, greenbriar, pokeweed, Va. creeper, sumac, palmetto) are cold-month edibles. Nesting occurs April-August. 2-3 clutches of 4-5 splotched-aqua eggs are brooded by both parents. Dad fiercely guards nestlings, dive-bombing snakes, cats, dogs or humans, & relentlessly pecking the head of anyone who strays too near the roost!

Threatening with flapping wings

CEDAR WAXWING

● **March will-o-wisps,** Cedar Waxwings annually migrate north through Hilton Head just in time for The Heritage. These smallish (7") crested birds wear elegant blended brownish-amber plumage, with a contrasting black eye mask/throat patch & a yellow tail band. The species' last name describes waxy red knobs on the tips of the secondary feathers. Perhaps these help camouflage the bird amid red berry-laden limbs during feeding ——.

● **Listen, then look** to observe Waxwings. Their high, lisping, "pzee... pzee... pzee" floats in from woodland borders, marsh edges & orchards. Here tight flocks of 5-50 fly tree to tree... weaving & wheeling like swallows then descending in unison into upper branches. Cedar Waxwings do catch flies, 'skeeters & 'no-see-ums' in mid-air, & glean caterpillars (like cankerworms) from cultivated fields, benifitting farmers. But ripening fruits (cedar, holly, pyracantha) really attract them up the Atlantic flyway. They'll gorge on berries, passing large pits in tact in their droppings, thus planting "volunteer" shrubs & trees. When overripe fruits ferment & turn winey, gluttonous Waxwings get tipsy! They wobble on the perch or, blacking out, fall to the ground, perishing upon impact. Literally "dead drunk"!

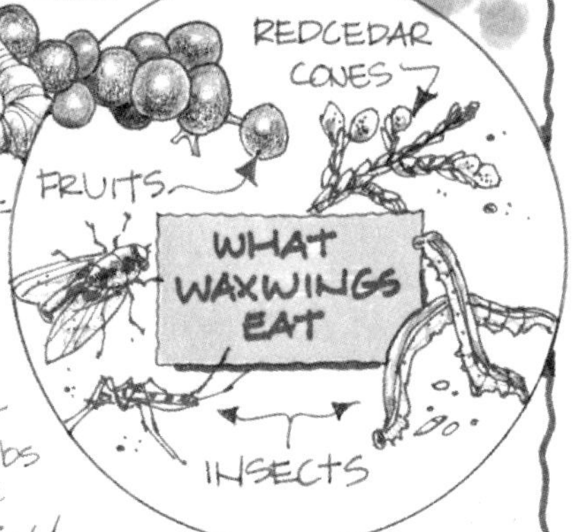

REDCEDAR CONES
FRUITS
WHAT WAXWINGS EAT
INSECTS

● **Poor pop.** Summer's male Waxwings work overtime to support 2 families. After the 1st June brood hatches, he again mates the female, builds her a new nest, feeds her on the roost, meanwhile foraging for the 3-5 chicks. He'll lug a whole cropful of fruits & disgorge them 1 by 1 into the youngsters' gaping mouths!

WAXWINGS BREED FROM NO. VIRGINIA TO NEW BRUNSWICK.

FISH CROW

Coastal cacklers, Fish Crows are small cousins to the familiar Common Crow. Our 14" all-black 'Fishers' are found on beaches/tideflats & in sloughs/swamps foraging both flotsam & fresh eats (inset, below). Autumn's Fish Crow colonies swell to 50-100 birds which raze tree tops, vines & fairways for ripe palmetto, poke, grape, magnolia, bay & holly fruits. To know the Crow, just listen for its nasal "uh-oh!" call.

Palms, cedars & pines are favorite May nest sites. 3-7 brown-spotted eggs are laid in a weave of sticks, pine straw & moss.

Fish Crow capers unfortunately includes nest-robbing. These blackleg bandits haunt spring song-bird clutches/heron rookeries. When roosting parents fly off, they boldly swoop down & devour the eggs! Sometimes angry parents are seen chasing Fish Crows from the nursery, pecking their heads in mid-air! A more honest living is made hunting clams, crabs, shrimp & crawfish. Striding swash lines, they dig out & crunch burrowed creatures with their strong beak, then tear out the meat using long, nimble claws. Fish Crows also eat their namesake. Dashing down 20 feet into swarming schools, they snatch fish in their bills & lug the quarry back to their own hungry nestlings!

• **Largest members of the blackbird family.** Boat-tailed Grackles measure 13½" (♀) to 16½" (♂). The male's head & throat are iridescent greenish-blue, its lower body black. Females are sooty brown above, buffy brown below. These birds are known by their long (6½"), keel-shaped tail. Noticeably fanned-out toward the tip, the "boat-tail" is a sure fieldmark.

• **This "saltwater blackbird"** is a permanent resident of coastal beaches, marshbanks & mudflats. Here it nimbly trods the slimy muck ... getting support from wide-spreading toes & balance from the big tail... & catches insects with flying leaps!

Longish legs enable Boat-tails to wade belly-deep in creeks, where they submerge heads in search of fiddler crabs, shrimp & fingerling fish. Grubs, grasshoppers & palmetto berries are upland edibles.

Note: The long Boat-tail swivels side to side.

CRUSTACEA
FISH
PALM FRUITS
INSECTS

• **Fall-Spring this species travels in 'sexist flocks'** (all male or all female). Hordes alighting in oak limbs are heard gurgling a harsh "churr-churr-cheep-cheep" grackle gutteral, set to the overhead rythym of flapping wings. Females visit male flocks to breed freely in March. With no true pairing between mates, brooding chores fall mainly upon the mother. Bulky nests of bunched twigs, rootlets & bark peelings "chinked" inside with mud & grass are stuffed in small trees/shrubs, below 40 ft. Boat-tails roost in colonies. The 3-5 brownish-drab eggs are camouflaged with dark blotches. Hatchlings resemble females, males wear glossy black colors by October...

SONGS OF SPRING
...OUR FIRST BIRD CAROLS!
AB
• By early March the effect of ever-longer days will stimulate birds here to croon, cry & cackle. Spring bird songs... those repeated melodies males warble to herald claimed territory & attract a female (& at times signal danger, or flocking directions)... will trickle in at 6:00 AM & last 'til noon. Then most day-feeders pipe-down for mid-day hunting & rest. Tho' some of these choristers boast 20-30 tunes apiece, their loudest songs should be familiar to all Islanders who enjoy the Music of the Spring sky...
• CARDINAL.. streams out, "Swee-eet!", or "chu-chu-chu-chu!" from grape vines & hardwoods...
• TUFTED TITMOUSE.. The small crested culprit behind the "S'you... S'you...", coming from the tree tops...
• CAROLINA WREN.. Our State bird, rings out a 3 syllable, "whee-udle, whee-udle, whee-udle!". Loud for its size, this Wren always sings 3-4 times in a row...
• CAROLINA CHICKADEE.. Sings a timid, "chick-a-dee-dee"...
• RED-SHOULDERED HAWK.. Screams, "kee-ahhh!" from 100 ft. up...
• RED-WING BLACKBIRD.. Echoes a liquid, "O-kal-a-re-eee" in marshes.
• BOAT-TAILED GRACKLE.. Gurgles, "chur-chur-chip-chip" from Oak crowns...
• CHUCK-WILL'S WIDOW.. Calls, "Ch'k-Will's-Widow!" after sundown...

WINTER GUESTS

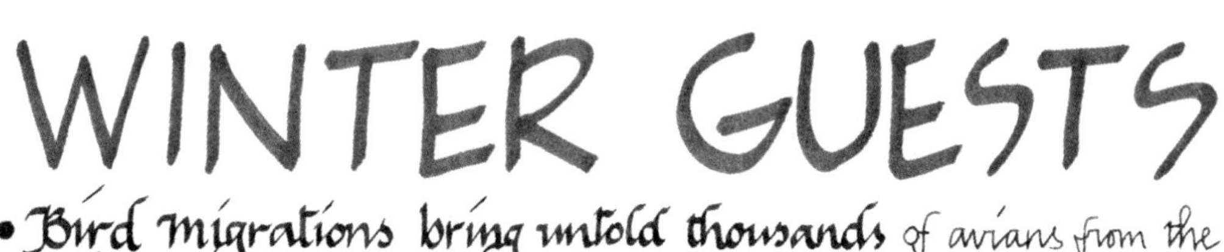

• **Bird migrations bring untold thousands** of avians from the north country to overwinter here. Navigating along the Atlantic Flyway, a popular coastline-aerial-transit route, are these common birds of the sea, beach or inshore waters —

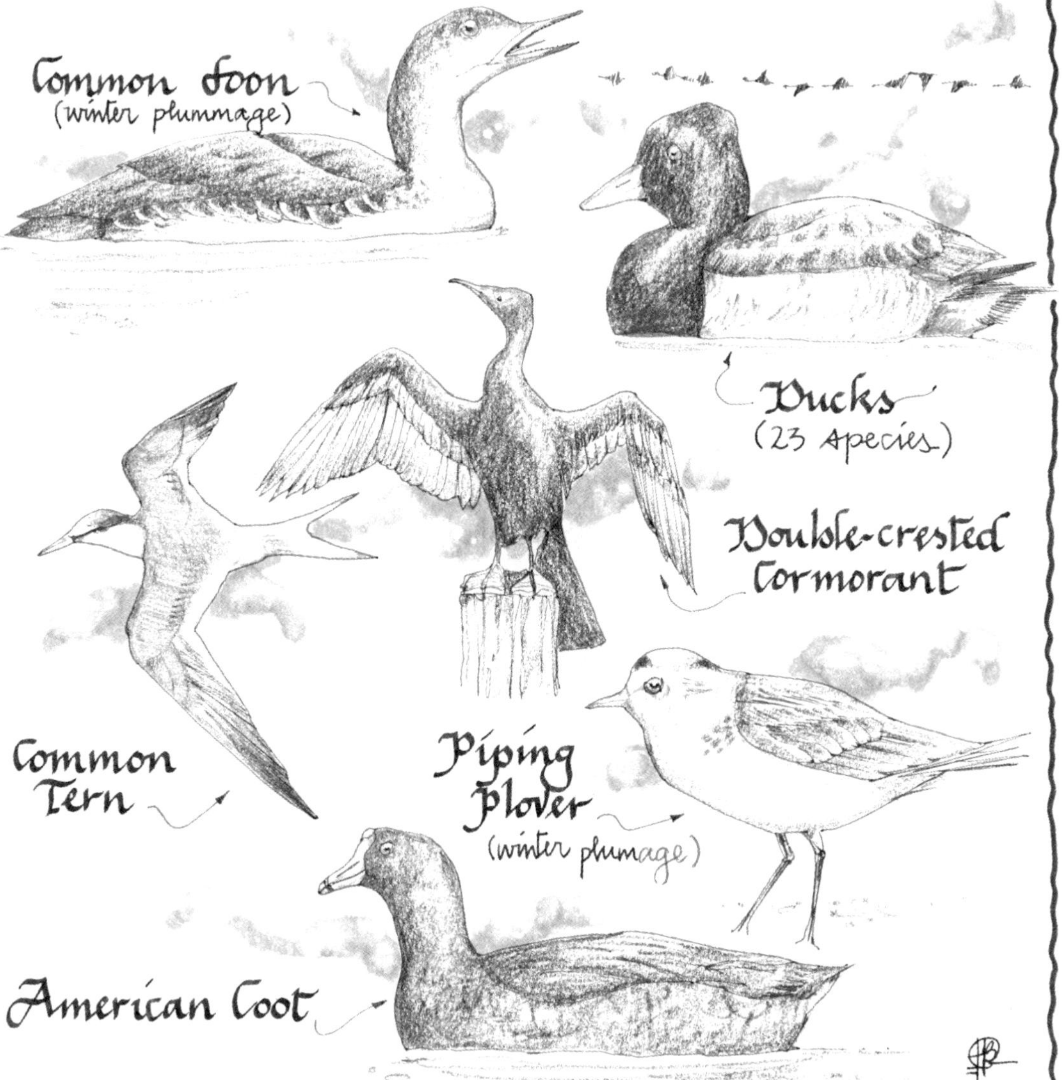

Common Loon
(winter plummage)
Ducks
(23 species)
Double-crested Cormorant
Common Tern
Piping Plover
(winter plumage)
American Coot

WINTER GUESTS
~Part II
• Winter's marsh borders, shrubby hammocks & seed-strewn roadsides abound with populations of these well-known migratory birds...
Tree Swallow
Cedar Waxwing
Winter Wren
Kestrel
White-throated Sparrow
Yellow-rumped Warbler
Rusty Blackbird
(often seen flocking with Starlings & Grackles.)

WHALES

OF SOUTH CAROLINA

• **20 species of whales** have been identified in our Carolina waters or on the shores, according to the Charleston Museum. Most whales seen here are migrants. They swim up & down the coast, pursuing fish schools & traveling to breeding grounds. Remember, whales are mammals & must breath air to live. The hissing spout of a "blow" is a thrill to ocean & inshore boaters. The pheromenon is the animal expelling condensed moisture & carbon dioxide from its blowhole before inhaling rapidly. Note: The largest recorded S.C. whale was a 70 ft. fin whale which stranded at Myrtle Beach, 1921 ___.

OUR 3 MOST COMMON WHALES

① **BOTTLENOSED DOLPHIN**: 8-12 ft. Grayish above, paler below. The "bottlenose" extends out from its bulbous forehead. Travels in pods of 2-10, normally. Common year-round.

② **PILOT WHALE**: 14-28 ft. Entirely black. Note the high fore-head & recurved dorsal fin. Travels in large schools.

③ **PIGMY SPERM WHALE**: 9-13 ft. Black above, pale below. A broad fore-head protrudes over a narrow lower jaw.

• **Beaching... why whales strand themselves ashore & die.**

① Illness & old age result in drowning.

② These air-breathing marine mammals weaken & drown during storms at sea.

③ As they chase fish thru' shoals, they may run aground on sandbars. The ebbing tide causes them to die of sun exposure on sand/mud flats.

④ Parasites like roundworms (right) infect the ear sinuses & may interfere with the whales' "echolocation" sonar navigation ___..

BOTTLE-NOSED DOLPHIN

Dolphin have an extended jaw or "beak". Porpoise jaw is snub-nosed.

• **A sleek gray fin** slicing salty waters in the Atlantic or estuaries pinpoints a nearby Bottlenosed Dolphin. This 7-12 ft., steel-colored whale may weigh up to 500 lbs. Boaters here watch them surface almost at arm's length for air. With a loud, "whoosh!," they hastily inhale air thru' their blowholes, then submerge their melon-shaped heads. Streamlined as a missle, Dolphins cruise shoals for squid, fish (mullet, menhaden, herring, anchovies...) & crabs... streaking 20-45 m.p.h. after prey! 80 to 88 conical teeth lining the "bottlenose" beak are used to grasp food which is turned in the mouth & swallowed whole—.

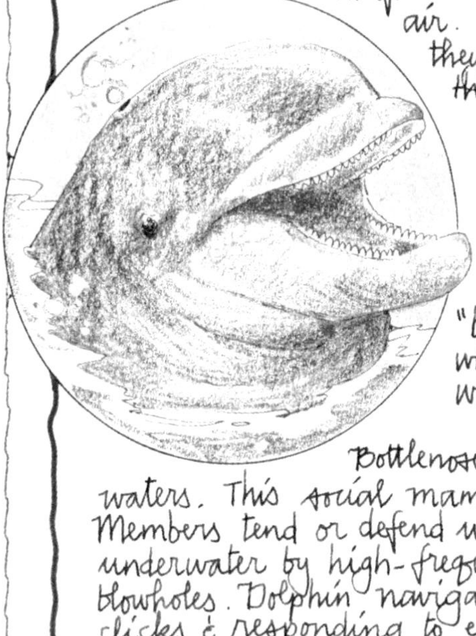

• **Nature's bodysurfers,** Bottlenoses cavort in ships' wakes & nearshore waters. This social mammal travels in "pods" or herds of 4 to 6. Members tend or defend wounded, sick or young. They communicate underwater by high-frequency squeaks & whistles emitted thru' their blowholes. Dolphin navigate & locate food by making gutteral clicks & responding to echoes made when the sounds rebound from objects. This built-in sonar is known as "echolocation".

• **Entering the waterworld tail first**, 2 ft. calves are soon strong swimmers. Mother nurses her "only child" & teaches it fishing skills the 1st year. Adults may live to a ripe old age of 30 years!

Females carry the fetus 1 full year!

PORPOISE OR DOLPHIN?

• **"Porpoise" is a coastal slang word...** a catch-all name locals use to describe any of the smallish cetaceans (toothed whales) swimming offshore or inshore waters here. But what folks call a "porpoise" may in fact be a Dolphin, an entirely distinct species of whale. Or mention "Dolphin" to a fisherman. He'll swear you're referring to colorful game fish! So, just what is a porpoise? What is a Dolphin? Shown below, the two marine mammals are noticeably different.

Porpoise

Atlantic Harbor Porpoise

• 4-6 ft. Smaller than the Dolphin. Black back, pink sides, whitish belly. Appears blunt-nosed, its jaw not extending out from the skull. Dorsal fin is triangular. Teeth are spade-like. Range: No. Atlantic waters south to Delaware coast.

Dolphin

Atlantic Bottlenosed Dolphin

• 7-12 ft. Larger than the porpoise. Gray color. Its 3" snout or beak extends from the skull. Dorsal fin has a curved-back shape. Teeth are conical. Range: Common from Cape Cod to Florida.

Note. **The Fish, Dolphin**, also called Dorado, or Mahi Mahi by Hawaiians, shows a blunt forehead, rainbow colors and a long dorsal fin. This leaping, fast-swimming fish is a highly sought game species of southern seas...

OTTER
●Four feet of furry fun, our sleek "River Otter" rolls & cavorts in back creeks/marsh pools, swimming smoother than dolphin, cruising as quiet as 'gators. Surprise comes to fishermen & dock walkers here when an Otter pops its whiskery muzzle out of the water, jerks around its bullet-shaped head in greeting & then sinks away in a trail of bubbles. Identify these big (25 lbs.) weasel cousins by their thick insulating coat of rich brown fur fading to tan underneath & that chunky, foot long tail ——"
TRACKS
FISH
CRABS
TURTLES
BIRD EGGS
●Tho' they bed down on land, Otters are supreme swimmers. Webbed feet & a rudder-like tail powers 'em along at 12 mph. They can stay submerged for ½ mile & easily capture slow moving, non-game fish & mud-crawling prey. Our ever-curious river rascals use their nimble fingers to steal Willet/Rail eggs; or pluck crabs from commercial traps. But here lurks danger... the Otter may ensnare in the wires & drown... it can hold its breath just 4 min.! Safer sport is "bellywhooping", the family's game of skimming down mudbanks 20-30 times on well-greased belly fur, chattering with loud Otter glee!
●In March, 2-3 silky black pups are born blind in dens, in hollow logs/trees or grassy clumps. At 3 mos. timid babies are taught to swim when mom piles 'em on her back & then takes a deep dive. Float... or else! At 8 mos. youngsters range off from home.

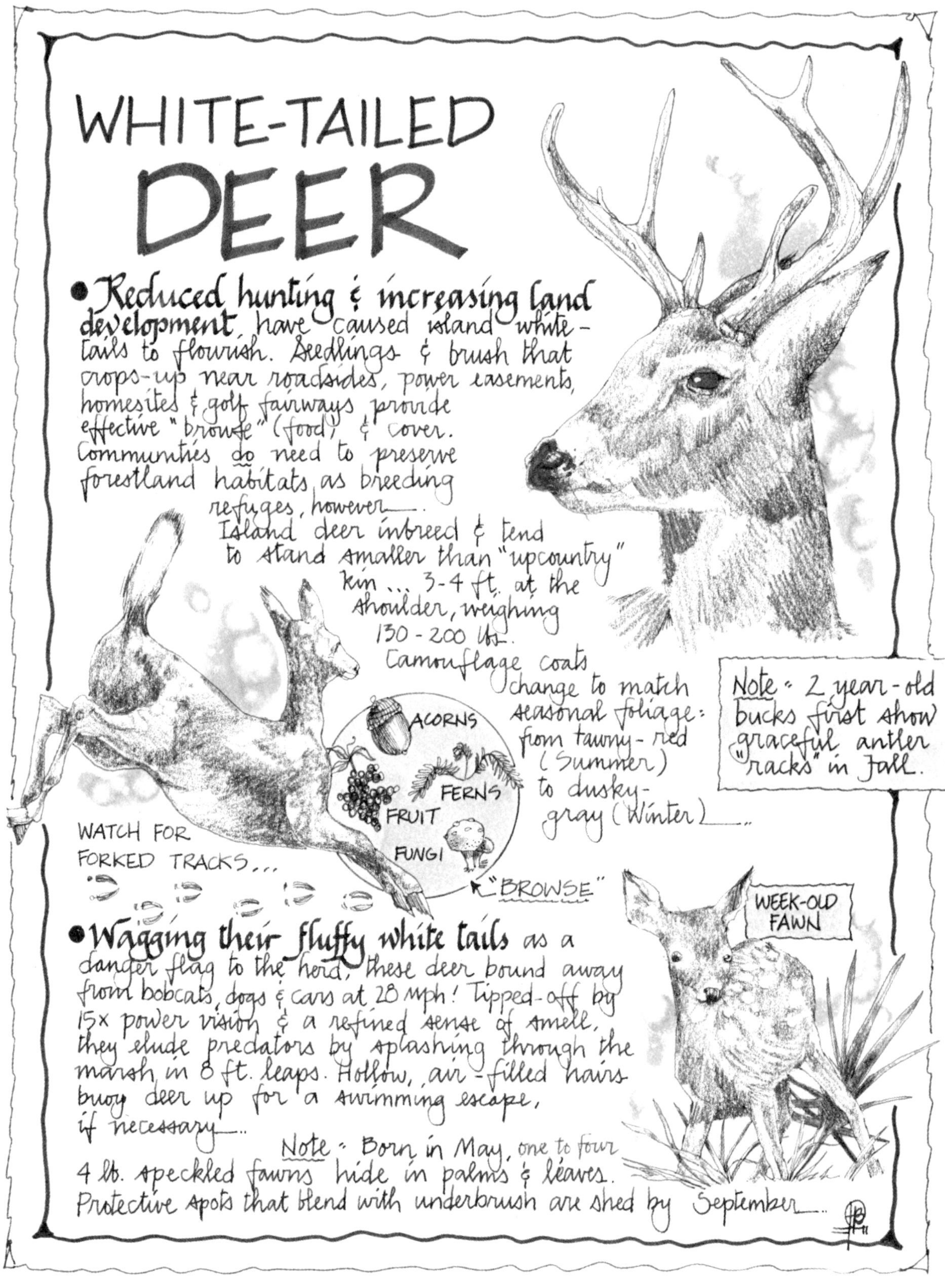
WHITE-TAILED DEER
• Reduced hunting & increasing land development have caused island white-tails to flourish. Seedlings & brush that crops-up near roadsides, power easements, homesites & golf fairways provide effective "browse" (food) & cover. Communities do need to preserve forestland habitats as breeding refuges, however...
Island deer inbreed & tend to stand smaller than "upcountry" kin... 3-4 ft. at the shoulder, weighing 130-200 lbs.
Camouflage coats change to match seasonal foliage: from tawny-red (Summer) to dusky-gray (Winter)...
Note: 2 year-old bucks first show graceful antler "racks" in Fall.
ACORNS
FERNS
FRUIT
FUNGI
"BROWSE"
WATCH FOR FORKED TRACKS...
WEEK-OLD FAWN
• Wagging their fluffy white tails as a danger flag to the herd, these deer bound away from bobcats, dogs & cars at 28 mph! Tipped-off by 15x power vision & a refined sense of smell, they elude predators by splashing through the marsh in 8 ft. leaps. Hollow, air-filled hairs buoy deer up for a swimming escape, if necessary...
Note: Born in May, one to four 4 lb. speckled fawns hide in palms & leaves. Protective spots that blend with underbrush are shed by September...

'COON!

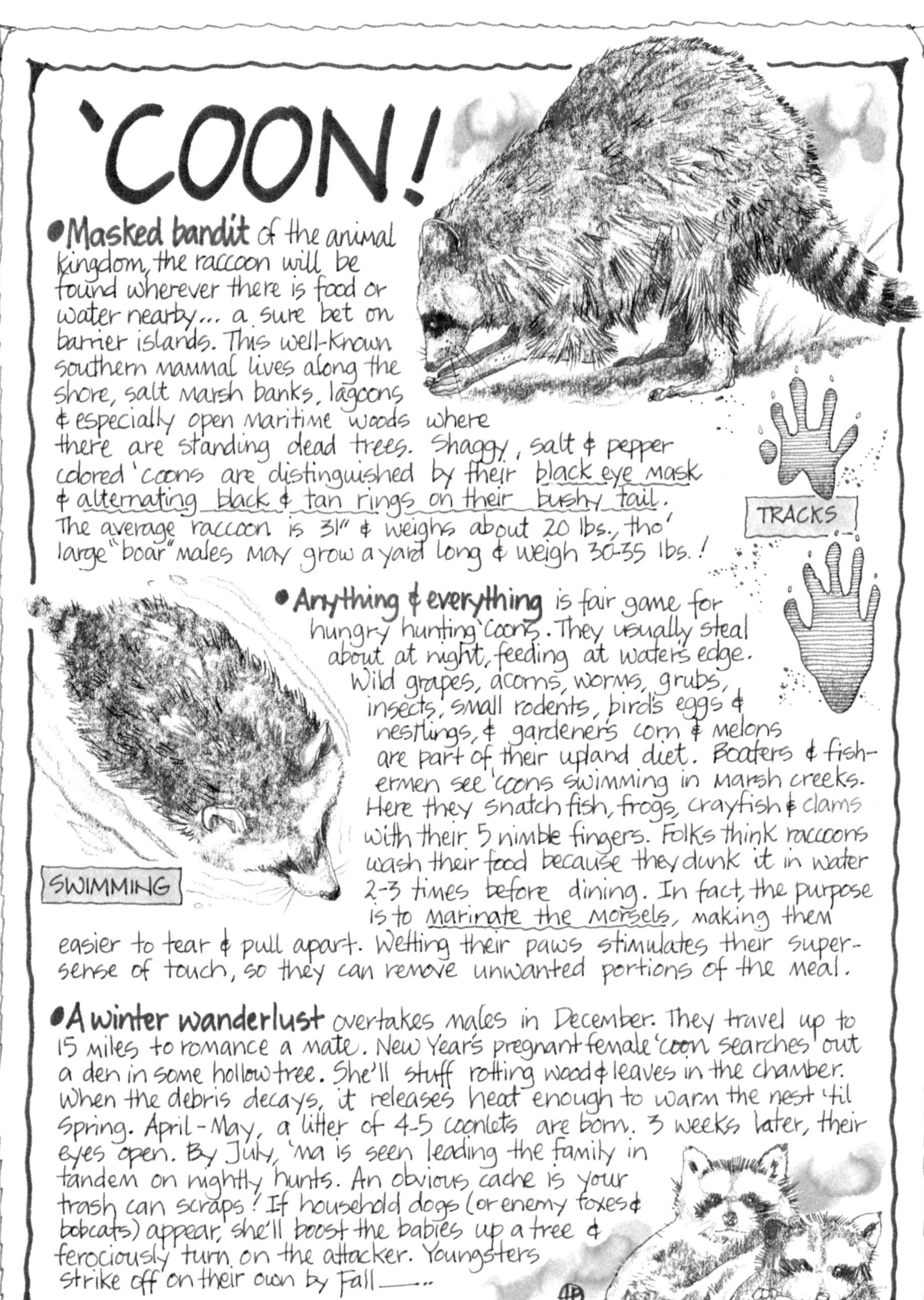

• **Masked bandit** of the animal kingdom, the raccoon will be found wherever there is food or water nearby... a sure bet on barrier islands. This well-known southern mammal lives along the shore, salt marsh banks, lagoons & especially open maritime woods where there are standing dead trees. Shaggy, salt & pepper colored 'coons are distinguished by their black eye mask & alternating black & tan rings on their bushy tail. The average raccoon is 31" & weighs about 20 lbs., tho' large "boar" males may grow a yard long & weigh 30-35 lbs.!

• **Anything & everything** is fair game for hungry hunting 'coons. They usually steal about at night, feeding at water's edge. Wild grapes, acorns, worms, grubs, insects, small rodents, bird's eggs & nestlings, & gardener's corn & melons are part of their upland diet. Boaters & fishermen see 'coons swimming in marsh creeks. Here they snatch fish, frogs, crayfish & clams with their 5 nimble fingers. Folks think raccoons wash their food because they dunk it in water 2-3 times before dining. In fact, the purpose is to marinate the morsels, making them easier to tear & pull apart. Wetting their paws stimulates their super-sense of touch, so they can remove unwanted portions of the meal.

• **A winter wanderlust** overtakes males in December. They travel up to 15 miles to romance a mate. New Year's pregnant female 'coon searches out a den in some hollow tree. She'll stuff rotting wood & leaves in the chamber. When the debris decays, it releases heat enough to warm the nest 'til Spring. April-May, a litter of 4-5 coonlets are born. 3 weeks later, their eyes open. By July, 'ma is seen leading the family in tandem on nightly hunts. An obvious cache is your trash can scraps! If household dogs (or enemy foxes & bobcats) appear, she'll boost the babies up a tree & ferociously turn on the attacker. Youngsters strike off on their own by Fall——..

GRAY FOX
"DOG OF THE TREES"
●Unlike its field, farm & poultry-loving red cousin, the gray fox is our forest fox. And its more common on the barrier isles. This bushy-tailed, 10 LB. canine is a stalker, not a runner. It'll scamper up a leaning oak, fast as a cat, when chased. Long, sharp claws on each paw provide the purchase. A "salt & pepper" coat, tinted with red on the neck, legs & flanks, & a black-tipped tail with an ebony streak ontop, blends this 40" long fox into its bark & branch backdrop. Note its eyes are adapted to night hunting & the pupils contract into slits in sunlight
●Gray foxes prowl evenings, hunting voles, marsh rabbits, nesting birds, frogs & even lizards. Tracking like a "pointer dog", they creep close, then capture prey with a frenzied pounce. the predator gobbles its meal on the spot, leaving a mere hunk of skin, or a pile of feathers behind at the "table". To sweeten their diet, gray foxes feast on persimmon, grapes & blackberries during summertime.
NOTE: COMPARED TO DOMESTIC DOGS, FOXES SHOW SMALLER, MORE POINTED MUZZLES, MORE SLANTED EYES, LARGER POINTED EARS and A MUCH FULLER TAIL.
FRONT
HIND
NOTE THE SIZE OF CLAWS ON THE PAWS...
●Chilliest January is mating season for gray foxes. Dad helps his vixen scratch & scrape out a den in a hollow log or tree. Here, 3-5 pups are born blind. They are weaned by March. Whelps at 2 months tag after parents on hunting forays. By autumn, the family scatters. But adults are life-long lovers: they may cozy up for nearly a decade___.
PUP AT 4 WEEKS

COTTON RAT

● **Rats running by your toes** on the walk to the beach may be a startling experience, but is no oddity in Nature. For the grassy dunes as well as marsh borders/overgrown fields are the domain of the Hispid Cotton Rat. Named for its grizzled fur (hispid means "bristly hair"), the common 8-14" rodent is blackish-brown above, tawny-white below. The tiny ears are barely visible 'neath the shaggy coat. Note this rat's tail is short, less than ½ its body length.

● **Day & night,** Cotton Rats scurry along surface runways in a never-ending quest for food. Their tramped trails are found in sheltered hedgerows; small heaps of chewed grass stems border the little paths. Grasses & herbs are the rat's main menu, tho' insects & the eggs or chicks of quail & chuck-wills-widows are attacked in season. Long, sharp incisor teeth pierce shoots, stems, leaves, seeds & even egg shells or bones. One Hispid's home range is less than 200' across... therefore it eats heartily in small spaces. For farmers, resident rats are a menace to sweet potato, sugarcane, corn, tomato & squash crops.

TRACKS

1"

● **Nature's meat machines,** super-fertile Cotton Rats breed year-round. Females can birth 5-6 ratlets, 9 times annually. Within a week, young leave home... a burrow or matted grass "nest." Now they will breed at just 6 weeks of age! Only 1 natural factor controls furry hordes from entirely overrunning the Island (a balance of 10-12 rats dwell per acre)... predators. Ravenous rat hunters include hawks, owls, snakes & bobcats (see inset, left). On resorts such as Hilton Head, rodent populations are directly related to the numbers, or lack of predators which are eliminated by land-developments mindlessly clear-cutting their woodland or marsh habitats in favor of golf cources, multi-family housing & cosmetic landscaping.

A Conservation Ethic

A 1986 study by the National Oceanic and Atmospheric Administration determined that the Atlantic coastal region between New Jersey and Florida is blessed with nearly 2 million acres of beaches, salt marshes and productive mudflats. But not one square foot of our tidelands should be taken for granted. No part of nature, no matter how vast, is immune from degradation through human neglect, carelessness and pollution. The truth is, the environment needs help from you and me. Here are 10 ways to make a difference.

• **Sea oats: Love 'em and leave 'em.** The beautiful grasses with the dangling golden seed heads build dunes and slow beach erosion. It is against S.C. law to pick, pluck or prune sea oats. Take photos, not plants.

• **Tread lightless around turtles.** Threatened loggerhead sea turtles lay eggs annually on Southeastern beaches. Please leave a nesting female alone (*never* shine a flashlight on her). If you see signs of a nest, call the local turtle protection project in your area. On Hilton Head Island, call Project Turtle Watch at 803/842–9197. If you don't have a sea turtle conservation group in your town, call your state wildlife department and ask how to start one. Folks in beachfront dwellings should turn off outdoor lights and shade illumination from second-story windows.

• **Watch, don't feed, the dolphins.** Atlantic bottlenosed dolphins are highly evolved, intelligent marine mammals. They have been skillfully hunting fish and squid for 70 million years. Feeding dolphins may be entertaining (and profitable) for humans, but at the animal's expense. The practice provides unhealthy food and passes on human germs. Worse, enticing the animals trains them to beg. The secret to learning about dolphins is to live and let live—without handouts.

• **The same goes for the 'gators.** Feeding alligators is definitely dangerous. The practice teaches the toothy reptiles to think of humans as a food source. Consider the consequences.

• **Sand dollar etiquette.** Sand dollars, those flat cousins to starfish and sea urchins, are favorite finds for beachcombers. But they are living animals. They play their integral part in the food chain of the ocean bottom (sand dollars recycle bottom nutrients and are food for fish and rays). If you find a live green specimen, study it and then toss it back into the water. Dead 'dollars, sunbleached white, are O.K. to keep.

• **Keep off dunes and bluffs.** Ocean dunes are natural bulkheads that protect the woods and homes from storm floods. High bluffs and steep mud banks on the marshside of the island also fend off tidal surges. Always use designated walkways and boardwalks to cross these areas. They are habitats, not playgrounds.

• **No wake, please.** The number one cause of destruction of oyster beds and erosion on inshore bluffs is waves from passing boat wakes. Boaters, go slow past shellfish colonies, docks, and obviously crumbling cliffs—whether waters are posted or not.

• **Fishing lines can be fatal.** Brown pelicans, gulls and terns can be permanently crippled and even killed by discarded monofilament fishing line and hooks. Loggerhead turtles can become tangled and drown. Never, never cut tangled lines and allow them to float free.

• **Trash: Pack it out.** On any given day, visitors toss almost 2 million pounds of garbage on the shorelines in the U.S., Canada and Mexico. That amounts to nearly 7,000 pounds of junk per mile. In order, the mess includes plastics, glass, cigarette butts, metal cans and rings and foam cups. Let's follow a simple rule: When you go down to the sea, pick trash up and pack it out.

• **Control your pets.** Cats and dogs have a bad habit of chasing and killing wild animals for the fun of it. Attach bells to your felines. And leash your dog when you pass through natural areas. Better: Keep pets indoors. Remember, wildlife has first rights.

A wise and familiar saying goes: "We have not inherited the earth from our parents; we have borrowed it from our children." I take this to mean that the coastal environment, and that of the wider world beyond, is not ours by right. Using our hearts and brain power, it is our privilege to protect all things natural for generations to come.

Let's get started today.

Toward The Horizon

The first thing vacationers here want to do is go down to the beach. There is something timeless about watching the sea. Out on the azure expanse, the swells roll and dip with the winds. Approaching shore, they change form, curving upwards with a foaming crest before slamming down and spraying shoals and flats below with a shrapnel of shell bits, quartz, and salt. Again and again the endless sea pushes in rhythmically, forcefully. This is nature's guarantee.

Most islanders are islanders because they have sought out the beauty of an environment surrounded by the sea. It is only natural that more and more persons would seek this beauty as well. Development, some planned and some uncontrolled, follows demand for housing and office space. A town emerges. Pavement, traffic and clustered "units" spring up where untrammeled forests and wetlands once thrived. Terms such as "non-point source pollution" and "sewage outfall" are commonplace in an islander's vocabulary. The first-timer, who once vacationed here and has since moved the family to the isle, often doesn't visit the sea for weeks, complaining of the demands of business.

Now more than ever, we, like this typical "hurried man," need to get back to nature. When the day's stress is at peak, when on-the-job burnout reduces us to a state of apathy, we must visit the sea like a newcomer. We slip off our shoes and warm sand caresses our toes. As the breeze pushes the hair back off our tired face, the sun soaks deeply into the skin. The salt air swirls about us with a moist and soothing embrace. The din of our automobile has been forgotten against the roar of rushing surf.

We all need to encounter something much larger than ourselves to regain our sense of place in the scheme of the universe. When we come to the sea, we are confronted with a natural power beyond comprehension. Against it, our responsibilities and worries diminish into a healthier, happier perspective.

To be sure, it is the destiny of Hilton Head Island to grow as a community. Yet, enmeshed with our development as a townscape, must be the rising commitment to preserve our tideland resources. They influence and benefit our lives in every way, but are impacted by the activities of man. As we expand as a populace, let us never forget our natural heritage: the beaches and marshes. They are the products of the sea's sculpting hand on the island.

Each of us will be remembered not so much for the way we altered the landscape here for short term profit, rather by how well we saved the beauty of Hilton Head for our children. The future of this island, and barrier islands like it, rests in the hearts and minds of those who would conserve our coastal environment. Have you visited the beach today?

INDEX

R

S

T

U

W

Y

References

Amos, William. **The Life of the Seashore.** New York. McGraw-Hill. 1966
Amos, William and Amos Stephen. **Atlantic and Gulf Coasts.** New York. Knopf. 1955
Arnold, Augusta Foote. **The Sea Beach at Ebb Tide.** New York. Dover. 1968
Bent, Arthur Cleveland. **Life Histories of North American Marsh Birds**. Assorted Vols. New York. Dover Publ. Co. 1963
Bergeron, Eugene. **How to Clean Seashells.** St. Petersburg. Great Outdoors Publishing Co.1971.
Berrill, N. J. and Berrill, Jacquelyn. **1001 Questions Answered About the Seashore.** New York. Dover. 1957
Berrill, N. J. and Berrill, Michael. **The Life of the Sea Islands.** McGraw-Hill. 1969
Brockman, Frank C. **Trees of North America.** New York. Golden press. 1968
Brown,Vinson, **Knowing the Outdoors in the Dark.** Harrisburg, Pa. Stackpole Books. 1972
Brown, Vinson, **Reading the Woods.** Harrisburg, Pa. Stackpole Books. 1969
Bustard, Robert. **Sea Turtles...Their Natural History and Conservation.** New York. Taplinger Publ. Co. 1972
Butler, Nancy. **The Subtropic Coast.** Hilton Head Is., S. C.
Calder, Dale. **A Guide to Common Jellyfishes of South Carolina.** Charleston, S. C. South Carolina Sea Grant Consortium. 1977
Cathcart, Nancy. **The Natural History of Hilton Head Island, S. C.** Savannah. Printcraft Press. 1981
Chapin, Henry. **The Remarkable Dolphin.** New York. Young-Scott. 1954
Cobb, Broughton. **A Field Guide to the Ferns.** Boston, Mass. Houghton Mifflin Co. 1956
Collingwood, G. H. and Brush, Warren D. **Knowing Your Trees**. Washington D. C. The American Forestry Assoc. 1964
Conant, Roger. **A Field Guide to Reptiles and Amphibians.** Boston, Mass. Houghton Miffling Co. 1958
Cousteau, Jacques. **The Ocean World of Jacques Cousteau.** 20 Vols. Hartford, Ct. The Danbury Press 1973
Crowder, William. **Seashore Life Between the Tides.** New York, Dover. 1931
De Carli, Franco. **The World of Fish.** New York. Abbeville Press. 1975
The Editors of Life. **Life Nature Library.** Assorted Vols. Time, Inc.
Elman, Robert. **The Living World of Audubon Mammals.** New York. Grosset & Dunlap. 1967
Everside, Arnold. **A Guide to Common Whelks.** Carleston, S. C. South Carolina Sea Grant Consortium. 1957
Gosner, Kenneth. **A Field Guide to the Atlantic Seashore.** Boston. Houghton Mifflin. 1979
Gray, William. **Friendly Porpoises.** New York. A. S. Barnes Co. 1964
Guggisberg, C. A. W. **Crocodiles...Their Natural History, Folklore and Conservation.** Harrisburg, Pa. Stackpole Books. 1972.
Jacobson, Morris and Franz, David. **Wonders of Jellyfish.** New York, Dood & Mead. 1978
Kaplan, Eugene. **Southeastern and Caribbean Seashores.** Boston. Houghton Mifflin. 1988
Lee Rue, Leonard III. **Pictorial Guide to the Birds of North America.** New York. Thomas Y. Crowell Company. 1970

Lee Rue, Leonard II. **Pictorial Guide to the Mammals of North America.** New York. Thomas Y. Crowell Company. 1967

Lilly, John, M. D. **Communication Between Man and Dolphin.** New York. Doubleday. 1978

Lilly, John, M. D. **Lilly on Dolphins.** New York. Anchor Books. 1975

Lilly, John, M. D. **Man and Dolphin.** New York. Doubleday. 1961

Lineaweaver, Thomas and Backans, Richard. **The Natural History of Sharks.** New York. Doubleday. 1969

Longstreet, R. J., ed. **Birds in Florida.** Tampa, Fla. Trend House. 1969

Martin, Alexander C., Zim, Herbert S., Nelson, Arnold L. **American Wildlife & Plants, A Guide to Wildlife Food Habits.** New York. Dover Publications, Inc. 1951

Marshall, Olga. **Ocean Life.** New York. MacMillian. 1971

McClane, A. J. **Field Guide to Saltwater Fishes of North America.** New York. Holt. 1974

McKay, Francis P. **Let's Go Shelling.** St. Petersburg, Great Outdoors Publishing Co.

Meinkoth, Norman. **The Audubon Society Field Guide to North American Seashore Creatures.** New York. Knopf. 1981

Morton, Julia F. **Folk Remedies of the Low Country.** Miami, Fla. E. A. Seemann Publishing Inc., 1974

Murie, Olaus J. **A Field Guide to Animal Tracks.** Boston, Mass. Houghton Mifflin Co. 1954

Pearson, Gilbert T., ed. **Birds of North America.** Garden City, N. Y. Garden City Books. 1917

Petry, Loren. **A Beachcomber's Botany.** Chatham, Mass. Chatham Conservation Foundation. 1968

Schwartz, Frank. **Sharks of North Carolina and Adjacent Waters.** Morehead City, N. C. North Carolina Department of Natural and Economic Resources. 1975

Robbins, Chandler S., Bruun, Bertel and Zim, Herbert S. **Birds of North America.** New York. Golden Press. 1966

Sprunt, Alexander. **Carolina Low Country Impressions.** New York: The Devin-Adair Co. 1964

Sprunt, Alexander. **South Carolina Bird Life.** Columbia. Univ. of S. C. Press. 1949

Von Frisch, Karl. **Animal Architecture.** New York. Harcourt Brace Jovanovich. 1974

Wallace, George, J. **An Introduction to Ornithology**. New York. The Macmillian Co. 1955

Zinn, Donald J. **The Handbook for Beach Strollers from Maine to Cape Hatteras.** Chester, Ct. The Pequot Press. 1975

Zim, Herbert S., et al. **Golden Nature Guides.** Assorted Vols. New York. Golden Press.

Notes

Notes